Community Engagement in African Universities

Perspectives, Prospects and Challenges

Edited by
Julia Preece,
Peggy Gabo Ntseane,
Oitshepile MmaB Modise
and Mike Osborne

niace

promoting adult learning

Published by NIACE

© 2012 National Institute of Adult Continuing Education
(England and Wales)
21 De Montfort Street,
Leicester,
LE1 7GE

Company registration no. 2603322
Charity registration no. 1002775

NIACE has a broad remit to promote lifelong learning opportunities for adults.
NIACE works to develop increased participation in education and training, particularly
for those who do not have easy access because of class, gender, age, race, language
and culture, learning difficulties or disabilities or insufficient financial resources.

You can find NIACE online at www.niace.org.uk

Cataloguing in Publications Data

A CIP record for this title is available from the British Library

ISBN 978-1-86201-599-9 (print)
ISBN 978-1-86201-600-2 (PDF)
ISBN 978-1-86201-601-9 (ePub)
ISBN 978-1-86201-603-3 (online)
ISBN 978-1-86201-602-6 (Kindle)

Cover design by Book Production Services

Designed and typeset by Cambridge Publishing Management, Cambridge, UK

Printed and bound in the UK

Contents

Acknowledgements

The editors would like to thank The University of Botswana for hosting the ninth PASCAL International Observatory Conference, which was the original inspiration for this book. We would also like to thank Paulette Bowman from the Northern Illinois University for her tireless efforts to format the final manuscript for submitting to our publishers, NIACE.

Lastly, we should like to thank David Shaw and NIACE for giving us the opportunity to access an international publisher to publish a book on Africa.

Author biographies

Idowu Biao is professor of lifelong learning at the University of Botswana. Previous positions have been deputy director at the Institute of Extra-Mural Studies at the National University of Lesotho and professor of lifelong learning at the Department of Adult and Continuing Education, University of Calabar, Nigeria. His research interests include the development of learning resources for out-of-school learners and gerontology. Recent publications include *Comparing Pioneer African Institutes of Extra-Mural Services* (2010), published by Lambert, and 'Human development index literacy as a new social development theory', in *International Critical Thought* (2011).

Opha Pauline Dube is a global environmental change (GEC) scientist and associate professor at the University of Botswana. She has contributed as a lead and coordinating lead author in the IPCC WGII assessments. She currently serves as vice chair of the International Geosphere-Biosphere Programme where she leads a synthesis on GEC and least developed countries. She has published on indigenous knowledge and on institutions and practices, and contributed to a number of GEC science plans including the Southern Africa GEC and Food Systems initiative and the GEC research sponsors Belmont Challenge, 'To deliver knowledge needed for action to mitigate and adapt to detrimental environmental change and extreme hazardous events'.

John Robert Ikoja-Odongo is professor of library and information science at the East African School of Library and Information Science, Makerere University. His research interests are information behaviour studies, knowledge management, publishing studies and indigenous knowledge. He is currently conducting a bibliometric study on HIV/AIDS in Uganda and is also engaged in a study of the information-seeking behaviour of pastoralists of Uganda.

Abel G. Ishumi is professor of education at the University of Dar es Salaam, based in the Department of Educational Foundations, Management and Life-long Learning of the School of Education. He has taught courses in sociology and philosophy of education, as well as conducted research and published in the same and related areas. A selection of his previous publications includes *Philosophy of Education: An Introduction to Concepts, Principles and Practice*, co-edited (Dar es Salaam University Press, 2002) and *Tracer Studies in a*

Quest for Academic Improvement, co-edited (DUP, 2004). He is currently involved in a research/writing project on fifty years of education in Tanzania, 1961–2011.

Peter Kearns is principal of Peter Kearns and Associates, and intellectual director of the PASCAL International Exchanges, a project of the PASCAL International Observatory that promotes online exchanges of information and experience between cities across the world. His research interests include policy and strategies to foster lifelong learning and build inclusive and sustainable learning cities and communities. His book publications include *VET in the Learning Age: The Challenge of Lifelong Learning for All* (1999) and *Building a Learning and Training Culture: The Experience of Five OECD Countries* (2000), both published by NCVER, Adelaide.

Oitshepile MmaB Modise is a senior lecturer in the Department of Adult Education, University of Botswana. She has close to 30 years of experience as an educator, more than a decade as a trainer/educator at university level and on-the-job training, as well as manager and researcher. Her research interests include community development, non-formal education, higher education and industry. She has published in international journals including the *International Journal of Lifelong Education, Western Journal of Black Studies* and *Australian Journal of Adult and Community Education*.

Chadzimula O. Molebatsi is a human geographer-cum-urban planner and teaches in the Department of Architecture and Planning, University of Botswana. His most recent research is on the question of governance and the democratisation of the urban planning process. He has published in the areas of urban planning, environment and community development.

Dama Mosweunyane is a lecturer in the Department of Adult Education of the University of Botswana. He previously worked for non-governmental organisations, where he held positions as programme officer and programme coordinator. His research interests are poverty eradication, community development, sustainable development and organisational management. He has co-authored a research-based publication entitled, *Perceptions of Citizenship Responsibility Amongst Botswana Youth*, published by Lentswe La Lesedi (2004).

Mpoki J. Mwaikokesya is a PhD candidate at the School of Education, University of Glasgow, and a lecturer in the Department of Educational Foundations, Management and Life-long Learning in the School of Education at the

University of Dar es Salaam. His PhD thesis is on the examination of under-graduate students' development of lifelong learning attributes in Tanzania.

Dorothy Nampota is associate professor of science education and direc-tor of the Centre for Educational Research and Training at the University of Malawi. Her research interests include education and poverty reduction, envi-ronmental education and non-formal education. She has published in education journals including *International Review of Education*, *Compare*, *African Journal of Research in Mathematics*, *Science and Technology Education* and *Malawi Journal of Education and Development*. She has contributed chapters in several books.

Peggy Gabo Ntseane is associate professor in the Department of Adult Edu-cation of the University of Botswana. She has been head of the department and national coordinator of international research partnerships, including the PASCAL/PURE research project, as well as being involved in textbook production projects. Her research work and publications are in gender and development, HIV/AIDS, indigenous knowledge systems and transform-ational learning. Her current research topics are culture and transformational learning, and adult education and regional engagement.

Frances O'Brien's disciplinary backgrounds are in social work and higher education. She has undertaken and promoted service learning in various com-munity–university engagement initiatives. She is now involved in the aca-demic development of educators in the higher education sector and pursues scholarship in university–community engagement, curriculum development, teaching and learning, and higher education institutional issues.

Dr George Ladaah Openjuru is the dean, School of Distance and Lifelong Learning, of Makerere University. He has coordinated a number of research and development projects funded by DFID, including a current project 'Learning for empowerment through training in ethnographic research'. His research interests include formal and non-formal adult education, focusing on adult literacy edu-cation and lifelong learning in higher education institutions. He is presently the chair of Uganda Adult Education Network. His publications include a co-edited book, *Everyday Literacies in Africa: Ethnographic Studies of Literacy and Numeracy Practices in Ethiopia*, published by Fountain Publishers (2009).

Mike Osborne is professor of adult and lifelong learning at the University of Glasgow, director of its Centre for Research and Development in Adult and Lifelong Learning, and co-director of the PASCAL Observatory on place management, social capital and lifelong learning. His main research interests are: widening participation in higher education; teaching and learning in higher education; the VET/HE interface; and the development of learning cities and regions. Recent publications include a co-edited book, *Perspectives on Learning Cities and Regions: Policies, Practice and Participation*, published by NIACE (2010).

Julia Preece is professor of adult education at the University of KwaZulu-Natal in South Africa. Formerly director of a research centre at the University of Glasgow, she has also worked in universities in Lesotho and Botswana. She has published extensively in the areas of lifelong learning, adult education and gender, and community engagement. Recent publications include *Lifelong Learning and Development: A Southern Perspective* published by Continuum (2009) and an edited book, *Community Service and Community Engagement in Four African Universities*, published by Lentswe La Lesedi (2011).

Wapula Nelly Raditloaneng is associate professor in adult education in the Department of Adult Education at the University of Botswana. She is a multidisciplinary sociologist, and an adult and health educator. Her areas of research and publication include gender, the social context of adult and continuing education, HIV/AIDS, poverty and literacy issues. She has been the country coordinator for two international research projects.

Michael Tagoe is senior lecturer at the Institute of Continuing and Distance Education, University of Ghana, Legon. His areas of research and publication include lifelong learning, adult literacy, HIV and AIDS, leadership, and the cultural context of adult and continuing education. He has published in education journals such as the *International Journal of Lifelong Education, Journal of Health and Human Services Administration, Ghana Journal of Literacy and Adult Education, Journal of Organizational Transformation and Social Change* and the *Journal of Asian and African Studies*. He has contributed a chapter on lifelong learning in *Transitions from Education to Work: New Perspectives from Europe and Beyond*, published by Palgrave Macmillan (2009).

The African university and community engagement in context

Julia Preece, Peggy Gabo Ntseane, Oitshepile MmaB Modise
and Mike Osborne

Introduction

> *In the mid-19th century, in the transition from the slave trade to the imposition of colonial rule, those who were asking for an African university saw the mission of the university as the mental liberation of the African from the shackles that slavery and religious dogma had imposed. Hence they wanted a secular university, emphasizing African and classical studies, science and technology. What they got were Fourah Bay College and Fort Hare. In the colonial period, they saw the mission of the university as the renaissance of Africa, emancipation from colonial rule and the establishment of African nations able to take their place in the 'comity' of civilized nations of the world. In the period of decolonisation, they saw the university as part of the effort to bring the nation into being, having the same mission as the nation, that is mental, economic and political de-colonisation. After independence, the university people found that they were no longer the ones defining the mission: the state did and universities took their cue from that to define their role. It was the state that crystallized the mission as Development.* (Ajayi et al.,1996, p. 187)

The above extract summarises the changing fortunes of African universities over a period of approximately one hundred years. This chapter elaborates on that summary, contextualising the specific historical circumstances pertaining to higher education in African contexts and positioning the African university within contemporary world debates that give rise to a renewed global emphasis on universities and the notion of 'engagement'.

We start with the origins of the university in Africa and a reflection on the philosophical heritage of learning within the African continent. We move chronologically through some key milestones that have influenced the development, mission and fortunes of higher education in African countries before moving to the current context. We then discuss the different ways in which the authors of this book position and describe their selective experiences or perspectives of the university's engagement mission in the current century. A section on regionalism and engagement places the book within debates around lifelong learning and the notion that universities have a role to play within learning regions or cities. Linked to that is an introduction to the notions of community engagement and service learning, which have become popular in southern Africa, followed by a brief discussion of some critiques of these concepts. Finally, this chapter outlines the structure of the book as a whole and how the subsequent chapters contribute to that structure.

Early beginnings

Only a handful of publications have traced the evolution of African universities (Ngara, 1995; Lulat, 2005; Ajayi et al., 1996) though these can be supplemented by country-specific references, literature on lifelong learning in Africa, UNESCO and World Bank publications and more recent debates about higher education and globalisation (Teferra and Greijn, 2010; Association of African Universities, 2004; Zeleza and Olukoshi, 2004). The continent's unique experiences of slavery, missionary interventions, colonialism, post-colonialism and externally imposed development discourses created a distinctly disruptive identity for African universities and populations at local, national and regional levels. The legacy of these periods in history continues to impact on contemporary efforts by institutions to position themselves on the global stage.

The oral tradition of learning in African contexts is now well articulated (Fordjor et al., 2003; Amutabi and Oketch, 2009). It consisted of age-related, holistic and graded learning where all community members were socialised into cultural, philosophical, occupational and moral roles by various members of their community with the aim of serving the needs of society. Experts in medicine, science, religion and philosophy would travel between communities, thus creating a community of oral scholars with a designated status of wisdom, based on their reputation and experience. But the epistemological basis of the learning was essentially spiritual, rather than following the Cartesian rationality of Western thinking: 'its epistemology placed emphasis not so much on rationality as on the deeper meaning and the power of words, particularly the names of things' (Ajayi *et al.*, 1996, p. 4). While such forms of knowledge construction are gaining more credence in current thinking (Ntuli, 2002), the colonial enterprise created a disjuncture between traditional African thought and Western thought, and destruction of any natural evolution of an African knowledge base in its own right, with consequences for African identity and scholarship.

Ajayi *et al.* (1996, p. 5) provide the most comprehensive record of university origins in Africa, highlighting the continent's pre-colonial written contributions to international knowledge as well as its oral traditions for higher learning. They show that the roots of the university as a 'community of scholars' can be traced to the Alexandria Museum and Library during the third century BC in Egypt. A strong influence on early scholarship was the monastic life, which attracted teachers and religious guides to live together as contemplatives while, in the Islamic tradition, as Muslims moved across Africa, madrasas served similar purposes. These early traditions were severely disrupted from the fifteenth century onwards by European slave traders, who introduced highly selective Western-style elementary schools at trading stations to serve the slave trade. During the nineteenth century, further educational interventions by Western missionaries served the interests of spreading Christianity. An example of a higher education institution for this purpose was Fourah Bay College, founded in 1826 in Sierra Leone. Colonial expansion rapidly followed with subsequent education systems modelled on European institutions.

Among the anglophone colonies, the British Advisory Committee on Education in the Colonies established a more formalised education system in 1923, which included a few university colleges strategically positioned to serve the administration needs of the colonial masters. By the 1930s, selective higher education was identified as a strategy to undermine traditional chieftainship leadership under the hegemonic guise of responding to increased indigenous demand for educational expansion. In 1837, the British government, in anticipation of future decolonisation, sponsored the De La Warr Commission for East Africa, followed in 1945 by the Asquith and Elliott commissions, 'so as to produce an elite of good quality leaders' (*ibid.*, p. 55) for West and Central Africa.

3

Thus a number of university colleges were established under the parenthood of British universities and many of these introduced adult education and extramural departments. This followed the British tradition of outreach and extramural work as part of the university's mission to educate the wider public, including provision of literacy programmes (Amutabi and Oketch, 2009, pp. 78–9). The trend was to create one regional or national university to serve the nation. Early universities included Fourah Bay College in Sierra Leone; the University of Cape Town, founded in 1952; University College, Gold Coast, Ghana, founded in 1949; and the Nigerian University College, Ibadan, founded in 1948. Later additions during the 1960s included the University College of Rhodesia; the University of Kenya; University College, Nairobi; and the University of Zambia.

Similar initiatives took place in francophone and lusophone Africa, but with less emphasis on adult education. For instance, the Université Cheikh Anta Diop de Dakar (UCAD) was established in Senegal in the same period and linked to the University of Bordeaux with programmes that mimicked the French system (Crossman, 1999). In this book, chapter 7 makes reference to the Arabic and French influences in Senegal.

However, enrolments in these institutions were generally pitifully low and the number of universities was very limited. Benneh *et al.* (2004), for instance, state that in 1960 there were only six universities in sub-Saharan Africa, though Sawyerr's (2004) observation that 18 out of 48 countries had universities or university colleges in the same period suggests that many of the universities were serving more than one country.

During the 1960s, the height of decolonisation, a number of initiatives took place to promote the Africanisation of universities and the establishment of new universities or new campuses of existing national universities. Key milestones are outlined below.

In 1961, the Conference of African States at Addis Ababa was organised to plan for African educational development at primary, secondary and higher education levels (UNESCO, 1963). Each country was required to prepare higher education development plans with a focus on increasing enrolments. In 1962, a UNESCO conference in Tananarive on the development of higher education in Africa (UNESCO, 1963) focused specifically on the role of higher education for social and economic reconstruction, with an expansion plan up to 1980. Because of the need to share limited resources, the Association of African Universities (AAU) was initiated in 1967 with a view to establishing regional cooperation in the promotion of Africanised universities and appreciation of African culture and heritage (Ajayi *et al.*, 1996). Chapter 8 in this book reports on recent collaborative projects that were funded by the AAU to this end.

The notion of 'Africanisation' essentially embraced two concepts – the transfer of ownership of curriculum and management of higher education institutions and also the redirection of mission to address national and regional development needs. The Africanisation process has become an ongoing project, largely because African nations have never really been in charge of their own development mission. A number of chapters in this book, for example chapter 5, refer to the African knowledge base as an issue in this respect.

The African university and its mission

At the point of independence, the African university was faced with multiple challenges. First, many countries inherited extremely poor infrastructures. Botswana in 1966, for instance, had only 12 km of tarred road, 22 university graduates and 100 secondary school leavers (Obasi, 2011). Second, the colonial regime had divided and ruled African nations in ways that had fuelled tribal rivalries rather than supporting natural boundaries. Third, the education that was available had been modelled on Western academic curricula designed for the narrow administrative needs of colonial civil servants. This issue is referred to in a number of chapters but particularly in chapter 3 by Modise and Mosweunyane. Universities were largely staffed by expatriates and even those who were local citizens had usually been educated overseas. Fourth, African universities required international assistance to achieve their development tasks. Fifth, the newly constituted governments were keen to take ownership of their own institutions after being subject to so many years of external rule. Universities became parastatals. The indigenous academic population supported this aspiration in the face of opposition from expatriate staff who were keen to promote the traditions of academic freedom and keep the university in the British model of separation from the state (Ajayi *et al.*, 1996).

These tensions continue to be played out in the mission of African universities. For instance, most national university vice chancellors are appointed by governments based on political affiliation. Their chancellors are usually the national president or sovereign head of state and politicians continue to view with suspicion any critical appraisal by higher education institutions of government itself. Many universities are therefore subject to government control over senior staff appointments, curriculum content, research and publications.

During independence, the African university focused on serving national development needs, contributing to building national identity and developing an African-based scholarship that would contribute to an African knowledge base. It was recognised, however, that the task was so large that universities would need to work cooperatively and required international assistance. Thus the UNESCO conference of 1962 made this commitment:

> *While wishing to make its full contribution to the universal stock of knowledge, African higher education must aspire to give African peoples their rightful place and to cement African unity forever. Towards this end, the African university must regard itself as the cultural centre of the community in which it is placed and the guardian and proponent of its artistic, literary and musical heritage ... in view of the fact that until recently education in Africa has been largely oriented towards the culture of foreign peoples, the African university must correct this imbalance by adapting the content of both its teaching and research specifically towards African problems ... by the progressive africanisation of the staff ... Far from becoming ivory towers detached from the society in which they are situated, higher education institutions in Africa must be in close and constant touch with society, both through their extra-mural departments and through all those activities which can contribute towards preserving the African heritage ... In order to perform their tasks effectively, African universities must enjoy traditional academic freedom to the fullest extent possible.* (UNESCO, 1963, p. 12)

In many ways, therefore, the African university was positioned to respond to the very same mission of engagement for development that characterises today's discourses. Indeed, there are examples during the 1960s and 1970s of highly focused engagement activities where governments steered universities towards nation building. One of the most famous examples is that of Julius Nyerere in Tanzania, who recorded his development goals in the Arusha Declaration of 1967 (Ajayi *et al.*, 1996, p. 118). Nyerere's socialist approach insisted on direct links between the university and village communities. Academic and government staff were often interchangeable.

Students were required to contribute to community service during long holidays and village leaders' assessment of their behaviour would contribute to their academic qualifications. The university also provided a range of adult education opportunities for the wider population. Similar initiatives took place in Uganda with Makerere University, which is discussed in chapter 9.

Further international efforts within Africa attempted to promote a home-grown version of the African university. The AAU, for instance, organised a workshop in Accra in 1972, 'Creating the African University':

> *The truly African university must be one that draws its inspi-ration from its environment; not a transplanted tree, but one growing from a seed that is planted and nurtured in the African soil.* (Cited in Ajayi *et al.*, 1996, p. 91)

This resulted in 1973 in what came to be known as the 'Yesufu model' (Ngara, 1995), which attempted to formulate a mission for the African university:

> *It follows that an emergent African university must, henceforth, be much more than an institution for teaching, research and dissem-ination of higher learning. It must be accountable to, and serve, the vast majority of the people who live in the rural areas. The African university must be committed to active participation in social transformation, economic modernization, and the train-ing and upgrading of the total human resources of the nation, not just of a small elite.* (Yesufu, 1973, p. 41, cited in Ajayi *et al.*, 1996, p. 112)

Yesufu identified six main functions of the African university, which includ-ed promotion of social and economic modernisation, intercontinental unity and international understanding, as well as manpower development. Ngara (1995), however, states that the mission was not formally adopted by Afri-can universities. He offers his own mission adaptation of the Yesufu model which includes, in addition to teaching and research, 'fostering moral values and raising social consciousness' plus 'consultancy' and 'other community focused activities' (Ngara, 1995, p. 31). Like Yesufu, he argues that the liberal ideology of pursuit of knowledge for its own sake was not enough in a devel-opment context; 'universities should ... be mindful of the needs of society' (*ibid.*, p. 40).

The tension arises, however, in interpreting by whom and for whom 'development' is carried out. Furthermore, the long-term development project in itself has been subject to the rise and fall of international economic fortunes and changing visions for higher education on the African continent by leading aid agencies. Ade Ajayi *et al.* (1996) and Lulat (2005), among others, highlight the roller-coaster nature of development as a discourse and how its fluctuating interpretations interfaced with the changing value placed on higher education's ability to contribute to development at different points in time.

Changing fortunes

There was evidence of significant expansion and progress in higher education and national development throughout the first two decades of independence, and Benneh *et al.* (2004) report that universities increased in number to 120 across Africa by 1980. However, by the late 1970s, a number of factors contributed to the beginning of a decline in fortunes that would have far-reaching consequences for Africa's progress. Political instabilities across some countries were exacerbated by a crisis in the oil price, economic decline and growing debt from nations in receipt of financial aid. Higher education in this context was viewed as an expensive project, particularly because campuses had been constructed as residential villages for staff and students and there was a continuing, expensive dependence on expatriate staff and their ongoing repatriation costs. The World Bank response was to redefine the role of higher education. It was no longer defined as a 'public good' but instead was seen as a 'private good' that no longer deserved international support, under the rationale that African universities were elitist and did not produce a sufficient rate of return on investment (Sawyerr, 2004). Throughout the 1980s and 1990s, structural adjustment policies resulted in new definitions of development and relevance, an emphasis on vocationalism, privatisation of public services, including education, and a refocus of funding support on basic education (Association of African Universities, 2004; Sawyerr, 2004). Universities were left to fund themselves. The resulting decline in standards, resources, infrastructure, pay scales and research outputs produced a legacy of brain drain and demotivated staff who increasingly used research time for individual, paid consultancies.

In contrast to European and global discourses for lifelong learning, and an expanded higher education sector within a neo-liberal discourse of the market and rapid globalisation, African and other developing nations were increasingly being subjected to a limited development vision for basic education (Torres, 2003; Preece, 2009).

Towards the end of the 1990s, there was recognition that Africa's declining fortunes – poverty, hunger, droughts and food insecurity, disease, low life expectancy, HIV and AIDS, undeveloped industrial base, illiteracy, refugees, and so forth (Ngara, 1995) – were limiting trade expansion opportunities for the economically advanced world. Attention once more turned to a new development vision for Africa that would ostensibly be more partnership oriented, with national ownership of development agendas. A number of events coincided just prior to the turn of the millennium to bring higher education back into the fold for this new vision.

Within the continent itself, the Africa Regional Council of the International Association of University Presidents (IAUP) was established in 1997 and held its first conference in Accra in 1998, supported by the AAU, among others. Its aim was to promote development partnerships with the private sector and civil society – once more turning towards university engagement (Benneh *et al.*, 2004). In South Africa, these trends were supplemented by the new post-apartheid White Paper for Higher Education (Department of Education, 1997), which explicitly referred to the need for South African universities to develop community service learning opportunities for students in an effort to encourage cultural tolerance and citizenship responsibility.

Coinciding with the Accra conference, the UNESCO-sponsored Conference of Ministries of Education for African Member States (MINEDAF) was held in Durban with the title 'Lifelong Education in Africa: Prospects for the 21st Century'. The Durban Statement of Commitment placed Africa firmly in the frame for lifelong – as opposed to basic – education:

> *We commit ourselves to an expanded role for education which should be a lifelong process, a continuum which transcends schooling systems and which focuses on the building of a learning society.* (UNESCO, 1998a, Vol. 4)

This focus would be repeated in the organisation's subsequent conference four years later (UNESCO and MINEDAF, 2002).

At the same time as the first MINEDAF conference, a preparatory event for UNESCO's first World Conference on Higher Education was held in

Mumbai by university adult educators. They made a strong plea for the role of adult education for active citizenship, as expressed in the Mumbai Statement (Mauch and Narang, 1998). The UNESCO World Conference, in its world declaration on higher education, included this in its expanded vision for higher education:

> *The core missions of higher education systems (to educate, to train, to undertake research and, in particular, to contribute to the sustainable development and improvement of society as a whole) should be preserved, reinforced and further expanded, namely to educate highly qualified graduates and responsible citizens and to provide opportunities for higher learning and for learning throughout life. Moreover, higher education has acquired an unprecedented role in present-day society, as a vital component of cultural, social, economic and political development and as a pillar of endogenous capacity-building, the consolidation of human rights, sustainable development, democracy and peace, in a context of justice. It is the duty of higher education to ensure that the values and ideals of a culture of peace prevail. (UNESCO, 1998b, p. 138)*

Thus the concepts of lifelong learning and university engagement were linked in a way that could be used to position higher education within social as well as economic discourses for development. African nations were represented at these conferences but it was the initiatives at the turn of the century that really began to shape the path for Africa's higher education system.

A key factor at this time for African countries was the construction of a global development agenda. In 2000, the Millennium Development Goals became internationally agreed development targets for education, gender equality, health and economic growth. The targets failed to include adult or higher education (even though it is clear that adult and higher education are necessary resources to achieve the targets) but they paved the way for an ostensibly new development relationship with Africa. In 2002, the African Union (AU) was reconstituted from its former Organisation of African Union (OAU). It called for an increased focus on revitalising higher education in Africa (Shabani, 2010). A New Partnership for Africa's Development (NEPAD) was adopted by the UN General Assembly in 2002 as the main framework for collaboration between Africa and the UN (referred to in chapter 6). Its aim is to encourage cooperation between African nations so that an African peer review system forms the basis for international development aid agreements in the form of poverty reduction strategy papers. However, this new strategy is still heavily dependent upon African nations prioritising their goals according to neo-liberal principles in order to attract international aid (Preece, 2009). Chapters 6 and 9 provide evidence of this being played out in practice.

Other events followed, leading to the revitalisation of interest in higher education in Africa and including an agenda that focused more on social purpose. In 2005, for instance, the British Commission for Africa contributed to the refocused attention on Africa's development needs, and subsequent US and UK higher education funding has concentrated on capacity-building partnerships with African universities. More recently there has been an African Regional Conference (UNESCO, 2009a) in preparation for the second UNESCO World Conference on Higher Education (WCHE) in 2009 (UNESCO, 2009b). The African regional conference delegates issued a conference statement, which served as one of the inputs to the 2009 WCHE. The statement concluded with the need to focus on seven key areas, including one related to 'relevance, efficiency and effectiveness':

> *Under this theme, items include the demand for supporting higher education institutions to serve priority needs, for including African indigenous knowledge into higher education, for ensuring that values of peace, conflict prevention and resolution are taught, for fostering a culture of ICT, for promoting democratic values, sustainable development as well as the Millennium Development Goals and for strengthening higher education governance and management.* (UNESCO, 2009a, item 2)

In a complete turnaround from the World Bank's declamation during the 1980s of higher education's contribution to the 'public good' (Ajayi *et al.*, 1996), the 2009 UNESCO WCHE once more places higher education firmly on the development map:

> *The past decade provides evidence that higher education and research contribute to the eradication of poverty, to sustainable development and to progress towards reaching the internationally agreed upon development goals, which include the Millennium Development Goals (MDGs) and Education for All (EFA). The global education agenda should reflect these realities. Higher edu-*

11

cation institutions, through their core functions (research, teaching and service to the community) carried out in the context of institutional autonomy and academic freedom, should increase their interdisciplinary focus and promote critical thinking and active citizenship. This would contribute to sustainable development, peace, wellbeing and the realization of human rights, including gender equity. (UNESCO, 2009b, Communiqué, section 3, p. 14)

Other World Bank publications (2000, 2009) concerned with higher education in Africa inevitably focus on the role of higher education for economic development. However, the imperative of the South African post-apartheid reconstruction agenda for universities has created a discursive space that higher education also serves wider social needs within a broad lifelong learning framework for human development (Council for Higher Education, 2001).

The scene is therefore set for higher education in Africa to respond to global discourses and debates about the university's role in regional and community engagement. Nevertheless, the legacy of international influences on the curriculum and the locus of training for many African academics – along with ongoing state control (where the state's development plans are themselves controlled by external funding agendas) – still impinge on the African vision. The Africanisation of universities remains only a partially fulfilled aspiration, with very little evidence of its influence on the global stage (Teferra and Greijn, 2010). Similarly, evidence of the university's relationship with civil society and other development partners is poorly recorded in the public domain, partly as a result of continued infrastructure constraints in many universities, but also because Western publication outlets show little interest in the African story. This publication is one attempt to redress that imbalance and provide a space for African dialogue.

The current context for university engagement

As is often the case, the most dominant voices for university engagement emanate from countries in the Organisation for Economic Co-operation and Development (OECD), particularly the USA, Australia and countries in Europe. The PASCAL International Observatory has focused strongly on this topic throughout the world, through its PASCAL Universities for a Modern Renaissance (PUMR) and PASCAL Universities for Regional Engagement (PURE) initiatives.[1] It thus provides a unique platform for African universities to contribute to public debates on engagement through cyberspace. There are also other more conventional communications, such as this book and the conference held in the city of Gaborone as a dissemination event for the PURE projects.

The nature of engagement on the African continent is necessarily context specific, though there are some common constraints that impact on regional and more local collaborations. Some of these reflect universal issues such as the tension between higher education's role as a knowledge producer for its own sake (mode 1 knowledge) and its perceived contribution to producing mode 2 'socially robust' knowledge (Gibbons, 2006). Other issues reflect the post-colonial heritage and development priorities of international aid for Africa. In other words, the situation of civil society organisations and institutions that are competing for similar pots of money from donor agencies, and the need to respond to top-down donor development agendas, do not make it easy to collaborate on home-grown, bottom-up priorities that may fail to synergise with current development discourses. Moreover, government influences on university autonomy and academic freedoms continue to create uneasy power relations between local governance structures and their universities in some instances.

Nevertheless, universities across the world share an interest in contributing to the global repositories of scholarship, and African universities are increasingly seeking to have a place on the international stage (Teferra and Greijn, 2010). The remainder of this chapter reviews selective literature from the 'global north' and Africa relating to the various notions of engagement at regional and community levels, as a precursor to introducing the different experiences of authors in this book.

Regionalism and engagement

The concept of a learning region or learning city has gained credence particularly in the new millennium. It is contextualised in the discourses of globalisation as a response to increased mobility, growth of knowledge-intensive economic sectors, global communication networks and increasingly multicultural city populations and intensity of communication systems. The rationale is seen as emanating from a need to invest in education as a lifelong process and develop 'the urban population's capacity to act and express themselves … and join in the production of the future' (Bélanger, 2006, p. 21).

Bélanger describes the approach to developing a learning city as 'an overarching strategy to change learning behaviour; harnessing of economic, political, educational, cultural and environmental structures for human development' (*ibid.*, p. 25), using lifelong learning as the organising principle. An earlier book in this series covers this territory in some detail (Longworth and Osborne, 2010).

In the northern hemisphere, the terms 'learning city', 'learning region' and 'learning community' have emerged as concepts that attract a certain interest in debate at all levels of government since they potentially provide a vehicle for uniting a broad range of formal and non-formal providers of education at all levels (Gustavsen *et al.*, 2009). More than 50 cities and regions in the UK have at one time or another described themselves under one of those labels, as have cities in other countries of Europe, such as Gothenburg, Rotterdam, Dublin, Kaunas, Limerick and Brno. In Germany, more than 70 'learning regions' were established in the period 2002 to 2006. Espoo leads an informal Finnish network of some 20 'learning municipalities' and, in Italy, a Learning Cities Association is growing from its roots in the province of Puglia.

It is also a phenomenon in other parts of the world. Beijing participated in the PALLACE Global Learning Regions project (Longworth and Allwinkle, 2005), and all cities and towns in Victoria (Australia) have become learning cities and towns. In other parts of the world, such as Canada and the USA, learning region activity has been developed under the notion of 'smart cities'. Cities such as Vancouver and Victoria in British Columbia, Canada, are notable in that respect.

Although the majority of Africa's population still lives in rural areas, urbanisation is an increasing phenomenon and the continent is predicted to have a majority living in urban areas by the year 2030 (Hinrichson, 2010). On the African continent, however, there are few national or urban infrastructures that sufficiently cater for such population growth. For instance, lifelong learning is rarely an organising principle in policy documents. As a result of various externally imposed development agendas, lifelong learning in many African countries is reduced to literacy education (Aitchison and Alidou, 2008), so the political infrastructure simply does not exist for such collective action. Furthermore, as Walters asserts, the politics of development in African contexts are constantly shifting:

> *In the South African case, there is a continuum of development discourses which jostle for position from socialist, to social demo-*

> *cratic, to neo-liberal, which are mobilised by different constitu-*
> *encies within government, civil society, business, and labour. There*
> *is an ongoing contest for hegemony of one development approach*
> *over another.* (Walters, 2007, p. 287)

She also asks whether it is possible to interpret and develop the notion of learning region or city in 'contexts of widespread poverty and social polarisation' (*ibid.*).

Walters (*ibid.*, pp. 277–8) identifies five essential characteristics of a learning city or region. They are summarised as a world-class education and training system; high levels of collaboration and networking; a world-class, accessible information system; high value placed on all forms of learning, non-formal, formal and informal; and high levels of social cohesion.

The question for Africa, then, is to ask whether such characteristics need to be in place before the learning region project begins, or whether a learning region initiative might attract sufficient funding and political support to accelerate the move towards these characteristics. Walters' description of the Western Cape initiative – a research project to develop indicators for assessing the extent to which learning is monitored in the region – suggests that a process of research can raise awareness of the issues and possibilities as well as enlist political support. Nevertheless, she highlights the need for more than political support if the project is to translate into reality:

> *If the vision of the learning region is to be a lever for change*
> *then more than political buy-in is required. It needs translation*
> *into budgets and programmes which challenge government de-*
> *partments, at local, provincial, and national levels, to move 'out*
> *of their silos', and engage in the 'border skirmishes' which may*
> *follow.* (*ibid.*, p. 287)

Since Walters' description of the learning region initiative in the Western Cape, African notions of learning cities and learning regions have been emerging slowly. For instance, the eThekwini Municipality in Durban, South Africa, is positioning itself as a learning city through the recent launch of the Municipal Institute of Learning (MILE). There are plans to establish memorandums of understanding with local higher education institutions, the University of KwaZulu-Natal, the Durban University of Technology and the Magosuth University of Technology. MILE has structured its approach on four learning pillars – 'capacity enhancement, learning partnerships and networks, collaborative research and municipal technical support' (Mile.org, 2010).

Other initiatives are highlighted in this book, sometimes speculative ones (chapters 6 and 7) and sometimes reflecting the pragmatics of the beginnings of a formal partnership between university and city (chapters 2, 3, 4 and 5). In the context of Dakar in Senegal, Kampala in Uganda and Dar es Salaam in Tanzania, Kearns and Ishumi describe the challenges of promoting learning cities in cultural contexts of poverty. This once more raises questions about the transfer of European models into African cultural contexts that are often controlled by external development agendas and refers to the role of civil society and informal learning structures in stimulating bottom-up learning. In Botswana, where a formal agreement has been signed between the city council and the University of Botswana, the emphasis has been on the need for widespread consultation and engagement of a whole range of stakeholders (chapter 2).

The concept of engagement at a more *local* level, however, is more developed on the African continent – particularly in South Africa, but increasingly further afield. In some cases this is the result of the university's colonial legacy of extramural work; in other cases, it is in response to funded initiatives by the AAU to support capacity building and collaboration across African universities.

Community engagement and service learning

Although most university mission statements and strategic plans refer to 'community service' as a core feature of university activity, it is only within the South African context that it is enshrined in government policy (Department of Education, 1997), primarily as a strategy to redress the inequities of the former apartheid regime.

The notion of community engagement has been a rapidly 'moving feast' over the past decade. It is encapsulated in a variety of terminologies, ranging from 'outreach' to 'community service' and 'community service learning'. It can be interpreted to mean an individual philanthropic exercise of 'doing good' in response to a community need or a more collaborative partnership to address a community identified issue or problem. The philanthropic approach, implicitly enshrined in many university mission statements under the notion of 'service', has recently evolved into the notion of engagement as a mutual learning project and a means of contributing to the knowledge society, particularly in the form of 'mode 2' knowledge (Gibbons, 2006; Preece, 2011a). Mode 2 knowledge is broadly associated with practice-based research where the locus of the problem is in a context that requires a multidimensional approach to its solution. It is seen as being constructed collaboratively in a transdisciplinary way (Muller and Subotzky, 2001) in contrast with traditional, discipline-based knowledge, classified as 'mode 1' knowledge. The association between community engagement and the construction of knowledge is linked to the notion of a 'scholarship of engagement' (O'Brien, 2008). This is further discussed in chapter 11 of this book.

In community engagement terms, mode 2 knowledge can be developed as a direct result of collaborative research between community members and members of the university (van Schalkwyk and Erasmus, 2011). For instance, new knowledge might emerge about the best way to develop pit latrines in remote rural environments as a direct result of working with village communities. In other cases, existing indigenous knowledge practices for creating organic fertiliser might be enhanced by access to scientific expertise in the university and vice versa. Such a project was developed by one of the ITMUA case studies (see chapter 8 and Biao *et al.*, 2011). Alternatively, new understandings might evolve as a result of interdisciplinary contributions to the multidimensional nature of poverty in rural or urban contexts. Oyewole (2010, p. 20) uses the term 'enabling knowledge' for this process of acquiring a better understanding of local knowledge for knowledge production that is relevant to African contexts.

The literature on community engagement is largely ideological, emphasising mutuality and reciprocity of relations between university and community participants (Wallis *et al.*, 2005; Oyewole, 2010; Naidoo and Devnarain, 2009). However, there are few learning projects that explore the nature of this mutuality, particularly in relation to knowledge creation. Some exceptions are the project discussed in chapter 8 of this book and its published report (Preece, 2011b) and Van Shalkwyk and Erasmus (2011). However, since community engagement projects are usually short term and depend on external funding, the value of their reciprocity and mutual benefit can be short-lived (Preece, 2011c). Some issues that have been discussed in the literature include the challenge to ensure equal power relations between essentially unequal partners (Camacho, 2004); the extent to which engagement contributes to lifelong learning (Preece, 2011c); and the issue of utilising indigenous knowledge systems (Brock-Utne, 2003). PASCAL launched an African hub in 2010 at the University of South Africa to facilitate progress on these and other issues in the region.

In the South African context, community engagement is most commonly applied in the context of 'service learning'. The definition of service learning most frequently referred to is the one described by Bringle and Hatcher:

> *Course-based, credit-bearing educational experience in which students (a) participate in an organized service activity that meets identified community needs and (b) reflect on the service activity in such a way as to gain further understanding of course content, a broader appreciation of the discipline, and an enhanced sense of personal values and civic responsibility.* (Bringle and Hatcher, 1995, p. 112)

There is an extensive literature around its concept as a form of experiential learning pedagogy (Bender and Jordaan, 2007), a process (Nduna, 2006) and a model of engagement with the specific goal of making the university curriculum more relevant (Hall, 2010). Tagoe and O'Brien (chapters 10 and 11 respectively) discuss these various elements of service learning within their specific country contexts and from different perspectives. Tagoe's chapter is an optimistic portrayal of the extension of traditional extra-mural work; in O'Brien's case service learning is critiqued in terms of power relations and processes, among other issues.

Critiques of the community engagement discourse

Community engagement in African contexts, in spite of its historical relevance to nation building, is not well embedded in universities. The competing claims of the globalised higher education agendas for internationalisation, competitiveness, discipline-specific research and income generation have a tendency to pull struggling universities away from, rather than closer to, their communities and regions. Service learning projects often resemble student placements with little interaction between the university institution and the placement organisation. These practical and ideological tensions are reflected in literature that questions both the purpose and mission of community engagement and service learning. Butin (2010), in the context of North America, highlights the pedagogical, political and institutional limits to service learning. Higgs (2002), in the context of South Africa, asks to what extent traditional concepts of university knowledge and institutional autonomy should be challenged by the more practical, utilitarian goals of mode 2 forms of knowledge production.

On a different note, Visagie (2005) questions the discursive hegemony of community engagement which serves to give an impression of new collaborations. These are either merely representations of what was already happening, but are now repackaged in the vocabulary of engagement, or serve to give credence to activities that are merely rhetoric rather than real practices for collaboration and change.

Finally, Higher Education Quality Council evaluations in the South African context (Anderson, 2010) suggest that community engagement and service learning are poorly coordinated in most universities, with inadequate quality assurance mechanisms or evaluation strategies to assess the impact of the work on the communities they serve. Chapters 8 and 11 refer to these concerns when analysing their empirical studies.

This book is divided into two parts. Part 1 focuses on learning cities and regions, and part 2 on community engagement and service learning. Each part is prefaced by a short introduction that summarises the respective chapters. A final chapter offers a thematic analysis of the overall context of the book in relation to prospects and challenges for Africa. It is not a complete picture. The dominant perspectives are those of anglophone Africa and only nine out of the continent's 54 countries are represented here. This book therefore makes a starting contribution to a topic that we still have much to learn about in relation to African contexts.

References

Aitchison, J. and Alidou, H. (2008) 'The development and state of the art of adult learning and education (ALE) in Sub-Saharan Africa', paper prepared for CONFINTEA VI regional conference, 'The power of youth and adult learning for Africa's development', Nairobi, Republic of Kenya, November.

Ajayi, A.J.F., Goma, L.K.H. and Johnson, A.G. (1996) *The African Experience with Higher Education*. Accra: AAU and Oxford: James Currey Publishers.

Amutabi, M.N. and Oketch, M.O. (2009) *Studies in Lifelong Learning in Africa: From Ethnic Traditions to Technological Innovations*. Lewiston, NY: Edwin Mellen Press.

Anderson, I. (2010) 'Community engagement as an area of specialization at the Centre for Adult Education, UKZN: An analysis of its context within state and higher education community engagement policy', appendix 4. Unpublished report. Pietermaritzburg: University of KwaZulu-Natal.

Association of African Universities, Working Group on Higher Education (2004) *Higher Education in Sub-Saharan Africa with Specific Reference to Universities*. Accra: AAU.

Bélanger, P. (2006) 'Concepts and realities of learning cities and regions', in C. Duke, L. Doyle and B. Wilson (Eds) *Making Knowledge Work: Sustaining Learning Communities and Regions*. Leicester: NIACE, pp. 18–39.

Bender, G. and Jordaan, R. (2007) 'Student perceptions and attitudes about community service-learning in the teacher training curriculum', *South African Journal of Education*, Vol. 27, pp. 631–54.

Benneh, G., Awumbila, M. and Effah, P. (2004) *African Universities, the Private Sector and Civil Society: Forging Partnerships for Development*. Proceedings of the first conference for the African Regional Council of the International Association of University Presidents (IAUP), Accra, Ghana 9–11 June 1999. Accra: Ghana University Press.

Biao, I., Akpama, S., Tawo, R. and Inyang, E. (2011) 'Calabar case study 1: Female farmers in a university-led agricultural training programme in Calabar, Nigeria', in J. Preece (Ed.) *Community Service and Community Engagement in Four African Universities*. Gaborone: Lightbooks, pp. 61–70.

Bringle, R.G. and Hatcher, J.A. (1995) 'A service learning curriculum for faculty', *The Michigan Journal of Community Service Learning*, Vol. 2, pp. 112–22.

Brock-Utne, B. (2003) 'Formulation of higher education policies in Africa: The pressure from external forces and the neo-liberal agenda', *JHEA/RESA*, Vol. 1, pp. 24–56.

Butin, D. (2010) *Service-Learning in Theory and Practice: The Future of Community Engagement in Higher Education*. New York: Palgrave Macmillan.

Camacho, M.M. (2004) 'Power and privilege: Community service learning in Tijuana', *Michigan Journal of Community Service Learning*, Vol. 10 No 3, pp. 31–42.

Council for Higher Education (CHE) (2001) *Reinstating the Public Good into Higher Education Transformation*. CHE discussion series 1. Pretoria: CHE.

Crossman, P. (1999) *Endogenisation and African Universities*. Brussels: Belgian Administration for Development Cooperation.

Department of Education (1997) *Education White Paper 3: A Programme for the Transformation of Higher Education*. Pretoria: Department of Education.

Fordjor, P.K., Kotoh, A.M., Kpeli, K.K., Kwamefio, A., Mensa, Q.B., Owusu, E. and Mullins, B.K. (2003) 'A review of traditional Ghanaian and Western philosophies of adult education', *International Journal of Lifelong Education*, Vol. 22 No 2, pp. 182–99.

Gibbons, M. (2006) 'Engagement as a core value in a mode 2 society', keynote address at CHE-HEQC/JET-CHESP Conference on Community Engagement in Higher Education. Cape Town, September.

Gustavsen, B., Nyhan, B. and Ennals, R. (Eds) (2009) 'Learning together for local innovation: Promoting learning regions'. Thessaloniki: CEDEFOP. Retrieved 2 April 2012 from http://www.cedefop.europa.eu/EN/Files/3047_en.pdf

Hall, M. (2010) 'Community engagement in South African higher education', in Council on Higher Education (Ed.) *Kagisano* No 6. Auckland Park: Jacana Media, pp. 1–52.

Higgs, P. (2002) 'Nation building and the role of the university: A critical reflection', *SAJHE/SATHO*, Vol. 16, pp. 11–17.

Hinrichson, D, (2010) '"The World Comes to Town", people and the planet 2000–2010'. Retrieved 2 January 2012 from http://www.peopleandplanet.net /?lid=26729andsection=40andtopic=44

Inman, P. and Schuetze, H.G. (Eds.) *The Community Engagement and Service Mission of Universities*. Leicester: NIACE.

Longworth, N. and Allwinkle, S. (2005) *The PALLACE Project: Linking Learning Cities and Regions in Europe, North America, Australasia and China*. Final report to the European Commission. Edinburgh: Napier University. Available from http://www.pallace.net

Longworth, N. and Osborne, M. (Eds) (2010) *Perspectives on Learning Cities and Regions*. Leicester: NIACE.

Lulat, Y.G.M. (2005) *A History of African Higher Education from Antiquity to the Present: A Critical Synthesis.* Westport: Praeger.

Mauch, W. and Narang, R. (Eds) (1998) *Lifelong Learning and Institutions of Higher Education in the 21st Century*. Report on the preparatory meeting for the World Conference on Higher Education (Paris, October 1998) of the International Working Group on University-based Adult Education, Mumbai, 20–24 April 1998. Hamburg: UNESCO Institute for Education, and Mumbai: University of Mumbai.

Mile.org (2010) 'Municipal Institute of Learning'. Retrieved 2 January 2012 from http://www.mile.org.za/Pages/default.aspx

Muller, J. and Subotzky, G. (2001) 'What knowledge is needed in the new millennium?' *Organization*, Vol. 8, pp. 163–82.

Naidoo, B. and Devnarain, B. (2009) 'Service learning: Connecting higher education and civil society – are we meeting the challenge?' *Southern African Journal of Higher Education*, Vol. 23, pp. 935–52.

Nduna, N.J. (2006) 'Locating and managing service-learning: A complex issue in higher education', *Southern African Journal of Higher Education*, Vol. 20, pp. 488–502.

Ngara, E. (1995) *The African University and its Mission*. Roma: Institute of Southern African Studies, National University of Lesotho.

Ntuli, P.P. (2002) 'Indigenous knowledge systems and the African Renaissance – laying a foundation for the creation of counter-hegemonic discourses', in C. Odora Hoppers (Ed.) *Indigenous Knowledge and the Integration of Knowledge Systems*. Claremont: New Africa Books, pp. 53–66.

Obasi, I.N. (2011) 'Botswana at 45'. Retrieved 2 January 2012 from http://all africa.com/stories.2011100400794.html

O'Brien, F. (2008) 'In pursuit of African scholarship: Unpacking engagement', *Higher Education*, Vol. 58, pp. 29–39.

Oyewole, O. (2010) 'Africa and the global knowledge domain', in D. Teferra and H. Greijn (Eds) *Higher Education and Globalisation: Challenges, Threats and Opportunities for Africa*. Maastricht: Maastricht University Centre for International Cooperation in Academic Development (MUNDO), pp. 19–32.

Preece, J. (2009) *Lifelong Learning and Development: A Southern Perspective*. London: Continuum.

Preece, J. (2011a) 'Higher education and community service: developing the National University of Lesotho's third mission', *Journal of Adult and Continuing Education*, Vol. 17 No 1, pp. 81–97.

Preece, J. (Ed.) (2011b) *Community Service and Community Engagement in Four African Universities*. Gaborone: Lightbooks.

Preece, J. (2011c) 'Nurturing lifelong learning in communities through the National University of Lesotho: Prospects and challenges', *International Journal of Lifelong Education*, Vol. 30 No 6, pp. 713–32.

Sawyerr, A. (2004) 'Challenges facing African universities', *African Studies Review*, Vol. 47, pp. 1–59.

Shabani, J. (2010) 'Regional and international academic and research cooperation in Africa', in D. Teferra and H. Greijn (Eds) *Globalisation and African Higher Education*. Maastricht: Maastricht University, pp. 51–62.

Teferra, D. and Greijn, H. (2010) 'Introduction' in D. Teferra and H. Greijn (Eds) *Globalisation and African Higher Education*. Maastricht: Maastricht University, pp. 1–7.

Torres, M. (2003) 'Lifelong learning: A new momentum and a new opportunity for adult basic learning and education (ABLE) in the South', *Adult Education and Development Supplement*, Vol. 60, pp. 1–240.

UNESCO (1963) *The Development of Higher Education in Africa*. Report of the conference on the development of higher education in Africa, Tananarive, 3–12 September 1962. Paris: UNESCO.

UNESCO (1998a) 'The seventh conference of ministers of education of African states (MINEDAF VII Final Report, Durban, South Africa, 20–24 April

1998)'. Retrieved 2 January 2012 from http://unesdoc.unesco.org/images/0011/001133/113382e.pdf

UNESCO (1998b) World conference 1998, *Final Report of the World Declaration on Higher Education*. Paris: UNESCO.

UNESCO (2009a) *Thematic Studies Synthesis, Realized in the Context of the Task Force for Higher Education in Africa*. Paris: UNESCO.

UNESCO (2009b) *Conference Statement*. World conference on higher education, 'The new dynamics of higher education and research for societal change and development', UNESCO Paris, 5–8 July 2009. Paris: UNESCO.

UNESCO and MINEDAF (2002) 'Issues and strategies for the promotion of adult education in the context of lifelong learning, part II'. Retrieved 2 February 2008 from http://portal.unesco.org/education

Van Schalkwyk, F. and Erasmus, M. (2011) 'Community participation in higher education service learning', *Acta Academica*, Vol. 43 No 3, pp. 57–82.

Visagie, J. (2005) 'Deconstructing the discourse of community service and academic entrepreneurship: The ideological colonisation of the university', *Acta Academica*, Vol. 37 No 1, pp. 222–37.

Wallis, R.L., Wallis, A.M. and Harris, C.M. (2005) 'How universities can enhance sustainable development through successful engagement with their regional communities'. Retrieved 8 August 2011 from www.engaging communities2005.org/abstracts/Wallis-Robert-final.pdf

Walters, S. (2007) 'Building a learning region: Whose framework of lifelong learning matters?' in D.N. Aspin (Ed.) *Philosophical Perspectives of Lifelong Learning*. Dordrecht: Springer, pp. 275–92.

World Bank (2000) *Higher Education in Developing Countries: Peril and Promise*. Washington, DC: World Bank.

World Bank (2009) *Accelerating Catch-up: Tertiary Education for Growth in Sub-Saharan Africa*. Washington, DC: World Bank.

Zeleza, P.T. and Olukoshi, A. (Eds) (2004) *African Universities in the Twenty-first Century, Vol. 1, Liberalisation and Internationalisation.* Dakar: Council for the Development of Social Science Research in Africa CODESRIA.

PART 1

LEARNING CITIES AND REGIONS

This part of the book looks at the experiences of authors in Botswana, Tanzania, Senegal and Uganda in relation to the emerging concept of learning cities and regions in African contexts. The chapters highlight the challenges for resource-starved contexts but also emphasise the need for such initiatives to recognise and synergise with indigenous values and practices – in other words, the need to avoid uncritical international transfer of ideas.

Botswana is one of the few countries in Africa that has set up a formalised relationship between a university and its host city. The first chapters in this section highlight different aspects of this relationship. For instance, Ntseane, in describing the formalisation of the University of Botswana agreement with Gaborone City Council (chapter 2), stresses the need for wide consultation. She identifies four themes on which the partnership chose to focus as a result of a needs assessment between relevant partnership stakeholders. Two of those themes are discussed in subsequent chapters (urban planning by Molebatsi and environmental issues by Dube).

The university's formal memorandum of understanding with the City of Gaborone was established in the context of PASCAL's global PURE project. Modise and Mosweunyane elaborate in chapter 3 on partnership relations between the city and university – a concern that also emerges in Ntseane's chapter. They suggest ways in which the University of Botswana might rebrand itself to become a more engaging university but also shake off the heritage of its colonial past in a way that establishes an African, rather than northern, knowledge base. The rebranding includes the development of socially relevant research and also entails developing human and social capital to serve the country's labour market needs. However, the chapter also positions the university within the globalisation 'market competitiveness' agenda. This aims to ensure the repositioning of an African agenda that is relevant to its stakeholders but does not divorce itself from the neo-liberal agenda, thus allowing the university to compete on a level playing field with northern universities.

Molebatsi, in chapter 4, develops the general rebranding argument of Modise *et al.* to focus on nurturing a specific relationship between one university department and the city council urban planning sector. He describes the contextual issues for urban planning within the city at the needs assessment stage and explores the potential for university/city collaboration, revealing both challenges and opportunities for development.

Chapter 5, by Dube, explores another thematic area of the relationship between the University of Botswana and Gaborone City Council – that of the environment. The chapter outlines the changing environmental issues globally and in Botswana in particular, highlighting the mismatch between externally imposed commercial structures and traditional environmental resource management activities. This mismatch results in new inequalities and learning needs: 'Traditional management styles have been disempowered and the newly introduced ones lack capacity, are not adapted and have generally failed to take on board indigenous systems and practices.'

Dube argues for more lifelong learning (including research and knowledge dissemination) to facilitate local understanding of these changes – a role to which the University of Botswana could contribute in partnership with relevant agencies. She emphasises the need to synergise northern practices with African knowledge bases to facilitate a more organic interrogation of local knowledge systems in the face of globalisation. The failure to do this has resulted in further vulnerability in socio-ecological systems. In this context she challenges African higher education to be an 'agent of change facilitating migration away from the unsustainable, persisting disjointedness in African society between indigenous and modern systems.' She asks for a closer relationship with the African tradition of holistic and practice-based learning, but in a way that embraces the more complex context of contemporary globalisation issues that impact on a regional and global scale.

Mwaikokesya analyses the Tanzanian context in chapter 6 more speculatively, looking specifically at the collaborative role that universities can play in contributing to economic growth within a city or region. He also emphasises the link between indigenous African education that was both holistic and practice oriented, referring to the historical model promoted by the late President Julius Nyerere in Tanzania, who focused on synergising relations between higher education, lifelong learning and the wider society. Mwaikokesya places this issue within the current African policy context of NEPAD, which is an African partnership peer review system designed to secure funding support from international donor agencies. Mwaikokesya provides some examples of regional inter-university networks in Africa, before focusing on the city of Dar es Salaam in Tanzania. Mwaikokesya, too, emphasises the challenges of limited resources as well as the pedagogical systems within universities themselves that hinder partnership development. He finishes with suggestions for how universities might work more collaboratively with other actors such as libraries, and redesign their pedagogical systems to focus on learning rather than education.

The final chapter (Kearns and Ishumi) introduces the PASCAL International Exchange (PIE) online discussion forum designed to facilitate the sharing of ideas and experiences on topics related to the concept of engagement. There are three contributions from Africa and this chapter summarises those papers. The chapter positions the concept of learning cities and regions within a lifelong learning framework where cities are presented as places for informal, non-formal and formal learning. Cities are seen as a hub for resources, mutual exchanges, links to local government and a source of culture. In African contexts, cities are relatively new but also becoming more cosmopolitan. Kearns and Ishumi highlight the fact that rapid urbanisation results in challenges for planning, environmental issues, health, transport, housing, poverty and unemployment. This is the only chapter that refers to a francophone country, Senegal. The authors note that there are similar urbanisation issues for India and other emerging economies, and suggest that an African network of learning cities/regions might benefit from sharing experiences. Following the Botswana theme, they emphasise the need to develop learning cities that draw from cultural contexts and traditions that do not mimic the North.

2

Pathways to an engaged university and learning city: The case of the University of Botswana and Gaborone City

Peggy Gabo Ntseane

Introduction

In the increasingly globalised context, those concerned with higher education institutions' role in contributing to regional development have much to learn from the insights and experiences of the 'Third World' context engagement processes. This chapter looks at an example of engagement in an African context, in this case, Botswana. Discussions with stakeholders and other scholars regionally and internationally have emphasised the need to assess higher education activities in relation to issues of quality, relevance, equity and impact, and especially to assess the way that they affect immediate communities, cities and regions.

Puuka observes that there have been many initiatives across the countries in the Organisation for Economic Co-operation and Development (OECD) to mobilise higher education to support regional 'economic, social and cultural development' (Puuka, 2008, p. 151). Higher education institutions in developing countries such as those in Africa also realise the need to contribute to the debates that will subsequently lead to such engagement. However, given their contextual differences from other higher education institutions and regions of the world, there are still concerns to be addressed that must inform the processes of engagement. For instance, in the case of Botswana there are definitional questions such as, what is engagement and who defines it? As Inman and Schuetze (2010, p. 3) rightly observe, 'in the absence of clear and accepted boundaries, political or geographical, cultural or historical, what defines [regions]?' Furthermore, how does a university's mission and operation change to accommodate its new role of engaging in the development of its neighbouring community or region?

Cognisant of the reality that the new role of engagement had to be relevant and sustainable, the University of Botswana (UB) and its key stakeholders concluded that the process of engagement in this context would have to start with wide consultation and consensus.

Another aspect was that the engagement strategy adopted would have to be relevant to existing regional and national development strategies – namely, Botswana's national long-term strategic development plan (Republic of Botswana, 1997); Gaborone City Council development plan 2020 (Republic of Botswana, 2008); and the University of Botswana strategic plan (University of Botswana, 2008). This approach was essential, not only for ensuring that the engagement strategy for UB and Gaborone City Council was relevant, but also to ensure ownership, which was perceived as critical for its sustainability.

This chapter also sheds light on the processes and benefits of a pathway that recognises the value of international partnerships with experienced higher education institutions and their engaged regions and cities. According to Longworth, the reasons for becoming a learning city or community are 'not only economic, they are also political, cultural and environmental, social and personal' (Longworth, 2006, p. 6).

There are many interpretations of the concept of a 'learning city', but in this chapter the concept should be understood as 'a mechanism for providing a skilled and adaptable workforce, and for fuelling innovation and knowledge creation, and therefore for creating the learning or knowledge society' (Jones, 2010, p. 325).

Based on the benchmarking that was done through the PASCAL Universities Regional Engagement (PURE) research project, the pathway to a learning city in the Botswana context identified employment among small, micro- and medium-sized enterprises (SMMEs); environmental sustainability; culture; and planning as major themes to start the engagement practice. This chapter presents the results of the UB/PURE needs assessment study. It demonstrates how active participation (starting where people already are in terms of development strategies, activities, needs and challenges) and commitment from the city managers, policy makers, politicians, employers and employees (as well as the vast majority of citizens themselves) were essential to establishing ownership of this engagement strategy.

While the UB/City of Gaborone partnership has resulted in a strategic plan for engagement, it is aware of the initial challenges. This chapter identifies the challenge of financing collaborative projects in a context where city institutions, organisations and projects are sponsored by government and where there is restricted access to information and communication technology. These and many other challenges specific to the four themes are discussed in relation to their implications for lifelong learning and development of higher education and regional engagement.

The chapter concludes that the UB and Gaborone City Council engagement pathway is one of many pathways and argues that if regional engagement is the way to go then universities must be willing to change by unlocking their doors to more sections of the population. Other elements for engagement include networking with other universities globally, initiating innovative strategies and satisfying the needs of stakeholders and ordinary people as well as having the ability to manage and sustain best practice.

The Botswana context

According to the last census of 2011 (Central Statistics Office), Gaborone City has a population of 233,135. It is worth noting that villages on the periphery of Gaborone have experienced rapid growth and their populations have more than doubled. This has policy implications for the city. For instance, there are added pressures on provision and distribution of goods and services such as water, food, electricity, sewage, employment, education, health and housing. Poverty also remains one of the development challenges for the city. Environmental issues include lack of renewable energy targets, traffic congestion and refuse disposal challenges. The impact of HIV/AIDS in the city is the ever-increasing number of orphans, the increased pressure on health resources and the negative impacts on the workforce (Tsheko *et al.*, 2007). Finally, the City of Gaborone has the responsibility of contributing to the development and promotion of national, regional and international cultural ties. Informed by this city context, Gaborone City Council saw that partnering with UB for regional engagement would have considerable benefits, including research that would inform development strategies to enhance the quality of the environment, promote human well-being and create employment.

The University of Botswana was established on 1 July 1982 and is closely linked to the national development process of Botswana itself. According to the UB Public Affairs Department (University of Botswana, 2008, p. 8), its special functions are 'to engage in improving the quality and in expanding the quantity of the human resources needed for development, and to act as the repository of the collective knowledge and experience of the nation and the world.'

Universities have traditionally embraced three missions – teaching, research and community service. In relation to the third mission of community service (as outlined in chapter 1), UB has realised that it has hitherto merely been giving lip-service to this function. The UB strategic plan of 2008 included the learning city concept within a priority area of engagement, and the university management has engaged in partnerships that would help the UB community and stakeholders better understand the third mission of universities, especially those operating within a regional context. Concepts related to this mission that have attracted attention include 'the learning city/regions', 'regional engagement' and 'community engagement', to name just a few. As part of a restructuring exercise to ensure that the UB teaching and learning programmes are relevant to the needs of stakeholders, efforts were also made to discuss with stakeholders the need for higher learning institutions to promote the concept that universities must be engaged with their region and conversely that regions would consider universities as one of their greatest assets for development agendas in their respective contexts.

While it was important to embrace the third mission concept, it soon became very clear to UB that an understanding of this concept had to be context specific if it was to inform the development agenda. A comprehensive search of the literature revealed that different definitions emphasised different levels of engagement, depending on the geographic region and functions of the university or other higher learning institution. For instance, Inman and Schuetze (2010, p. 4) observe that, in the USA, land-grant universities see regional development as their mission, while research-based universities are likely to insist that their mandate to service is 'global aggregation of knowledge rather than local application.'

In the context of developing countries, such as in southern Africa – where universities are still in their infancy and where the practical implementation of the third mission of universities is largely sponsored by government – engagement might be thought of as service to the community. UB management decided to adopt a participatory model of engagement as a member of the PURE project, rather than the more conventional service model as discussed in chapter 1.

Public consultation and engagement

In 2008, UB held its first stakeholders' meeting. Partners from the international community were invited to a discussion on the third-mission concepts such as 'learning city' and 'regional engagement'. Two main questions were raised:

- While individual staff and students may undertake community service, could participants see ways in which they could incorporate this work into their teaching and research?
- What is 'regional engagement' in an African context where a 'community', let alone a 'region', is a multifaceted concept based on notions of place, functions of the university, external interests and needs as well as on funding issues and incentives made available to a specific university?

Participants resolved that UB should participate in the PASCAL engagement activities with the main purpose of learning from other PASCAL partners that had relevant international experience. A two-year memorandum of understanding was signed between UB and PASCAL's administrative coordinating institution, the University of Glasgow. As a result of this partnership, UB now had access to information networks such as learning clusters, engagement tools (the benchmarking data collection instruments for regional, institutional and organisational audit) and conferences hosted by any of the 15 regional members of PASCAL.

The meeting also resolved that it was timely for UB to start a systematic, transparent, relevant and practical approach to its 'third mission' in order to be seen as a responsible resident of its immediate community, the City of Gaborone. Since concepts such as sustainability, relevance and ownership of the engagement exercise were emphasised, it was agreed that the City of Gaborone personnel would also participate in the UB/PASCAL partnership activities. UB and the City of Gaborone signed their memorandum of understanding (MoU) on 2 March 2009. Its main purpose was to allow UB to contribute officially to the implementation of the Gaborone City Council development plan and implement UB's strategic plan. Beyond that, it emphasised the need to mobilise resources to turn Gaborone into a learning city through engagement priority goals. For example, one goal is to develop enterprises through knowledge engagement and transfer that will make Gaborone City economically vibrant while preserving its cultural and historic heritage.

A major activity was the PURE project through which a 'needs assessment for UB's regional engagement' would be carried out by a research team made up of experts from UB and relevant departments from Gaborone City Council. The stakeholder consultation meeting had identified four main themes as a focus for the needs assessment study, as mentioned earlier:
- Environmental sustainability
- SMMEs
- Culture
- Planning.

This initial needs assessment was crucial because the expected outcomes would include:
- A definition of the concept of 'regional engagement' which would be relevant to the higher learning institutions context.
- An inventory of current UB/City of Gaborone engagement activities.
- Identification of needs and interest in further engagement which would be relevant to the City of Gaborone's development agenda.
- Identification of thematic areas for the UB/City of Gaborone partnership strategic plan.

Acknowledging that contexts and practices for university engagement may vary with geographic location and institutions of higher learning, UB management and its stakeholders believed they could learn a great deal from experiences elsewhere, hence their participation in PASCAL, which connects four continents of the world, namely, Europe, the Americas, Australia and Africa.

At this stakeholder meeting, UB was commended for its civic initiative which came at the height of historic changes in the demographic, economic, technological and political conditions that affect colleges and universities in southern Africa. Public consultation (local workshops and hosting of the PASCAL conference in December 2010) on the proposed UB engagement strategy was essential for giving potential beneficiaries, the UB community and other higher education institutions in the country and Africa an opportunity to participate and have a voice in defining the issues. This is in line with the Government of Botswana's development principles of democracy, unity, peace, self-help and consultation (Government of Botswana, 2003).

The next section briefly describes the role of participation in UB's pathway to engagement.

Collective agreements

As a result of the first consultation meeting with key stakeholders, described above, it became very clear to UB management that beneficiaries of higher learning institution academic programmes are no longer only interested in lifelong learning, but are also interested in economic, social, political, cultural and environmental benefits that have implications for everyone's quality of life. This confirms the Commission of the European Union's (2000) position that:

> *Lifelong learning is no longer just one aspect of education and training; it must become the guiding principle for provision and participation across the full continuum of learning contexts.*
> (Cited by Longworth, 2006, p. 1)

Botswana PURE research team workshop

The first activity to ensure collective participation in mapping the way forward for the UB/Gaborone City Council regional engagement pathway was a workshop made up of UB and Gaborone City Council research experts. Its purpose was to confirm that the research team understood the concepts 'third mission of universities' and 'engagement', and to examine the PASCAL benchmarking tools and decide how to use them.

It was agreed that the PASCAL tools could be suitable for university academic staff, but were too complex for the broader population. However, it was resolved that they would serve as an excellent reference point, and could be adapted to produce a context-specific instrument or set of instruments that could then be used for the Botswana PURE needs assessment study. The research team used their experience and expertise to propose eight thematic areas to present to stakeholders who would have a say in selecting the final four themes (already outlined above).

PURE research stakeholders' workshop

Another activity was the UB and Gaborone City Council stakeholders' workshop. Participants included PASCAL/PURE project coordinators from Glasgow, the Botswana PURE research team (UB and Gaborone City Council), stakeholders from the organisations with a mandate related to the proposed thematic areas, UB management, representation from UB departments likely to be involved in the study, and local leadership (politicians and chiefs). The purpose of this workshop was to explain the concepts related to 'engagement' to a bigger audience of stakeholders. The research team perceived this to be important because the organisations and institutions represented were potential respondents to the Botswana PURE needs assessment study. The workshop also provided an opportunity to consult stakeholders on the selection of themes for the study.

Focus groups were held with relevant personnel to further inform the research team about practical and pertinent issues in each area. Members of the focus groups were given an opportunity to provide input on the data-collection instrument adapted from the PASCAL benchmarking tools. It was perceived as important that the pathway to an engaged UB adopted a bottom-up approach to ensure that the outcomes were sustainable in a context where development projects are carried out in consultation with residents of communities who are also the major agents of changes in their lives.

Collaboration/networking

The Botswana engagement pathway process benefited from the contribution of international collaborative partnerships, especially the experience and guidance of PASCAL and its partners in other regions of the world. Through the PASCAL/PURE project, a Southern Africa PURE Review Consultation Committee was formed with membership from PASCAL, the National University of Lesotho and the University of South Africa (UNISA).

The committee discussed and validated ideas for UB/Gaborone City Council partnership engagement. As a member of PASCAL, the UB and Gaborone City Council had the opportunity to attend international conferences and hear about experiences from Europe, America, Australia and Africa. UB also had the opportunity to host the ninth PASCAL International Conference in 2010. The major impact of this activity was to encourage participants to forge ahead with the engagement preparations and plans, especially the UB/Gaborone City Council partnership. Stakeholders from Botswana, southern Africa and other regions in Africa, the UB community, students from the region and local leaders (chiefs and politicians) had the opportunity to hear and discuss engagement issues with those who have relevant experience of them.

It is expected that the newly established engagement path is particularly relevant to Botswana's regional context but appropriate contributions from elsewhere are also still valued. As Akbar observes:

> *People must enter the world of scientific and scholarly analysis from the path of their historically and culturally developed perspective. These perspectives are not counter to the universal truth but simply access the universal through the window of one's particular worldview.* (Akbar, 1991, p. 248)

The Botswana engagement preparation process started well, with political, cultural and academic commitment attested by wide consultation, needs assessment and international benchmarking validation. The next section looks at the implementation and presents the results of the needs assessment study that would inform the UB/Gaborone City Council engagement activities.

The Botswana/PURE needs assessment study results

The aims of the needs assessment survey were to:
- Assess the perception by external stakeholders of the level of consultation that UB engages them in on matters pertaining to environmental sustainability, economic activities (especially those related to SMMEs), cultural issues and planning activities
- Audit the perception, by strategic units within UB, on the level to which the institution engages the external stakeholders on matters pertaining to the identified thematic areas.

Methodology
To achieve the first aim, a list was drawn up of stakeholders in Gaborone with strong links to the four themes. This came from the internet, UB and Gaborone City Council collaboration networks, Botswana Telecommunication Corporation (BTC), and the non-governmental organisation (NGO) directories. Then semi-structured questionnaires were prepared to collect the data required for the themes. A total of 125 stakeholders were identified, representing themes

from the NGOs, central government, the parastatals, the private sector and Gaborone City Council. A response rate of 80 per cent was achieved, which was regarded as adequate to provide a meaningful overview of the level to which UB was interacting with its external stakeholders since Gaborone is still a relatively small city. In order to facilitate basic and valid statistical procedures, the raw frequencies were translated by a simple multiple of ten. This chapter provides only summaries.

To realise the second aim, four UB institutional offices that capture information pertaining to the University of Botswana were identified. These were the offices of Research and Development, Deputy Vice Chancellor Academic Affairs, Institutional Planning and Public Affairs. In addition, relevant faculty and department staff and student representatives participated in the study. These were from the departments of Environmental Science; Culture, Sports and Recreation; Architecture and Planning, and Business. The student association on the main campus was also involved, as were respondents from the commercial sector (the wholesale and retail trade, real estate).

Findings of the PURE needs assessment study

The needs assessment study showed that (in order of importance) stakeholders expect higher learning institutions such as UB to provide public education, carry out research and consultancy, partner with other organisations in the country, and provide in-service training for diverse development agendas. When asked if they were aware of a UB mandate to engage stakeholders, it was mostly stakeholders from central government who were aware. Others included commercial enterprises and real estate, city council employees and NGOs.

Although there were examples of previous collaboration between UB and external stakeholders in promoting development activities to support the thematic areas, it was generally observed that further work was needed if the UB engagement pathway was to be more relevant. Both the proceedings of the stakeholder workshops and the assessment study results revealed that the collaboration that takes place is fragmented and is confined to research activities and student practicums (Ntseane, 2010).

Perceived areas of potential collaboration identified by stakeholders included public education, research, in-service training (such as short courses by request) and sharing of resources. When asked to identify UB's weaknesses in collaboration, participants stated that UB was too academic and did not consult sufficiently: 'We never know what UB is doing behind or next to our fence,' said one stakeholder.

Finally, participants were asked to identify what they see as threats for future collaboration with UB. The responses were: lack of funding (68 per cent of responses), competition from upcoming institutions (22 per cent), and lack of commitment on the part of the diverse organisations of the City of Gaborone (10 per cent) – especially relating to the private sector and the SMMEs that struggle to survive.

Findings from the needs assessment show there is a general lack of knowledge about the university's operational system for sustainable development in the thematic areas. This lack of consensus reflects an absence of coherent and consistent goals, policies and collaboration programmes. Stakeholders believe an engagement strategy is needed because what has been done so far has been sporadic and uncoordinated.

Given the results of the needs assessment, what are the implications for higher education institutions and regional engagement in the Botswana context? The next section presents the perceived opportunities and potential challenges for the UB pathway to learning city engagement.

Challenges and opportunities for the proposed UB learning city engagement strategy

Overall, an analysis of the needs assessment study results and UB's preparation for engagement shows both opportunities and challenges. The key stakeholders and organisations representing the four themes perceive four main opportunities for a successful UB/City of Gaborone learning city strategy.

The first opportunity relates to perceived mutual gains in access to resources. UB and the City of Gaborone, central government, the private sector and NGOs welcomed the idea of a partnership as something that will improve service delivery and production on their part. The university mentioned the possibility of accessing resources for intensifying research in areas that matter to organisations. For example, market-based production and finance management research were identified by the Faculty of Business staff and students as activities likely to be financed by the City of Gaborone business community. Furthermore, through student internship programmes, the business community in return saw the benefit of the university providing access to techno-logical innovation and ideas and hands-on practice. This finding confirms the literature (Varga, 1997) which concluded that private organisations are likely to increase their financial or other support to universities when such collaborations take place. Furthermore, projects that involve university–industry links attract increased government subsidies.

Second, it was perceived that an engagement strategy between higher education institution research departments and Gaborone City Council would increase interest in community-based research. For example, instead of being the object of academic research, the Department of Environmental Affairs would be in a position to define the focus and the methodology of the research topics in its area of expertise. As one environmental specialist put it, 'in fact where possible, we could even budget for such research if it is seen as critical for the implementation of the City Development Plan.'

Third, stakeholders from fields related to adult education (such as vocational and basic education) highlighted the potential to widen participation and diversification of teaching modes. For instance, the Department of Out-of-School Education Training (DOSET), the vocational training institutions and NGOs believed that an engagement partnership would result in the introduction of more academic programmes that could be undertaken flexibly and on a part-time basis.

Fourth, participants in this needs assessment study acknowledged that higher learning institutions have the capacity to develop competitive advantages in the local market as well as to create innovation. An example cited was in the area of SMMEs where the Faculty of Business, especially its Business Clinic, could facilitate capacity-building training to ensure that SMME clients acquire skills such as finance management, customer relations and marketing. Through assistance from the Faculty of Science and Technology, SMME production businesses could benefit from technological innovation initiated by students.

Based on these opportunities, the UB engagement pathway has generated commitment and enthusiasm, as attested by the signing of the memorandum of understanding and promises of collaborative research by UB and Gaborone City Council management. However, for universities to undertake engagement successfully, there must be changes in the way they are managed so that engagement moves from being the activity of individual academics to an institution-wide approach. This has implications for capacity building for both the higher learning institution and the region or community.

Challenges

The results of this study also revealed that there were challenges that would have to be factored in when the UB/Gaborone City Council partnership strategic plan was crafted. Five challenges were highlighted.

First, pressure of resources was identified as a major constraint because the central government budget does not highlight engagement as a funding stream for UB or the City Council. This point was illustrated thus: 'Currently both UB and government/City of Gaborone departments' budgets do not cater for engagement possibilities.' Another participant said, 'Without this financial commitment, and decreased budget cuts at times of economic crisis, the partners may pursue business as usual despite signed MoUs and proposed engagement projects.' This is a real threat even for the implementation of the pilot activities recommended in the UB engagement strategic plan. However, with a culture of collective working, the draft plan can be used to mobilise the business community, government and UB management to introduce a budget line for at least one or two engagement activities.

Second, it is possible that there is a lack of commitment to partnership engagement. Given the private sector's focus on profit making, sustainability concerns were raised. As one person put it, 'Some academic research even in the relevant area may not bring immediate returns expected by a profit-oriented organisation. This might impact adversely on having research as a priority for both funding and time.'

Third, the UB lecturers also questioned the sustainability of the UB/Gaborone City Council engagement activities, which would impact on how engagement could be institutionalised in the university. One academic articulated it thus: 'While UB frequently promotes service as a mission equal to teaching and research, this commitment is not reflected in the faculty reward system.' In the past, staff members who preferred to be involved more in service or applied scholarship were frustrated to the point where they had to give up this kind of work when they realised that it would not advance their careers.

Fourth, there remain questions about clarity of purpose. Although at first the coordinating committee thought it understood the concept of 'engagement' and how it was different from 'service to the community', once there were more than 50 stakeholders fully engaged in the deliberations, it became very clear that more time was needed to clarify the purpose of engagement in the various social dimensions identified by multiple and diverse stakeholders. Ultimately, UB and the Gaborone City Council stakeholders adopted the definition of 'engagement' in our context as:

> *A two-way process that makes the resources of the university accessible to external communities for their benefit and the resources of these communities available for the advantage of the university.* (Ntseane, 2010, p. 5)

Finally, the Botswana experience of benchmarking tools revealed that there could be difficulty in measuring highly complex engagement relations and processes. For example, after trying the tools with stakeholders, the Botswana PURE research team decided to adapt them to our context. This resulted in a shorter and more manageable tool for the study.

Similarly, the UB strategy will have to respond to the question 'how will engagement be measured?' Although the needs assessment benefited from the benchmarking approach, UB could expand this literature on measuring university engagement and include an appropriate, context-specific, measurement strategy in its proposed engagement strategy document. The literature (Lall, 2009) has distinguished different types of measurement such as audit, benchmarking and evaluation. According to Lall (*ibid.*, p. 75) the audit approach usually involves the description and simple measurement of interventions to see whether what was promised has been delivered. This approach is represented by surveys that rely on qualitative measures and templates of projects. The evaluation approach, on the other hand, is concerned with assessing whether the best outcome was realised and identifying best practices. This approach may include standard indicators, surveys and institutional reviews. The benchmarking type of measurement focuses more on the collection of information that allows an organisation to compare itself with others in ways that show a process of self-improvement. Thus this approach requires a combination of quantitative indicators and a comparative analysis of practices.

Even with these challenges, the needs assessment study analysis showed that both the UB/City of Gaborone partnership and 125 stakeholders that participated confirmed that higher education institutions such as UB can and should contribute to the development of the City of Gaborone and the nation at large.

Conclusion

Higher education has the potential to influence regional development because of its focus on research and its dominant position in training experts
and producing technologically innovative products. Moreover, the impact of
Gaborone City Council on the engagement partnership agenda was seen as
paramount, especially as a basket for collecting the social issues and problems that need research and development.

Another major finding of the Botswana PURE assessment study is that most
participants still view a university such as UB as a traditional education centre. The biggest impediment to successful collaboration, according to the participants, is having limited information about the university's purpose and activities. For example, analysis of data from the SMMEs theme revealed that
most firms in Gaborone do not know what the university does besides education. It was also an interesting revelation that university researchers and administration staff have only a limited understanding of business needs and the
potential business applications of their research. This conclusion is unfortunate
because there is an increasingly important role for universities and research
institutions as knowledge centres to improve and disseminate comprehensive
information to support regional development – which is the core business of
communities such as the City of Gaborone.

Finally, based on the findings of the four themes (environmental sustainability, culture, SMMEs and planning) it is recommended that the UB/Gaborone
City Council partnership strategic plan should consider appropriate thematic
policies for different development paths rather than a 'one size fits all' solution. Given the economic situation (for example, limited funding which has
been aggravated by the global recession), it was emphasised that the City
of Gaborone's regional development needs require an engagement partnership that will build on existing capacities rather than attempting to craft new
strategies.

References

Akbar, N. (1991) 'Evolution of human psychology for African Americans',
in R. Jones (Ed.) *Black Psychology*, second edition. Berkeley, CA: Cobb and
Henry Publications, pp. 99–123.

Central Statistics Office (2011) *Botswana Population Census Report.* Gaborone: Government Printer.

Government of Botswana (2003) *National Development Plan 9.* Gaborone: Government Printer.

Inman, P. and Schuetze, H.G. (Eds) (2010) *The Community Engagement and Service Mission of Universities.* Leicester: NIACE.

Jones, R. (2010) 'Learning cities: What do people think? Summary of a case study', in N. Longworth and M. Osborne (Eds) *Perspectives on Learning Cities and Regions: Policy, Practice and Participation.* Leicester: NIACE, pp. 323–35.

Lall, S. (2009) 'Why should we evaluate social enterprises?' in S. Lall, V. Somic, E. Schroeder and E. Schmidt (Eds) *Identifying Spatial Efficiency–Equity Tradeoffs in Territorial Development Policies.* Washington: World Bank, pp. 1–29.

Longworth, N. (2006) *Learning Cities, Learning Regions, Learning Communities: Lifelong Learning and Local Government.* London: Routledge.

Ntseane, P.G. (2010) 'PASCAL report to Gaborone region: PURE 2009–2010'. Unpublished report.

Puuka, P. (2008) 'The role of higher education institutions in building regional innovation systems', *Regional Science,* Vol. 9 No 2, pp. 271–86.

Republic of Botswana (1997) *Botswana Long Term Strategic Development Plan: Vision 2016.* Gaborone: Government Printer.

Republic of Botswana (2008) 'Review of Gaborone City development plan 1997–2021. Draft development plan'. Unpublished report. Gaborone City Council.

Tsheko, G.N., Bainame, K., Odirile, L.W. and Segwabe, M. (2007) *A Baseline Study on Psychosocial Support of Orphans and Vulnerable Children in Two Villages in Botswana.* Cape Town: HSRC Press.

University of Botswana (2008) *A Strategy for Excellence: University of Botswana's Strategic Plan to 2016 and Beyond.* Gaborone: University of Botswana.

Varga, A. (1997) 'Regional economic effects of university research: a survey'. Retrieved 2 April 2012 from http://www.rri.wvu.edu/pdffiles/surveyattila.pdf

3

Engagement with the city: A new paradigm for rebranding institutions of higher education

Oitshepile MmaB Modise and Dama Mosweunyane

Introduction

The competitive forces of the global knowledge and innovation-based economy since the turn of the twenty-first century have attracted a lot of debate from researchers and scholars. As a result there is increasing 'economic competitiveness and in response to declining public funding, universities have embarked upon a fundamental reassessment and redefinition of their outreach mission' (Franklin *et al.*, 2008, p. 206). The third mission of universities, community engagement, is an academic activity in which a university's teaching and learning are integrated with research activities that involve the community as genuine partners (Wallis, 2006). It is through 'engagement forms of teaching and research, [that] faculty connect their academic expertise to public purposes as a way of fulfilling the core mission of the academic institution' (Holland, 2005, p. 3). The authors share the sentiments that 'unless our institutions respond to the challenges and opportunities before them they risk being consigned to a sort of academic Jurassic Park – of great historic interest, fascinating places to visit, but increasingly irrelevant in a world that has passed them by' (Kellogg Commission, 1999, cited in Alperovitz *et al.*, 2008, p. 3). When universities engage with the complex problems in their communities, there are gains in terms of scholarship, teaching and learning. Interdisciplinary efforts gain academic vitality and public relevance that synergistically benefit each other (Franklin *et al.*, 2008).

Institutions of higher education the world over are faced with the challenge of branding themselves in a way that bridges the gap with stakeholders. The stakeholders feel much greater ownership of the university if they are able to translate the brand into a creative and tangible effort. It is on this basis that universities are making deliberate attempts to create awareness and engage the communities around them.

It is argued here that an important feature of professional institutions of higher learning is the ability to rebrand and maintain and enhance the brand. This chapter discusses how proactive engagement with stakeholders could be a useful tool for rebranding universities. First, the authors outline how universities in the political south have been moulded by post-industrial economic and political forces. Then we argue for demystification and de-institutionalisation of the university as we know it. Third, we discuss the changing voice of ordinary citizens in the university and the need to rebrand, using the University of Botswana as an example. Finally, we highlight the need to foster a process of dialogue over contemporary issues of national interest, finishing with some concluding remarks about the ongoing challenges for universities on the African continent.

African universities in the post-colonial era

Universities in Africa, including the University of Botswana, have not yet been able to establish their ideological base informed by realities that prevail in the continent. The African institutions of learning in the former colonies continue to be used by the political north to promote their agenda of subjugation, which is meant to obliterate the knowledge that Africans can identify with. Universities in Africa have served their colonial powers by focusing on non-African cultures and concepts. Consequently, African universities seldom promote indigenous knowledge that can foster African identity. It comes as no surprise that Mazrui (1980) once described universities in Africa primarily as institutions for the promotion of Eurocentric civilisation. He proposed that they should rewrite text books and reconstitute them to include African experiences. Years after the concern was raised, there are hardly any examples of departments or faculties in African universities that are consciously trying to restore the African heritage.

The universities in the continent of Africa not only failed to heed the call for Africanisation of knowledge, but have also ignored that which presented Africa as a continent of discovery. Brock-Utne (1999) cites Ki-Zerbo as having raised a concern that, well before the other continents, Africa was a producer of education and teaching systems which have since not been promoted or labelled as African. The author laments that it is all too often forgotten that Africa was the first continent to know literacy and to institute a school system. Thousands of years before the Greek letters 'alpha' and 'beta' were invented, roots of the world alphabet, and before the use of the Latin word *schola*, from which the word 'school' derives, the scribes of ancient Egypt wrote, read, administered and philosophised using papyrus. It is also important to appreciate that some authors, such as Sylvester (1999), note that despite the overwhelming reality of economic decline, unimaginable poverty, wars, malnutrition, disease, and political instability, African cultural productivity grows briskly. It is interesting that this appreciation of Africa's cultural uniqueness is promulgated by Christine Sylvester who is not an African and yet African academics ignore this reality.

Institutions in Africa, just like the countries in which they exist, are impecunious. This makes them consumers of northern resources and knowledge, which have been released with some conditionality – the most obvious of which is that all nations have been compelled to adopt 'civilisation' into their midst at the outset. The political north wanted to create a world after its own image (Ake, 1978). It is important to note that the African universities (which were moulded as institutions to promote Eurocentric culture) embraced this concept of civilisation and produced individuals who undermined their own culture, which was portrayed as barbaric by the powers from the political north. The institutions failed to recognise that the education of both the young and adult population in developing countries had more urgency and importance than education in developed and industrialised countries (Koma, 1974). This meant that African universities should have provided a form of education to accelerate the development of the continent. Instead, they mimicked those in industrialised countries, reproducing their structures and theories and responding to their research demands with research that was fully funded by northern countries.

It was a common belief among the colonial educationalists that a curriculum that stressed abstract knowledge was too complicated for Africans to grasp (Kelly, 1984). This view has resulted in the indigenous knowledge of African nations being undermined, if not ridiculed, by their universities. The universities in Africa have adopted attitudes from the political north, where universities generate knowledge *for* communities instead of *with* them, thus maintaining the traditional university attitudes that offer expertise rather than appreciation of indigenous knowledge (Inman and Schuetze, 2010).

In many cases, expatriates dominated the academic population of African universities, thus promoting even further the obtrusion of northern cultures and their capitalist values. This arrangement meant that the pre-colonial education system did not have any place within African universities. This education provided a link between general knowledge and practical life. It was linked to production, social life and culture, both through the use of mother tongue and through the incorporation of cultural practices such as games, dancing, music and sports (Brock-Utne, 1999).

The education provided by the University of Botswana, for instance, failed to focus on making its recipients critical thinkers who were prepared to deal with the maladies that besieged their respective communities, their nation and the international arena. It also failed to be guided by the great leaders from the African continent. For example, African universities did not respond to the words of Dr Julius Nyerere, as cited by Koma (1974), who stated that our education must ensure that the educated, as distinguished from the merely certificated, should know themselves to be an integral part of the nation and recognise the responsibility to give a greater service. Education must equip an individual with an inquiring mind to learn from what others do and reject or adapt it to his or her own needs. It must instil in the educated a basic confidence in their own positions as free and equal members of society, who value others and are valued by them for what they do and not for what they obtain (Koma, 1974). On the contrary, the academics in African universities cocooned themselves within their institutions, only emerging with briefcases to collect data from the impoverished in villages. The information collected through researches conducted in rural areas of Africa has only served to produce articles for northern journals and reports for northern libraries. It is notable, for instance, that one of the most comprehensive libraries on Africa is held by the School of Oriental and African Studies in the UK, rather than in Africa.

This colonial inheritance, which concentrated on education for an elite few, meant that African governments, even after independence, continued to neglect education both quantitatively – as evidenced by the numbers enrolled in schools – and qualitatively. This same education has since been blamed for being inappropriate and too dominated by colonial culture, and for spoiling the indigenous culture (Coleman in Watson, 1982). The same issue was observed in the Asian countries, such as Japan, where national survival by educated Japanese depended on careful study and emulation of the ideas and technology that gave Western colonial powers their advantages. Everything Western, from natural science to literary realism, was hungrily soaked up by Japanese intellectuals (Buruma and Margalit, 2004). Interestingly, however, the Asian intellectuals still managed to contribute significantly to the development of their continent compared with intellectuals in Africa. At the start of the twenty-first century, Africa is once again seen by many in the political north (and in the East) as marginal to world affairs, and increasingly so. As other parts of the old 'Third World', especially the rising economic powers of China and India, emerge onto the global stage, Africa seems to be left behind. Mired with poverty, debt, corruption and conflict, the continent is still perceived as 'particular', as 'beyond the pale' (Parker and Rathbone, 2007). African universities still remain closed to the ordinary people and have contributed little to the economic and political advancement of their continent. Some European academics have, out of frustration and guilt, left Africa and headed to their ideological homes in the political north (Narciso, 1999).

The migration of academics from the African continent to industrialised countries, and the continued exclusion of ordinary people from universities, have partly been made possible because Africans are educated in a manner completely divorced from their national roots. This form of training has served to maintain and promote the anti-national character of the current bureaucratic neo-bourgeois intelligentsia and its academics, resulting in a lack of confidence in the people of Africa, their capacities and 'genius', focusing instead on the continent's lack of ability and its corruption. These are phenomena related to the role assumed by colonial education, which refused to dissipate when the flags of colonising empires left the continent of Africa (Moumouni, 1968). The southern part of Africa is evidently most affected by European culture, as noted by Thompson (1982) who averred that Western culture made more pervasive inroads into the African societies of southern Africa than those further north.

Changing global expectations, however, are creating a window of opportunity for African universities to redress these issues from within. It is now time for universities in southern Africa to reverse past trends and engage with the nation's citizenry in this endeavour. The second part of this chapter discusses the current context for African universities, followed by a rationale for the rebranding process for higher education, with evidence of some favourable environments in which this could happen. It takes the University of Botswana as its exemplar, highlighting a variety of rebranding strategies that would link the university more closely to the needs of its capital city. The final section concludes with observations on some ongoing challenges for the continent as a whole in this respect.

Demystification and de-institutionalisation of the university as we know it

It is important that universities in the Third World, and in Africa particularly, close the gap between themselves and the wider population. However, African universities are faced with a daunting challenge because the continent is engulfed in serious development problems. What is even more imperative is that the prevailing development strategies and policies are re-examined carefully to determine why they have been difficult to implement and, more importantly, why they have not succeeded in reversing the crises, such as poverty, once they are implemented.

One problem for the universities in Africa is the obtrusion of conditionalities imposed by the World Bank and the International Monetary Fund and also by associated donors to the education sector. Donor policies, for example, have insisted on an increase in user fees at the universities in Africa and the reduction of funding support for books, food and tuition fees – making universities in Africa become places of learning only for the children of the well-to-do. Due to lack of resources, African universities are compelled to seek donor support for their departments, faculties and research institutes from more affluent universities in the north (Brock-Utne, 1999). This arrangement has distanced African universities from the ordinary people because they serve those northern universities they are linked to or those from which they beg resources. The north has used discourses in its post-colonialism drive to protect and spread northern culture through cultural hegemonic strategies and also to promote the ineradicable idea of north-centredness, sometimes simply conflated as 'west-centredness' (Yang *et al.*, 2006).

It is crucial that new alternatives be proposed (Mengisteab, 1996), which is a challenge that the academics in Africa cannot afford to ignore if they are to remain relevant to the continent. The demystification and de-institutionalisation of concepts is what has to form a starting point in working with cities. However, this requires reversal of the colonising plans that are built on the assumption that local people are unenlightened. The universities, just like civil society, should counter the plan to force them to obey the moralities and values set up by their external rulers (Yang *et al.*, 2006).

It is therefore important for African universities to insist that stakeholders buy into the idea of allowing them to become more responsive to the economic and political demands of the continent.

54

The call for African universities to become more responsive to the demands of the continent is not new: it was advanced at the UNESCO/Economic Commission for Africa conference of university leaders and outside participants in Tananarive, Madagascar in 1962. The consensus at the conference was that universities were a 'key instrument for national development', a concept that later gave rise to the notion of a 'developmental university' – that is, a university with its work and mission directed towards the attainment of concrete and demonstrable development goals. A decade later, at a workshop organised in Accra by the Association of African Universities (itself conceived at the Tananarive conference), African university leaders and policy makers who dominated the event agreed on the need to have African university problems defined and solutions proposed and implemented by Africans. The universities needed a truly 'African identity' in order to escape from colonial hangovers and become more imaginative and enterprising (Yesufu cited by Sawyerr, 2004, p. 3).

There is a need for African universities to embark on demystifying knowledge and to look at the appropriateness of their research if they are to escape from the overabundance of influence from the North. For example, research reports by scholars from African universities should be made more comprehensible, so that their content can be consumed not only by experts. Most importantly they should embrace indigenous knowledge and open universities to the general public for mutual education. People should be free to learn, say what they think and know what others think, to organise in furtherance of their common interests. The people's interests and desires can only be known when they are free and have access to channels to express them (South Commission, 1990). The African universities should therefore take the responsibility of creating the necessary channels for ordinary people to identify and communicate their interests.

The university and the ordinary citizen: why rebranding

You do not only want to be considered the best of the best, you want to be considered the only ones who do what you do. (Garcia, cited in Aarker, 2001, p. 192)

The general shift in development assistance over the last three decades – from state-directed to market-driven policies – has accelerated in the new millennium. This means that the responsibility for providing social services has increasingly shifted from government ministries to civil society and to private and commercial institutions. By nature, though to varying degrees, these are more sensitive to market demand and customer or beneficiary readiness to pay (Modise, 2005). The African university, for instance, no longer enjoys the monopoly of being the sole provider of tertiary education. There is increasing competition from other providers, including private and international universities, which now bring their programmes closer to the market. This has also increased the demand for accountability from the ordinary citizen who demands an education that addresses their pressing and felt needs, not just education for the sake of it. The African university can no longer afford the luxury of enjoying its ivory-tower status because of the imperative to position itself strategically. This involves articulating and promoting its public image and revitalising the way it is perceived by its stakeholders compared with the image of its competitors.

When discussing the scholarship of engagement in the context of America, Boyer (1996) argued that colleges and universities are one of the greatest hopes for intellectual and civic progress. For this hope to be fulfilled, the academy must become a more vigorous partner in the search for answers to our most pressing social, civic, economic and moral problems, and must reaffirm its historic commitment to the scholarship of engagement. While the authors are not advocating duplicating American education, these statements have some relevance for the African university. Scholarship of engagement is described as:

> *Through engaged forms of teaching and research, faculty connect their academic expertise to public purposes as a way of fulfilling the core mission of the academic institution.* (Holland, 2005, p. 3)

Furthermore, engagement should be seen as a mutual, reciprocal and collaborative relationship between a university and external partner. This is endorsed by Wallis (2006, p. 2), who argues that 'community engagement is now better defined as a two-way relationship leading to productive partnerships that yield mutually beneficial outcomes'.

This partnership should be purposeful and aimed at achieving specific results. While this engagement is for the public good, we must hasten to acknowledge that it also helps to project a positive public image of our institutions of higher learning. Our argument in this chapter is that engagement can serve as a useful tool for rebranding institutions of higher learning. The mutual, reciprocal and collaborative nature of the process adds to the knowledge base and practice of these institutions. It is the responsibility of institutions of higher learning to protect the image of their product, and an understanding of market needs can therefore assist in realigning their brand. In the midst of the rigour of current market competition, the African university is faced with the challenge of continuously injecting excitement into its operations and programmes. In order to succeed, the academy should shift from its one-way, ivory-tower, discipline-based, episodic relationships with its broader communities to engage with complex societal problems. This would increase universities' public relevance and enhance their role as partners in building stronger regions and communities (Kellogg Commission, 1999).

The benefits of building such partnerships are enjoyed both by the universities and the communities with which they engage. The benefits for universities are articulated by Wallis (2006) who identifies, among many other benefits: productive relations with communities; enhanced teaching and learning outcomes through increased opportunities for student experiential learning and internships; and improved research productivity. The benefits for the community include: research outcomes that are socially robust; transfer of knowledge to the community; economic growth; linking the community with the wider world; development of human and social capital; and sustainable development, to mention a few (Wallis, 2006; Garlick and Pryor, 2003).

Professional training programmes in African universities, especially in the southern African region, are being established and growing at a time when:

> ... those same universities are under increased fiscal and political pressure from governments to justify expenditures in terms of enrolments and actual contributions to development and when the nature of social demand for human service professionals is itself undergoing profound changes. (Modise, 2005, p. 5)

The University of Botswana

Botswana is making a transition from a resource-based economy to a knowledge-based economy. This transition inevitably places an increased demand on tertiary education for skilled graduate-level people capable of meeting the changing requirements of the labour market and of creating self-employment (Tertiary Education Council, 2005).

The University of Botswana (UB) envisions itself as a centre of academic excellence in Africa and the world. This vision is partially dependent on the partnerships that could be established with relevant stakeholders, including its host city, to promote sound education for students. UB's mission spells out its central purpose and shared values, and highlights the role of partnership in the provision of relevant education for national development as well as delivery of competitive and sustainable programmes. It is on this premise that the national Vision 2016 encourages 'smart partnerships' – an atmosphere of mutual engagement on matters of common interest in a manner that builds strong, lasting and satisfying relationships. These relationships among institutions will extend to all stakeholders including, in the case of the institution of higher learning, learners (as customers), employees and the communities in which it operates.

In line with the assertions in the first part of this chapter, UB has been accused in some quarters of producing a crop of functionally unemployable graduates who possess certificates without relevant education. The problem of unemployed graduates is an issue of concern. Proactive engagement with all stakeholders and implementation of educational values espoused in our vision and mission statements should include a commitment to increase the involvement of our stakeholders. Additionally, programmes have to be innovative and influential to connect universities, their alumni and the notion of service. Alumni associations help in strengthening community engagement through a lifelong relationship with the university, its students, and fellow alumni. The relationship could be sustained through meaningful service and leadership.

The most acute problem for which citizens demand resolution is the employability of graduates when they complete their studies. Universities are challenged to demonstrate to employers and other stakeholders that their graduates bring to the field a set of skills and knowledge that are demonstrably useful for addressing contemporary issues (Modise, 2005). One of the key activities is to benchmark – in other words, to compare performance with other institutions with a view to identifying ideas for improvement and formulating standards for operation. This exercise accords us the opportunity to identify the costs and performance levels of competitors and how they achieve them. It helps to identify our own shortcomings in light of the competition. According to Aarker (2008), a strategic positioning means that the strategy should reflect a long-term effort to gain advantage in the market over competitors.

Efforts to rebrand should assist in giving programmes a personality so that they are more memorable and better liked than those of competitors. Rebranding work should resonate with stakeholder needs.

There are clear expectations from policy makers, employers, parents and students that UB will produce employable graduates. This expectation reflects international trends in which higher education institutions are increasingly expected to produce graduates who can compete successfully in national and international labour markets and can be self-employed. There is therefore a need for dialogue among stakeholders to foster a sense of partnership and shared ownership of the curriculum.

Professional and alumni associations have the social capital and power to regulate their fields and foster the process of dialogue over contemporary issues of national interest. This adds value to the usual, practical reasons to acquire a qualification. It is therefore important for UB to ensure that it supports alumni and professional associations, includes internship programmes in all subjects and fosters a spirit of volunteerism as part of preparation for the world of work, life and active citizenship. In the case of UB, there are fragmented efforts across the university to enhance and take into account employability attributes. The new *Learning and Teaching Policy* (University of Botswana, 2008a) outlines graduate attributes for all programmes, which include entrepreneurship and employability skills. University departments have advisory committees that play a role on behalf of employer stakeholders. Some programmes organise annual careers fairs where both alumni and potential employers are involved and the university careers counselling unit offers careers fairs, meetings with employers and training in job-seeking skills. The Department of Institutional Planning conducts a series of regular surveys on UB graduate destinations and employer satisfaction. These initiatives are significant for cultivating partnerships and providing feedback to the university.

UB has in its strategic plan for NDP 10 'Providing relevant and high quality programmes' as its priority area number 2 (University of Botswana, 2008b, p. 11). This includes the goal of better preparing students for the world of work and implementing a graduate employability strategy. The graduate employability strategy has been formulated with input from all stakeholders, both internal and external. Among the findings of the studies carried out during the process of formulating the strategy in 2009, was that the private sector is more concerned with skills and behaviours than with specific knowledge. This is especially the case because knowledge in certain industries quickly becomes obsolete and the skill of acquiring new knowledge becomes paramount. It emerged that employers expect professionals to be at work on time and, in most cases, professionally attired. Characteristics such as a good work ethic and enthusiasm about the job are important whether at entry level or for senior managers. Better communication between academic staff and host organisations during student internships would go a long way towards establishing and reinforcing professional conduct.

We acknowledge efforts by institutions of higher learning to engage a variety of stakeholders. For instance, UB organised a stakeholder forum in 2007 with a view to strengthening engagement between employers and the university. The forum was meant to calibrate how best there could be collaboration to develop Botswana's human resource base. Perhaps the most effective interaction with potential employers will come through industry research as university researchers in all disciplines work closely with industry to develop innovations. Students at all levels could work under the supervision of such researchers, gaining the skills and exposure to enhance their employability (University of Botswana, 2008c).

However, there remain a number of challenges if African universities are to build a stronger engagement relationship with their cities.

Some ongoing challenges for African universities

Lack of resources will without doubt present two major, conspicuous challenges across the continent. The first challenge is that well-resourced universities in developed countries would benefit immensely from their expansion into Africa through part-time and online programmes. This situation would further aggravate the already deteriorating financial situation for African universities, which would not attract students who could avail themselves of alternative opportunities from Asian, European and American universities for both face-to-face and online courses. It is therefore important for African universities to make a funding appeal to governments, private entities and individuals within African countries.

It has been suggested that one option would be to introduce a small tax known as a Tobin tax. According to Singh (1999), Friedman (1970) and Shiller and Tobin (1999), this form of tax was proposed by the economist Professor James Tobin in 1972. It is a tax on short-term currency trades between countries.

The tax revenue from such currency trades could be earmarked to pay for the infrastructure of African universities; this should be done overtly to avoid further distancing universities in the African continent from the ordinary people. Such an injection of cash would enable increased student enrolment.

The second challenge relates to the lack of resources in African universities for research on topics that are relevant to their contexts. This further alienates universities from the ordinary African citizenry and compromises their important function to take part in the development of their countries. Academics within African universities often supplement their income with more lucrative roles outside their institutional mandates. This also means that well-resourced institutions in the political north may intensify their brain-drain drive, which could academically incapacitate African institutions, rendering them 'white elephants'. It is therefore important for the African universities to provide courses on patriotism and Africanism so that citizens of African countries can attach value to serving their own people and their continent rather than give the highest priority to the accumulation of wealth. The patriotism and Africanisation programmes may not bring returns immediately, but will in the long run discourage Africans from migrating to foreign countries for better remuneration and working conditions. Such programmes would also provide leaders with the qualities required to serve their continent with distinction, selflessness and industriousness.

The economic recession presents another challenge for African universities, which are in most cases impecunious – a condition that compels them to depend on external resources. There are negative implications in the areas of research and teaching in particular, since fewer resources are allocated for the purpose of generating knowledge and disseminating it. Most importantly, there is a need for the universities in Africa to research the best strategies for generating resources, including financial resources. As noted by Banya and Elu (2001), the issue of financing higher education in sub-Saharan Africa has not been given sufficient coverage in the relevant literature and the paucity of research can be partially attributed to the assumption that national governments finance higher education (Banya and Elu, 2001). It is crucial for African universities to seek partnership within African regions so that resources that are available for use by the universities can be shared. It is therefore imperative that African universities find the best approaches to liberate themselves from economic and political dependency. This means they should rigorously work towards bridging the gap that they have created over the years between themselves and the ordinary people. This will provide the necessary justification for them to receive resources from governments and donors within their countries for their activities.

Conclusion

This chapter has demonstrated that African universities have to reawaken to the challenges of rebranding themselves. Engagement is seen as a useful tool for rebranding in the sense that it brings socio-economic and cultural benefits and is a mutually beneficial process. The authors have articulated how the post-colonial era has had a profound influence on African universities and we emphasise the need to critically reshape them by recognising the responsibility to engage. We argue that the demystification and de-institutionalisation of concepts should be the starting point for engagement – for example, scholars from African universities should produce comprehensible research reports that could be utilised by communities. We conclude that for the African university to succeed in its engagement efforts, there should be dialogue with all stakeholders to ensure curricula are relevant to national development needs, and academics should be motivated to see their role more positively in this respect.

References

Aarker, D.A. (2001) *Strategic Market Management*. Hoboken, NJ: John Wiley and Sons.

Ake, C. (1978) *Revolutionary Pressures in Africa*. London: Zed Press.

Alperovitz, G., Dubb, S. and Howard, T. (2008) 'The next wave: Building university engagement for the 21st century'. Pre-publication version of article published in *The Good Society*, Vol. 17 No 2, pp. 69–75.

Banya, K. and Elu, J. (2001) 'Implementing basic education: An African perspective', *International Review of Education*, Vol. 43 Nos 5–6, pp. 481–96.

Boyer, E.L. (1996) 'The scholarship of engagement', *Journal of Public Service and Outreach*, Vol. 1, pp. 11–20.

Brock-Utne, B. (1999) 'African universities and the African heritage', *International Review of Education*, Vol. 45 No 1, pp. 87–104.

Buruma, I. and Margalit, A. (2004) *Occidentalism*. London: Atlantic Books.

Franklin, T.V., Sandmann, L.R., Franklin, N.E. and Settle, T.J. (2008) 'Answering the question of how: Out-of-region university engagement with an economically distressed, rural region', *Journal of Higher Education Outreach and Engagement*, Vol. 12 No 3, pp. 205–20.

Friedman, M. (1970) 'Comment on Tobin', *Quarterly Journal of Economics*, Vol. 84 No 2, pp. 318–27.

Garlick, S. and Pryor, G. (2003) 'Community and campus: Benefits of engagement in Sydney'. Sydney: Australian Government, Department of Transport and Regional Services.

Holland, B. (2005) 'The growing role of community engagement in US higher education', *B-HERT News*, Vol. 21, pp. 2–4.

Inman, P. and Schuetze, H.G. (Eds) (2010) *The Community Engagement and Service Mission of Universities*. Leicester: NIACE.

Kellogg Commission on the future of state and land-grant universities (1999) *The Engaged Institution*. Washington, DC: National Association of State Universities and Land-Grant Colleges.

Kelly, G.P. (1984) 'Colonialism, indigenous society and school practices: French West Africa and Indochina, 1918–1938', in P.G. Altbach and G.P. Kelly (Eds), *Education and the Colonial Experience*. London: Transaction Books, pp. 9–32.

Koma, K. (1974) *Education in Black Africa*. Mahalapye, Botswana: Secretariat of the Botswana National Front.

Mazrui, A. (1980) *The African Conditions*. Cambridge: Cambridge University Press.

Mengisteab, K. (1996) *Globalisation and Autocentricity in Africa's Development in the 21st Century*. Trenton: Africa World Press.

Modise, O.M. (2005) 'Labor market demand and incipient professionalisation in African adult education: Tracing graduates of University of Botswana adult education programs'. Unpublished PhD dissertation, Department of Educational Leadership and Policy Studies, University of Florida.

Moumouni, A. (1968) *Education in Africa*. London: André Deutsch.

Narciso, M. (1999) *Brain Drain in Africa*. Accra: Association of African Universities.

Parker, J. and Rathbone, R. (2007) *African History*. Oxford: Oxford University Press.

Sawyerr, A. (2004) 'Challenges facing African universities', *African Studies Review*, Vol. 47 No 1, pp. 1–59.

Shiller, R.J. and Tobin, J. (1999) 'The ET interview: Professor James Tobin', *Economic Theory*, Vol. 15 No 6, pp. 867–900.

Singh, K. (1999) 'Tobin tax: An idea whose time has come', *Economic and Political Weekly*, Vol. 34 No 18, pp. 1019–20.

Sylvester, C. (1999) 'Development studies and postcolonial studies: Disparate tales of the third world', *Third World Quarterly*, Vol. 20 No 4, pp. 703–21.

South Commission (1990) *The Challenge to the South: The Report of the South Commission*. Oxford: Oxford University Press.

Tertiary Education Council (2005) 'Tertiary education policy for Botswana: Challenges and choices'. Consultation paper. Gaborone: Tertiary Education Council.

Thompson, L. (1982) 'The parting of the ways in South Africa', in P. Gifford and R. Louis (Eds), *The Transfer of Power in Africa*. London: Yale University Press, pp. 346–50.

University of Botswana (2008a) *Learning and Teaching Policy*. Gaborone: Department of Institutional Planning, University of Botswana.

University of Botswana (2008b) *A Strategy for Excellence: University of Botswana Strategic Plan to 2016 and Beyond*. Gaborone: Department of Institutional Planning, University of Botswana.

University of Botswana (2008c) 'Task force, graduate employability strategy'. A task force commissioned by the University of Botswana, Office of the Deputy Vice Chancellor.

Wallis, R. (2006) 'What do we mean by community engagement?' Paper presented at the Informa Conference, Knowledge Transfer and Engagement Forum, Sydney, June.

Watson, J.K.P. (1982) *Education in the Third World*. London: Croom Helm.

Yang, G., Zhang, Q. and Wang, Q. (2006) 'The essence, characteristics and limitation of post-colonialism: From Karl Marx's point of view', *Frontiers of Philosophy in China*, Vol. 1 No 2, pp. 279–94.

4

Needs assessment for collaboration between the University of Botswana and Gaborone City Council: Urban planning sector

Chadzimula O. Molebatsi

Introduction

The concept of 'engaged university' or 'university–community engagement' features prominently in contemporary higher education debates (OECD, 1999; OECD, 2001; Inman and Schuetze, 2010). Broadly defined, the term refers to the relationship between institutions of higher learning and the different stakeholders that constitute communities within which the institutions are situated.

The concept of engaged university offers universities an opportunity to reflect on their role in the development of the regions within which they are situated. 'While universities are located in regions, questions are being asked about what contribution they make to the development of those regions' (OECD, 1999, p. 9). According to Florida (1995, p. 258), 'learning regions function as collectors and repositories of knowledge and ideas and provide an underlying environment or infrastructure that facilitates the flow of knowledge, ideas and learning'. Universities, particularly in developing countries such as Botswana, can play a major role in the creation of their learning regions and a knowledge-based economy.

In the case of Botswana, discussions on university–community engagement featured prominently in the University of Botswana (UB) policy discussions in 2003 as part of the strategic planning process. The first UB strategic plan, *Shaping our Future: University of Botswana's Strategic Priorities and Actions to 2009 and Beyond*, was released in 2004 (University of Botswana, 2004). The next, *A Strategy for Excellence: University of Botswana's Strategic Plan to 2016 and Beyond* was prepared in 2008 (University of Botswana, 2008). Both documents made clear pronouncements on engagement as one of the university's priority areas. As defined in the 2004 strategic plan, community engagement was conceived as including:

> *Establishment of local community learning hubs using technology to link local communities and the university and providing learning opportunities covering different areas of interest for various interest groups and to function as a community resource for innovative ideas.* (University of Botswana, 2004, p. 5)

The 2008 strategic plan was even more clear on engagement objectives, one of which was to 'establish a programme of development and capacity building to establish Gaborone as a 'learning city' (University of Botswana, 2008, p. 14). The preparation of the UB strategic plan was in line with global trends in strengthening university engagement and creation of learning regions and cities.

Dempsey (2010, p. 361) provides a useful typology for analysing university–community engagement. The classification is based on what Dempsey identified as 'shifts in the wider landscape of higher education' that justify the popularity of community engagement efforts. Dempsey argues that these shifts are driven by sets of financial interests and incentives. First, universities embark on community engagement to address negative impacts of neo-liberal economic policies. Second, community engagement can be understood in terms of universities' attempts to demonstrate their relevance to different publics. Third, community engagement could be driven by the funding cuts experienced by most state-funded universities. In response to dwindling financial support from public funding, university researchers choose topics that are of interest to outside sponsors. The fourth and last motivation for community engagement is what Dempsey describes as a 'return to a deep tradition of civic engagement' (*ibid.*, p. 362). This is akin to traditional outreach programmes that several universities have embarked on at some stage in their history.

Dempsey's view on engagement as cushioning the negative impact of neo-liberal economic policies is of particular interest to the present chapter. While this could be true, an equally persuasive interpretation could be advanced that such efforts are genuine attempts to address the injustices spawned by central-ised and non-inclusive policy formulation structures. In the field of education, this is particularly evident in Paulo Freire's transformative pedagogy (Freire, 1970). In the urban planning discipline, John Friedmann's view of planning as 'social mobilisation' points to the possibility of engagement as a genuine attempt at creating a more democratic and just society (Friedmann, 1987). This is the context in which we can begin to understand university–commu-nity partnership that focuses on marginalised communities.

In this chapter, we understand engagement as offering an opportunity for the creation of inclusive and participatory democracy in which groups have access to the decision-making processes. Access to information and partici-patory democracy is central to urban planning – the subject of the present chapter. Emerging urban planning concepts promote values such as democ-racy, justice, freedom and equality (UN Habitat, 2009). The chapter discusses the results of a needs assessment study for collaboration between UB and Gaborone City Council in the area of urban planning. We argue that UB could significantly contribute to addressing the marginalisation inherent in the current urban planning processes in Gaborone. Marginalisation should be understood in terms of the centralised nature of the development planning process in Botswana. Despite government rhetoric on decentralisation, both policy formulation and implementation remain the preserve of public sector bodies (Molebatsi, 1994).

Evidence produced in the chapter shows that currently the general public in Gaborone City is not well informed on planning-related matters. The chapter re-veals that while UB has data on various planning issues, Gaborone City Council suffers from a dearth of planning data. The study also reveals areas on which the university–community engagement efforts in urban planning could be built. These areas include case study-based courses in the Department of Architecture and Planning (DAP), collaboration between individual DAP staff members and communities in Gaborone and a draft memorandum of understanding between the Department of Town and Regional Planning (DTRP) and DAP.

Background to the study: Gaborone

Gaborone, the capital city of Botswana with a population of about 233,135,[2] is currently one of the fastest-growing cities in the world (Central Statistics Office, 2011). Within the national urban hierarchy, Gaborone displays characteristics of a primate city with inordinate growth that overshadows that of other urban areas (Republic of Botswana, 1998). Like other cities in developing countries, Gaborone's growth is accompanied by major challenges that include traffic congestion, inadequate infrastructure, inadequate housing, shortage of land and urban decay. Successive development plans for Gaborone have attempted to address these challenges with varying degrees of success.

The first plan for Gaborone was the master plan of 1963, which was followed by planning proposals in 1971. Thereafter, a series of planning documents was prepared for different parts of Gaborone, which included Broadhurst I and II, the Gaborone growth study of 1978, Gaborone West structure plan of 1979 and Greater Gaborone structure plan, 1994 (*ibid.*). Attempts at guiding the growth and expansion of Gaborone, described above, were rather disjointed and addressed urbanisation challenges in a piecemeal fashion. Attempts to introduce a more holistic and coordinated plan for Gaborone came in 1997 with the preparation of the Gaborone City development plan 1997–2021 (Republic of Botswana, 1998).

In 2007, the Government of Botswana commissioned a review of the Gaborone development plan 1997–2021 (Republic of Botswana, 2008). The revised plan is an ambitious document with 13 goals and 49 objectives. In addition, it provided a vision statement that calls for a well-planned city that is caring, economically well managed, environmentally friendly and has a well-preserved cultural heritage. The review resulted in a highly innovative planning document which, if implemented, could revolutionise the urban planning process in Botswana by making it more inclusive and participatory.

The University of Botswana/Gaborone City PURE project

The findings presented in this chapter are part of a larger needs assessment study for collaboration between UB and Gaborone City Council as part of a two-year PURE project (University of Botswana, 2010). The study was conducted under the auspices of the university's Department of Adult Education (DAE) and researchers were drawn from the university and Gaborone City Council (Ntseane, 2010).

The following focus areas were identified for engagement and collaboration: culture; environmental sustainability; small, micro- and medium-sized enterprise (SMME) development; urban/physical planning; and lifelong learning

(University of Botswana, 2010). For the urban planning sector, the needs assessment study focused on the following specific objectives:

- Identify areas in which UB, through DAP, could collaborate with Gaborone City Council in the field of urban planning
- Document current collaboration between DAP and the community, on which future collaboration could be based
- Suggest ways to implement collaborative activities between UB and Gaborone City Council.

Methodology

The study employed two methods of collecting data: in-depth interviews and analysis of documents. The exercise was preceded by the identification of key stakeholders directly dealing with urban planning. These included government departments, private-sector property developers, consultancy firms, non-governmental organisations and academicians. A total of 25 individuals drawn from different planning organisations were interviewed. The revised Gaborone development plan 1997–2021 was used as a case study through which areas of collaboration could be identified. The contention was that the preparation process for the revised plan would reveal the challenges associated with urban planning in Gaborone and thus form the base for collaboration efforts between the university and the city council.

The interviews solicited information on the following: awareness of the review of the Gaborone City development plan 1997–2021 (Republic of Botswana, 2008); the roles different stakeholders played in the formulation of the plan; the adequacy of information dissemination on Gaborone; perceived urban planning challenges; the role of different stakeholders in addressing the challenges; and, finally, the role that respondents thought UB could play in the planning of Gaborone.

Areas of collaboration

From the interviews, key informants generally agreed that there should be collaboration between the university and Gaborone City Council. Respondents called for a more visible role for the university in the areas of research and assistance in charting the general direction for the city's development. According to the respondents, this could be realised through greater interaction between the teaching staff at the UB and City Council employees, and the expansion of outreach programmes. The form of collaboration espoused by respondents here reflects a more traditional conception of engagement where the university provides expertise to a receptive and passive audience in the form of the city council. This is more in line with the 'ivory tower' perception of the university.

In this study, however, additional areas for collaboration were defined as those that were beneficial to both parties. For UB, collaboration with Gaborone City Council would fulfil one of the key priority areas stipulated in successive UB strategic plans – that of engagement. For implementation purposes, the strategic plans were cascaded to faculties. As a result, the Faculty of Engineering and Technology (FET)[3] adopted 'strengthening engagement' as one of its priority areas. It was envisaged that engagement would greatly enhance FET's global competitiveness and this was to be realised through the formation of collaborative relations with strategic partners both locally and globally. With regard to collaboration with local industry, the FET strategic plan contends that collaboration will assist in 'turning research and development into entrepreneurial ventures' (Faculty of Engineering and Technology, 2008, p. 5). The strategic plan also viewed outreach programmes as a crucial part of the engagement drive: 'community outreach programmes extend our reach to broader segments of society and help create awareness and interest in engineering and the built environment at the UB' (*ibid.*). Lastly, the FET strategic plan calls for strengthening of relations with government bodies through which FET research will be aligned to the national agenda. Needless to say, the collaborative efforts outlined above would also greatly enhance the relevance of the curricula offered in FET.

For its part, Gaborone City Council would greatly benefit from the collaboration in the sense that the university, through DAP, would assist in addressing some of the major challenges facing urban planning in the city.

The needs assessment study revealed two major deficiencies in the current urban planning process through which the various development plans for Gaborone were produced. First, the process marginalises communities, resulting in limited participation in decisions that shape the growth and expansion of Gaborone. Thus there is limited awareness of the urban planning process among the citizens of Gaborone City. Second, Gaborone City Council does not have reliable planning data. We contend that the collaboration between UB and the city council could greatly help in addressing these two challenges. Below, we briefly discuss the nature and extent of the challenges identified in the needs assessment study.

Limited awareness of the urban planning processes

It emerged from the needs assessment study that generally there is limited awareness of urban planning processes among the different stakeholders in Gaborone. Key informants drawn from various stakeholders were asked about their familiarity with the revised Gaborone development plan (Republic of Botswana, 2008). Half of the respondents indicated familiarity with the plan and half described their familiarity as partial to non-existent. Respondents were also asked to rate the public's awareness of the plan. Over 70 per cent thought the public was partially aware of the revised plan, while 24 per cent thought the public was completely unaware of it.

Given the sectors from which the respondents were drawn, it can be argued that the levels of awareness of urban planning processes remain unsatisfactory and that policy formulation in urban planning therefore proceeds with little involvement from other stakeholders. Respondents contended that there was minimal communication and information sharing between city council officials and the general public. Communities in Gaborone remain uninformed about what is happening in the city in terms of urban planning issues. Respondents cited the case of major shopping malls being built and major roads constructed and reconstructed in the city without any effective communication channels through which the public could be informed about them.

Awareness of planning issues among different stakeholders in Gaborone has also been raised in research that focuses on planning and development control (see collections in Department of Town and Regional Planning, 1998). The Town and Country Planning Act 1977 requires that any form of development within urban areas receives planning permission. In addition, any form of development, such as house construction and issues pertaining to the distance of the housing structure from the plot boundaries (plot set-backs), has to comply with development standards as prescribed in the Development Control Code (Republic of Botswana, 1995). However, an examination of the low-income residential areas in Gaborone reveals that development in these areas is far from what is prescribed in the Development Control Code. Contravention of the Development Control Code has been explained in terms of ignorance of planning requirements on the part of the developers. We argue that, at present, the majority of developers in low-income residential areas only learn of the planning process requirements when they are told that they have developed without planning permission or violated the Development Control Code and building regulations. Standard practices such as producing physical planning pamphlets and brochures are not widely used in Gaborone.

Key informants were also asked to comment on the adequacy of the information dissemination methods currently employed by urban planning officials in Gaborone. There is currently over-reliance on public meetings as a way to disseminate information on planning issues. The meetings are convened for late afternoon and evenings. Public meetings at ward level were particularly used in the preparation of the revised Gaborone development plan and were poorly attended by the general public. They were dominated by ward development committee members[4] and area councillors and there was an assumption that these roles would help disseminate the information since they interact daily with the people. However, there are no mechanisms for ensuring that this is done effectively.

In addition to public meetings at ward level, key informants also suggested the following as ways to disseminate information: regular consultative meetings with communities at village level; regular interactive radio and television programmes; and use of noticeboards. As pointed out above, public meetings at ward level are often made ineffective as a consultative strategy by the low turn-out of residents.

Apart from the public meetings, the consultants for the revised Gaborone development plan introduced a website where the public could make submissions. Public participation was also sought through the services of the mobile phone operator, Mascom. Consultation strategies adopted for the revised development plan demonstrated that, with careful thought, participation in the plan preparation process could be greatly enhanced. However, the problem with the two methods is that they tend to be discriminatory; those who do not have access to modern technology (internet and mobile phones) are left out of the discussion.

From our interaction with members of the public in Gaborone, it is apparent that there is minimal information sharing between the city council and the general public. Trees that are as old as the city are brought down and traffic circles are turned into complex intersections regulated by traffic lights. We submit that the ordinary citizens of Gaborone are ignorant of such developments since there are no formal and effective channels for communicating about or contesting such projects. Crudely put, the assumption seems to be that 'if it doesn't directly affect you, then there's no need for you to know.'

Such sentiments run contrary to current calls for participatory urban planning methodologies and the advocacy for an informed citizenry. Effective communication and information sharing between the city council and the general public seems to be one area that could become the focus of the envisaged collaboration between UB and Gaborone City Council. Working with the city council, DAP could devise innovative strategies to improve information sharing between the city and its citizens.

Limited reliable planning data

Discussions with the city council's Urban Planning Unit revealed that there is a serious shortage of data on several planning issues. This includes informal sector activities, land-use changes and issues pertaining to development control. It is interesting to note that while there is a dearth of planning data at the city council, students and teaching staff at DAP have conducted studies on several planning topics that could be of use to the city council. These mainly take the form of student dissertations where substantial work has been carried out on the informal sector and land-use changes in Gaborone's central business district.[5] Currently there are no established mechanisms through which research in DAP can inform practice in the city council.

Similarly, there is no data bank at the city council. There have been several studies conducted on important topics such as urban poverty (Mosha, 1999a; 1999b), urban agriculture (Mosha, 2003), non-motorised transport (Mosha, 2006), yet there has been no attempt to extract and collate vital data from these studies for use in carrying out the city council's physical planning mandate.

Gaborone City Council has been slow in localising international debates on urbanisation and planning, sponsored by multilateral organisations such as the United Nations Centre for Human Settlements (UN Habitat). Since the 1976 Vancouver conference on human settlements (Habitat I), UN Habitat has released reports on several topical subjects. For example, in 1996 the UN Habitat global report on human settlements focused on the subject of 'An urbanising world' (UN Habitat, 1996). In 2008, a UN Habitat publication covered the important subject of 'Bridging the urban divide' (UN Habitat, 2008). In 2009, the focus was on 'Planning sustainable cities' (UN Habitat, 2009). More recently, in 2011, the UN global report covered the subject of 'Cities and climate change' (UN Habitat, 2011). There is no question that the reports discuss important subjects that should be of interest to urban planning authorities in Gaborone. Moreover, some of the case studies presented in the reports provide best practice against which planning authorities in Gaborone could benchmark. Localisation of the debates and best practice contained in the UN Habitat publications offer possibilities for an enhanced urban planning practice in Gaborone. With their exposure to these debates, researchers from UB could play an important role in assisting the city council.

Current areas of collaboration between DAP and local communities

The previous discussion focused on possible areas of collaboration between UB and Gaborone City Council. This section discusses areas where there is already some form of collaboration between the two which, we contend, could form the basis for the envisaged partnership. These include DAP courses based on case studies; collaboration between individual DAP staff members and communities in Gaborone; and a draft memorandum of understanding between DTRP and DAP. These are discussed below.

DAP courses based on case studies

DAP currently offers two courses that could form the basis for collaboration between UB and Gaborone City Council in the area of urban planning. These are based on case studies and are 'Settlement upgrading' (course code URP 311) and 'Settlement development planning' (course code URP 409) (University of Botswana 2009, p. 91).

The settlement upgrading course deals with the redevelopment of former squatter settlements and is offered at third-year level in the urban and regional planning programme. In 2010, the course used Old Naledi – a former squatter settlement on the outskirts of Gaborone – as a case study. As part of the project, students visited different offices within Gaborone City Council to collect information on different aspects of Old Naledi. Residents of Old Naledi were directly involved as they not only provided information but also suggested possible solutions to the planning challenges identified.

For its part, the settlement development planning course deals with the preparation of spatial development plans for either urban or rural settlements. In recent years, project areas for this course have been drawn from settlements within a 50 km radius of Gaborone. As in the case of the settlement upgrading course, students are expected to visit the study area, collect baseline data and interact with residents in identifying planning issues and possible solutions.

Both courses have great potential as a base for collaboration between the university and local communities in and around Gaborone. Not only do they bring students into direct contact with communities, but also they give residents a voice in planning their settlements. Collaborative efforts between UB and Gaborone City Council could identify ways to implement the proposed intervention strategies identified in both courses.

Collaboration between individual DAP staff and local communities

Individual DAP staff members have initiated collaboration with local communities in some of Gaborone City's low-income residential areas. In 2010, for example, three staff members started the Community Building Outreach Project in Old Naledi. According to the project brief, 'the idea is to work with local communities to address acute needs for housing accommodation'. This would be realised through building houses and community facilities or upgrading existing structures (Mokwete *et al.*, 2010, p. 5). This project coincided with the national call in Botswana to eradicate poverty (President Khama, inaugural address, 2009). There is great potential in this project to address the housing challenges faced by low-income groups in Botswana's urban areas.

Memorandum of understanding

In 2009, DTRP (in the Ministry of Lands and Housing) approached UB through DAP seeking assistance with planning-related issues. The department wanted to reach out to its stakeholders in a bid to enhance customer satisfaction. Initial discussions between the two parties led to the formation of a steering committee under the joint chairmanship of the deputy director, DTRP, and the head of department at DAP. To assist with identification of strategies through which urban planning could be improved, it was agreed that the starting point would be a national conference on urban planning in Botswana to bring stakeholders together to reflect collectively.

It was agreed that the DRTP–DAP efforts should be captured in a memorandum of understanding stipulating the nature and terms of collaboration. This enthusiasm was stalled by the resignation of the DTRP planning officer who had spearheaded the project and his replacement is still to be identified. What is commendable, however, is that there is willingness on both sides to enter into a collaborative working relationship.

Conclusions and recommendations

This chapter set out to identify areas that could form the basis for collaboration between UB and Gaborone City Council in the area of urban planning. We have argued that the current regional engagement efforts are well aligned with UB's strategic plan (University of Botswana, 2008), which emphasises links between the university and the communities in which it is located. The needs assessment identified limited awareness of the urban planning process among key stakeholders in Gaborone and this is one of the planning challenges faced by the city council. The needs assessment also revealed an absence of reliable data held by the city council on planning issues. It also emerged from the needs assessment study that some individual members of staff were already involved in development projects with local communities in Gaborone. DAP is also running some courses based on case studies which require the involvement of local communities.

We recommend two significant actions: the establishment of an urban planning clinic at UB and the formalisation of all informal links between individual members of staff and local communities. These are discussed in detail below.

Establishment of a University of Botswana urban planning clinic

The envisaged urban planning clinic will be modelled on the legal clinic in the Faculty of Social Sciences and the business clinic in the Faculty of Business. It will act mainly as an advisory and information centre and will assist individuals, groups and public sector bodies in planning-related matters. Information will be disseminated through the preparation and distribution of planning brochures and leaflets on topical planning issues.

Formalisation of all links between Department of Architecture and Planning staff and city officials or local communities

We suggest that all existing collaboration between DAP staff and local communities in Gaborone be formalised. Without introducing rigidity to the collaboration efforts, formalisation will entail documentation of the nature of the links and specification of the aims and success indicators. Once they are documented, it is envisaged that collaborative activities would be budgeted for as part of DAP's budget process. Currently, the budgeting process requires any additional budget item to be justified, and approval is based on the strength of the argument presented. Given that university–community engagement is one of the priority areas on UB's strategic plan, the request for a planning clinic is likely to be well received by the university authorities.

References

Central Statistics Office (2011) *Botswana Population Census Report*. Gaborone: Government Printer.

Dempsey, S. (2010) 'Critiquing community engagement', *Management Communication Quarterly*, Vol. 24 No 3, pp. 359–90.

Department of Town and Regional Planning (1998) National workshop on the review of the Town and Country Planning Act. Gaborone: DTRP.

Faculty of Engineering and Technology (2008) 'A strategy for excellence 2009–2011'. Unpublished faculty document, University of Botswana.

Florida, R. (1995) 'Toward the learning region', *Futures*, Vol. 27 No 5, pp. 527–36.

Friedmann, J. (1987) *Planning in the Public Domain: From Knowledge to Action*. Princeton: Princeton University Press.

Freire, P. (1970) 'The adult literacy process: A cultural action for freedom', *Harvard Educational Review*, Vol. 40 No 2, pp. 205–25.

Inman, P. and Schuetze, H.G. (Eds) (2010) *The Community Engagement and Service Mission of Universities*. Leicester: NIACE.

Mokwete, K., Umenne, S. and Morobolo, S. (2010) Unpublished proposal, Department of Architecture and Planning, University of Botswana.

Molebatsi, C. (1994) 'Towards understanding policy-practice disjunction in urban planning'. Unpublished PhD dissertation, University of Newcastle upon Tyne.

Molefe, J. (2003) 'Urban planning aspects of street vending in Gaborone City, Botswana', unpublished dissertation submitted for the award of M.Phil in Urban Planning, University of Botswana.

Mosha, A.C. (1999a) 'Mainstreaming of urban poverty: A case of Gaborone City, Botswana', in M. Ghachocho (Ed.), *Urban Poverty in Africa: Selected Countries' Experiences*. Nairobi: UNCHS/HABITAT, pp. 57–81.

Mosha, A.C. (1999b) 'Municipal responses to urban poverty: A case study of Gaborone', in S. Jones and N. Nelson (Eds), *Urban Poverty in Africa*, London: Earthscan, pp. 122–34.

Mosha, A.C. (2003) 'Focusing credit on urban agriculture in Gaborone: Botswana', Urban Agriculture Magazine, No 9, April, pp. 16–17.

Mosha, A.C. (2006) 'A review of the non-motorised transport pilot project, Gaborone City'. Review commissioned by the United Nations Development Office, Gaborone.

Ntseane, P. (2010) 'PASCAL report to Gaborone region: PURE work 2009–2010'. Unpublished report, University of Botswana.

OECD (1999) *The Response of Higher Education Institutions to Regional Needs*. Paris: Organisation for Economic Cooperation and Development.

OECD (2001) *Cities and Regions in the New Learning Economy*. Paris: Organisation for Economic Cooperation and Development.

President Seretse Ian Khama (2009) Inaugural address, 20 October 2009.

Republic of Botswana (1995) *Development Control Code*. Gaborone: Government Printer.

Republic of Botswana (1998) *Gaborone City Development Plan 1997–2021*. Gaborone: Government Printer.

Republic of Botswana (2008) *Review of Gaborone City Development Plan 1997–2021 Draft Development Plan*. Gaborone: Government Printer.

UN Habitat (1996) *An Urbanising World: Global Report on Human Settlements*. United Nations Human Settlements Programme. Oxford: Oxford University Press.

UN Habitat (2008) *State of the World Cities Report: Bridging the Urban Divide*. United Nations Human Settlements Programme. London: Earthscan.

UN Habitat (2009) *Planning Sustainable Cities: Global Report on Human Settlements 2009*. United Nations Human Settlements Programme. London: Earthscan.

UN Habitat (2011) *Cities and Climate Change: Global Report on Human Settlements 2011*. United Nations Human Settlements Programme. London: Earthscan.

University of Botswana (2004) 'Shaping our future. UB's strategic priorities and action to 2009 and beyond'. Unpublished report, Gaborone: University of Botswana.

University of Botswana (UB) (2008) 'A strategy for excellence: University of Botswana's strategic plan to 2016 and beyond'. Unpublished report, Gaborone: University of Botswana.

University of Botswana (2009) 'University of Botswana undergraduate academic calendar 2010/2011'. Gaborone: University of Botswana.

University of Botswana (2010) PURE research committee minutes of meeting held on 10 November 2010.

5

University engagement for environmental sustainability

Opha Pauline Dube

Introduction

An engaged process of knowledge acquisition, sharing and dissemination is mandatory under a system of global economic liberalisation, rapid techno-logical advancement and worldwide interconnectedness. Further, the record global economic growth witnessed over the past century brought with it immense pressure on environmental resources to the extent that human acti-vities are a threat to the very life-supporting systems on Earth. The search for sustainable pathways to provide adequate food, energy and water to an ever-increasing population, in the midst of gross inequalities and widespread poverty, demands more than ever that universities spearhead the lifelong learning process for sustainable environmental engagement at all levels.

To attain sustainable environmental engagement, current African generations are compelled to engage in expanded, multifaceted lifelong learning to keep up with the increased worldwide interconnectedness that has resulted in complex interactions with the environment (Kaplinsky, 2000; Martens and Raza, 2010). Expanded communication technologies have increased research opportunities tremendously in terms of options for gathering, processing, exchanging and transmitting information on the environment (Scott, 2000; Martens and Raza, 2010). This compels traditional higher education institutions to review their way of working and to recognise the need to keep up with rapidly changing technology, changing values on environmental resources and ways of generat-ing knowledge about these resources. Universities are forced to reach out and be part of a wider global learning community while struggling to maintain their prestigious position in society as custodians of knowledge (Scott, 2000).

It is increasingly recognised that sustainable environmental engagement will be secured where there is a balance between the desire to pursue economic growth, social needs in terms of equitable distribution of resources for over-all human well-being, and the need for environmental protection (Holden and Linnerud, 2007). This development framework has come to be associated with the concept of sustainable development. However, this is a highly contested concept that lacks clarity on practical implementation (Williams and Millington, 2004).

Higher education institutions are challenged worldwide to provide innovative ideas for practical implementation of sustained environmental engagement (Scandrett, 2002). This is more so for developing countries where the current development frameworks are either slow or failing but is also the case for developed countries that are grappling with high consumerism and the impending global threat of climate change. In seeking solutions to these fundamental issues of development and the conservation of natural resources, university community engagement through lifelong learning becomes important for higher education and society as a whole.

The goal of this chapter is to show that university engagement for lifelong learning is a critical factor in maintaining a sustainable environment in Africa and beyond. The chapter teases out globalisation-driven social and economic conflicts linked to environmental resources at local levels in an African context and the implications for the environment. It covers the role of higher education institutions in providing a knowledge base for social transition to more resilient frameworks and in this context reflects on lifelong learning at the University of Botswana.

Globalisation and sustainable environmental engagement

Inequalities, population growth and the environment

The wealth accumulation race and technological advancement characteristics of the free-enterprise development framework has in general produced grow-ing inequalities, unsustainable population growth and consumption patterns that are threatening environmental sustainability in different parts of the world (Kaplinsky, 2000; Adger *et al.*, 2009; Martens and Raza, 2010). This calls for wider engagement with society to reassess the meaning of development (Scandrett, 2002). For instance:

- Does material accumulation bring human well-being and happiness? If so, to what extent and at what levels of material accumulation?
- Is economic growth synonymous with development?
- How far can environmental resources sustain the ever-growing quest for more material accumulation and affluence, albeit to the benefit of the few?

The biggest challenge, for which the input of universities and research institutions is urgently needed, is a knowledge base that can help society to work out how to provide the growing global population with adequate energy, food and clean water while conserving natural resources for future generations (Reid *et al.*, 2010; ICSU, 2010). Lutz and Samir (2010) estimated that the world population will increase from its current 7 billion to 8–10 billion by 2050 and that most of this increase will be from developing countries where the negative side of globalisation is already reflected in a diminishing environmental resource base and in poverty.

A further complication is the mounting evidence of global warming (UNDP, 2007). Climate change is a classic example of the unsustainable nature of the free-market-based global economic growth experienced since the nineteenth century. The adverse effects of climate change will be most felt among developing countries, which have lower adaptive capacity due to widespread poverty which is exacerbated by a development framework that excludes locally adaptive systems in favour of imported knowledge systems (Bosetti *et al.*, 2008). Lifelong learning is essential for innovative locally based solutions to a web of socio-economic and environmentally linked problems that will emerge from a combination of climate change and already existing development challenges.

The anthropocene and sustainability on planet Earth

The concept of an anthropocene era is now taking root in science. This is the period when humanity is a central factor in changing the Earth on a scale comparable with some of the major events of the ancient past such as meteorite strikes, extraordinary volcanic outbursts and colliding continents (Goldberg *et al.*, 2003; Steffen *et al.*, 2007; Alasiewicz *et al.*, 2010). This epoch is represented by extinction of species, deforestation, an increase in invasive species, unprecedented wildland fires across continents, accumulated sediments, pollution and so forth (Dube, 2007; Alasiewicz *et al.*, 2010).

A number of questions arise from the anthropocene world for which continuous learning is needed and for which higher education institutions could have a significant role:

- To what extent can human well-being and life in general be sustained for future generations in this epoch?
- How might the anthropocene epoch end? (Stephens *et al.*, 2008; Folke *et al.*, 2010).

A transformational change in social-ecological systems is required. Among other things, it must include capacity to adapt to reduction in resource consumption and waste, increased efficiency in the use of the Earth's resources and aggressive reduction of inequalities to attain sustainability (Folke *et al.*, 2010; Smith and Stirling, 2010). The section below addresses global vulnerabilities at the local scale and the need for transformational change.

Social-ecological systems and need for lifelong learning

The term 'social-ecological systems' is increasingly being used to denote the inseparability of humans and ecological systems (see figure 1). It acknowledges the anthropocene epoch, indicating that there are no pristine systems without people nor are there social systems that can exist outside ecosystems. However, the social-ecological interactions are complex and demand lifelong learning to achieve sustainability.

The value of Earth's resources and sustainable environmental engagement

Sustainable environmental engagement is linked to the valuing of ecosystem goods and services and other naturally occurring material as perceived by society. Valuing environmental goods and services is a subject of ongoing debate that falls outside this chapter (Freeman III, 2003; Arntzen, 2003; Winkler, 2006). However, it is important to note that the process through which elements of different components of the Earth are considered to be assets associated with a certain value is partly socially constructed and goes beyond the need to meet basic human biological needs under social-ecological systems (Le Billon, 2001; Winkler, 2006). Le Billon refers to diamonds, which in nature are a useless stone but which have been socially constructed to become a highly priced resource through industrial processing, market manipulation and other value manipulation (such as relating diamonds to purity or love). Arntzen (2003) further notes the 'value paradox' where, for

86

Figure 1: Human and ecosystem interactions on the western side of the Okavango Delta floodplains in Botswana, 1996

The picture shows the benefits of flooding to farming. For instance, cattle can water and graze on floodplain grasslands while arable agriculture benefits from rich alluvial soils after floods have receded (as shown here by a maize molapo farm, floodplain cultivation and temporary dwellings used while looking after the crops). These activities influence surface water and moisture availability in the floodplain with implications for future channel flow, vegetation in general and aquatic plants and wildlife. (Photograph courtesy of O P. Dube, 1996)

example, an extremely valuable resource such as water has a lower price than diamonds. As a result, there is a need to consider for whom a certain resource is of value. This is a critical question which determines the focus of sustainable environmental management.

A conscious recognition of the value of environmental goods and services, and links between elements of the environment and links with human well-being (figure 1), will influence how people invest in the conservation of environmental resources (Winkler, 2006). It is through lifelong learning – to facilitate understanding of the externalities and public good of environmental resources – that society can appreciate the challenges and trade-offs needed to garner support to achieve sustainable environmental engagement, especially in a profit-driven market economy (Freeman III, 2003).

There is an increased realisation that the sustainable conservation of protected areas cannot be achieved without the involvement of communities (West *et al.*, 2009). In response, greater efforts have been made in different parts of Africa to bring community-based conservation (CBC) into pro-tected areas, for instance in Uganda, Botswana, Zimbabwe and Zambia (Musumali *et al.*, 2007). Communities support conservation and this was part of their traditional systems before they were disempowered (Arntzen, 2003; Ross, 2004; Musumali *et al.*, 2007). However, under the CBC engagement in the management of protected areas, communities are being required to

---

Box 1: Community-based natural resource management in Botswana – a change in value of natural resources and vulnerability

In the 1990s, community-based natural resource management was introduced in Botswana within the wildlife management areas that constitute 22 per cent of the land surface of the country. Local com-munities are granted the right to use the wildlife resources subject to government regulations such as the requirement to form a trust, prepare and adhere to a budget plan and apply for a hunting quota (Arntzen, 2003).

The implementation of community-based natural resource manage-ment has revealed many dilemmas (Rozemeijer, 2003). It strongly introduced the monetary value of natural resources in areas where knowledge and skills in such a value system are lacking. Remote areas, and their associated lack of development infrastructure, have limited ability to take full advantage of funds, which means that income is less likely to trickle directly to households.

Communities are not equipped to maximise these benefits, for example by entering into joint ventures with commercial tour-ist operators (Arntzen, 2003). Government support to build the required skills has been inadequate (Rozemeijer, 2003). Evidence has shown that only a few better-off members of the community have benefited, as have those who are traditionally most powerful, thus enhancing inequalities among communities. At the same time, communities have increasingly lost the direct use of these resources to tourism – for example, by not being allowed to hunt for their livelihoods those animals now deemed to be tourist attractions.

As a result, poverty persists in most remote areas of Botswana despite the existing potential to make use of natural resources.

---

change their perception of value of natural resources and adjust to a monetary-based value, which requires different managerial skills and mechanisms for distributing accrued benefits (see box 1). They are expected to effect this change within a rather short time, under limited and regulated control of these resources, which leads to increased vulnerability and raises further questions on the sustainability of protected areas (Aggarwal, 2006; West *et al.*, 2009). These challenges show that investing in lifelong learning through interaction with communities, and understanding their context within the global economy, is critical to sustainable environmental management and building resilience (Aggarwal, 2006; Adger *et al.*, 2009).

Commoditisation in the communal land-tenure system

Apart from in protected areas, globalisation has enabled communities around the world to generate income directly from selling local natural resources. Commercialisation of natural products for income generation by communities to meet basic needs has tended to breed over-exploitation of the resources (see box 2) (Kgathi *et al.*, 2005; Aggarwal, 2006). Others have linked this depletion to population pressure as more people cash in on the opportunity.

Greater engagement, for instance by universities, will help improve understanding of the community dynamics that lead to unsustainable harvesting when products are commercialised (Aggarwal, 2006). In the case of basketry in Botswana, the role of climatic factors needs more interrogation to determine whether anthropogenic climate change could be another factor that reduces supply (Dube, 2003). Fires are driven by climate and have escalated partly because of the tendency by government to disregard indigenous fire management practices, leading to the breakdown of these management systems (Dube and Mafoko, 2009). Also indicated in the basketry example is the role of elephants in making palm-tree leaves scarce, which raises the issue of wildlife management. Botswana has one of the largest elephant populations in the world (Moswete and Dube, 2011).

Communities that rely heavily on income from selling natural resources are usually part of a weaker segment of society, such as dwellers in remote areas or women lacking in literacy and without access to and understanding of markets. Such communities are subjected to unfair trading relations and therefore tend to sell their products at give-away prices, forcing them to labour harder to compensate for the loss.

Box 2: Basketry in Botswana – an example of commercialisation of an open-access natural resource

There has been a rise in the commercialisation of basketry in southern Africa (Terry and Cunningham, 1993). Most of this basketry activity falls under the informal sector, dominated by low-income women in remote areas. This activity is important for income generation. In 1990, basketry, mostly carried out in the Okavango Delta (Terry, 1994, quoted in Mbaiwa, 2004), accounted for 48 per cent of the jobs in the craftwork sector in Botswana. Botswana basketry has gained an international profile for its quality and appealing aesthetics, resulting in worldwide sale by upscale retailers (Tautona Times, 2011). This has been partly linked to the expansion of tourism.

However, local artisans do not enjoy the true value of their labour because of the low prices offered by commercial basketry dealers, who later sell at market value. Mbaiwa (2004) noted that a basket purchased by a dealer for less than US$10 could be sold in the market for around US$100 and found that the majority of weavers, about 60 per cent, were illiterate and over 40 years old, with limited capacity to run a modern enterprise.

Furthermore, commercialisation has led to overharvesting of basketry materials and the use of destructive harvesting methods under the open-access communal land-tenure system. The generation of income has also attracted other ethnic groups that have not previously specialised in this activity (Mbaiwa, 2004). Scarcity of raw materials for weaving, for example, palm-tree fibre (*Hyphaene petersiana*) and dye resources for decoration (*Berchemia discolor*) has been noted (Kgathi *et al.*, 2005). Over 90 per cent of basket makers acknowledge shortage of palm-tree leaves in Etsha villages and also scarcity of *Euclea divinorum* and *Berchemia discolor* tree species that produce dyes most favoured by international markets (Terry and Cunningham, 1993). Mbaiwa (2004) showed that weavers travel distances in the range of 15 to 45 km in search of palm leaves.

Scarcity has also been attributed to other factors such as destruction of palm trees by elephants, low rainfall, veld fires and high temperatures (Mbaiwa, 2004).

The increase in demand due to commoditisation usually occurs under communal land-tenure systems and is considered an informal activity, so there are no regulating measures in place (Mbaiwa, 2004). In general, traditional management systems have been disempowered and the newly introduced ones lack capacity, are not adapted and have generally failed to take on board indigenous systems and practices (Aggarwal, 2006). As a result, the noted depletion of resources is a signal of failure to establish sustainable environmental engagement in the face of changing values and new pressures. This failure exposes both natural resources and communities to exploitation, thus breeding deeper vulnerability (Aggarwal, 2006; Adger *et al.*, 2009).

Interfacing traditional and modern systems

The discussion above has shown the embedded problem of mismatch in the interface between traditional systems and modern ones. Increased vulnerability in Africa and many other developing countries has been linked to weakened structures of local institutions, organisations and knowledge bases as a result of globalisation, subsequently giving rise to further unrestricted globalisation. This has led to erosion of indigenous, more adaptive practices and their replacement by imported, usually Western, practices, some of which were not suitable or were not tested for suitability and have not been adapted to the local environment (Aggarwal, 2006; Dube and Sekhwela, 2007). Poor interfacing of conventional and local knowledge systems and practices has led to greater damage to the environment, eroding resilience in numerous parts of the developing world (Adger *et al.*, 2009; West *et al.*, 2009).

Inadequate lifelong learning and a lack of informed engagement across the education system in developing countries contribute to these consequences (Owuor, 2007; Nyamnjoh, 2008). For Africa, the introduction of the Western education system led to a deficiency in the level of engagement with African society and the undermining of African knowledge bases (Semali, 1999). It has deprived African society of the opportunity to apply and interrogate its knowledge in the face of globalisation, acknowledge its limitation, modify and develop it further and produce innovative, locally adaptive and environmental sustainable practices (Nyamnjoh, 2008). A Western-based education, the school system, isolated African children from their knowledge context – that is, from the family and community knowledge base – and starved them of a whole system of lifelong learning (Omolewa, 2002). This served to break down the system for transferring knowledge and skill, and erode confidence in African society.

Hence, for the basketry example in box 2, youth involvement is limited because weaving skills have not been learnt at family and community level and there is a belief that these skills are inferior (Mbaiwa, 2005). The lack of youth involvement is also partly because schools have failed to integrate these traditional skills into their curriculum, resulting in the so-called 'dualism' of modern and traditional systems in developing countries (Potts, 2007). There is a continued tendency by governments to maintain traditional income-generation activities, such as basketry in Botswana, under the informal sector, even where these activities show potential for global markets. This demonstrates the entrenched belief among policy makers, who are also informed by Western-oriented education, that these activities are inferior and in the final stages of survival despite their continued demonstrated resilience. In these informal unregulated sectors, exploitative practices thrive to the detriment of both people and the environment.

In many ways, Western-oriented education has weakened the African social fabric, dismantled management and organisation structures and eroded cultural values and beliefs that should have been developed to support sustainable environmental engagement. This has increased susceptibility to manipulation by market-driven forces and firmly entrenched the dependence of African economies on carbon-loaded economic frameworks of developed countries. This contributes to climate change and deepens vulnerability in social-ecological systems.

The emerging paradigm shift towards promoting education for sustainable development offers hope for a lifelong learning approach to community engagement that embraces the variety of knowledge systems available (Semali, 1999; Owuor, 2007).

Higher education and the challenge of environmental sustainability in Africa

Instruments for facilitating environmental sustainability
The challenge for higher education in Africa is to be an agent of change, facilitating migration away from the unsustainable disjointedness in African society between indigenous and modern systems. As noted by Stephens *et al.*

(2008), this is a call for a transition to a new pathway and more sustainable practices achieved through a delicate but calculated balance and integration of the competing demands of long-term change and short-term needs. The role of universities in facilitating this transition can be achieved through different interactive levels of learning (Stephens *et al.*, 2008), such as:

- Visioning: applying skills of abstract thinking learnt through synthesis, integration, and systems-thinking characteristic in universities to determine how to incorporate competing non-linear factors that challenge efforts towards sustainable environmental engagement. In this way higher education institutions will help define frameworks and provide strategic societal visioning to formulate future pathways
- Fact finding through problem-oriented research: engaging in real-world problem-based research on environmental sustainability issues and their inseparability from development in general and globalisation in particular. This will require coalition building such as engaging experts from different disciplines and other stakeholders in society
- Operational level: facilitating direct engagement on environmental challenges and mutual learning with society through curriculum and research, implementing environmentally sustainable outreach activities.

Lifelong learning for sustainable environmental engagement in Africa requires academic institutions to engage in the conceptualisation of social-ecological systems that goes beyond the student–teacher model of learning. It brings the classroom to the household and the community, to policy makers and stakeholders from different sectors – including engineering, civil society, and informal and formal business communities. It also means bringing these groups into the classroom (Semali, 1999; Holm, 2010). This should be a multi-dimensional interactive approach carried out on a more or less equal basis by the different actors with the aim of achieving 'co-production' of knowledge with society (ICSU, 2010). Such engagement is a challenge that requires huge transformation within the academic institutions themselves and demands a high degree of flexibility never witnessed before (Stephens *et al.*, 2008).

Both abstract and societal problem-oriented approaches to research and learning are critical. Societal problems are multidimensional by their nature, calling for learning to go beyond multidisciplinary approaches where a range of disciplines work on the same problem but with limited or no interaction. They also call for the need to go beyond an interdisciplinary approach, where many disciplines interact strongly and focus on developing integrated approaches. This approach may not necessarily engage the various segments of society outside the academic arena. A transdisciplinary approach is the most suitable, as pointed out by the International Council for Science (ICSU, 2010), because it cuts across social and natural sciences and orients lifelong learning to problems, practice, participation and process. For example, a river catchment assessment study may involve hydrological, engineering, ecological, socio-economic, demographic and population studies, geography and land-use data, and communities (such as arable farmers and pastoralists) residing in the area.

To some degree, the problem-oriented approach is synonymous with the case of African lifelong learning where learning was comprehensive, integrated and aimed at problem solving (Omolewa, 2002). But what is required now is far more complex than in the past, requiring not only interdisciplinary and integrated approaches but also a social and spatial dimension that encompasses household, community, district and national issues. Under globalisation, these are actively linked at regional and global scales and are highly dynamic (Adger *et al.*, 2009; Stephens *et al.*, 2008). This complexity calls for more effective programmes to facilitate co-production of knowledge through collaborative learning between academics, experts and the rest of society to encourage co-ownership of learning and resulting products. So far, there is no clarity within higher education institutions as to how this can be achieved.

Academic institutions still bear strong divisions between social sciences, humanities and natural sciences, and integration within each of these major blocks is still a challenge. Environmental issues continue to feature mostly in the natural science arena, a factor which has delayed the ability to address them comprehensively, given the critical role of socio-economic drivers in environmental degradation. One way to break these boundaries could be by developing transdisciplinary PhD and post-doctoral programmes (ICSU, 2010). Another would be to develop networks that are oriented to problems, practice, participation and process, as was the case of the Southern Africa Fire Network (SAFNet) in which biophysical fire scientists met social scientists (since fire ignition is human driven) and also engaged policy makers, fire users and fire managers (Dube, 2005).

The structure of funding for research at national, regional and international level has continued to be structured to match traditional disciplines. This has hindered integrated problem-oriented environmental research in transdisciplinary teams. Sponsors have a huge potential to foster change by offering transdisciplinary funding that encourages engagement of natural and social sciences with relevant stakeholders at local, national and international levels to address a particular environmental programme in an integrated way (ICSU, 2010).

Lifelong learning at the University of Botswana

There are several engagement activities in environmental sustainability at the University of Botswana (UB) which cannot be comprehensively covered here. The university national development strategic plan 10 (NDP10) cites the environmental sustainability value as one of its 13 identified values for planning:

> *By deepening awareness and ensuring environmental issues are incorporated into student learning and teaching and research, the development of environmentally sustainable campuses and through contributing to the environmental sustainability agenda in Botswana.* (Cited in UB Council 2008, p. 16)

An Environmental Sustainability Charter Working Group has been established, formed by representatives from different faculties and senior management, and stakeholders from government, the city council, non-governmental organisations (NGOs) and the business community. This is a sign of an attempt to engage UB in lifelong learning for environmental sustainability. It is an unproven initiative as yet, although it represents a high-level policy stand on the need for UB to be a model of sustainable environmental practices and also to engage society at large. These are roles that are increasingly being required of institutions of higher learning internationally (Stephens *et al.*, 2008).

Most universities, UB included, are located within cities where numerous environmental problems occur, such as waste disposal and sanitation, stormwater drainage, squatter settlements and so on. The different organisations dealing with these issues are also in close proximity, providing an opportunity for interactive lifelong learning in sustainable environmental management. The Department of Environmental Science in the Faculty of Science in UB, which offers programmes that cut across biophysical and human environment, has had several links with Gaborone City Council, with NGOs such as Somarelang Tikologo (Environmental Watch, Botswana), and government departments such as the National Disaster Management Technical Committee in the Office of the President and the National Climate Change Committee through the Department of Meteorological Services. These serve as a focal point for the United Nations Framework Convention on Climate Change (UNFCCC). All of these are based in Gaborone. The department has a memorandum of understanding with the Ministry of Environment, Wildlife and Tourism which has facilitated greater engagement with environmental issues of national interest.

In addition the Department of Environmental Science is actively engaged in regional and international environmental forums facilitated through its Botswana Global Environmental Change Committee (BGCC), formed in 1993 as a national committee of the International Geosphere-Biosphere Programme (IGBP). BGCC hosted SAFNet for seven years, which was instrumental in drafting the Southern African Development Community (SADC) fire protocol, thus providing a strong link to regional fire policy. BGCC members are also active in the Inter-Governmental Panel on Climate Change (IPCC) and in the UNFCCC climate change negotiations, such as the most recent in Durban in 2011. Similar engagements occur in other departments. UB has a number of research centres that address issues of national interest, such as the International Tourism Research Centre. However, research centres are currently underfunded and understaffed.

Informal channels are perhaps the most encompassing route for lifelong learning through community engagement that contributes to environmental issues in UB. This reflects the resilience of African social ties despite the influence of globalisation and Western values. Teaching and research in UB, as with other African universities, benefits from the remnants of the traditional African family and community-linked lifelong learning exhibited by the continued strong bond of both the student and lecturer to extended family, their villages and traditional lifestyles, as highlighted by Holm (2010) for UB academic staff.

The majority of environment-related engagement by UB staff with community, government, NGO and business sectors is voluntary. Although it forms part of the community service component of staff activity, it carries less weight for staff promotion than teaching and research activities. Holm (2010) noted the need for these activities to be strongly tied to research and learning. Growing student enrolments, leading to large classes, have limited innovative, socially engaged teaching. It is not uncommon for a practical second-year course in the Department of Environmental Science to have over 500 students. A rich research environment that stimulates abstract thinking is needed in UB to envision future environmentally sustainable systems.

Conclusion

This chapter highlights some of the complex interactions within social-ecological systems that occur at multiple scales, which cannot be disregarded if sustainable environmental engagement is to be attained under globalisation. The discussion outlines some challenges for developing the knowledge base required to guide society towards sustainable development through which environmental conservation can be realised. In developing countries, in particular, more adaptive systems have been overpowered by highly marketed off-site systems and this practice has led to the the erosion of resilience.

The discussion points to the inescapable need for lifelong learning in knowledge acquisition at all levels, and for use of this knowledge – which is difficult to achieve under the current strong disconnection between higher education and the practical world. Universities need to be fully engaged in social problems in terms of learning context and research focus to produce manpower and a knowledge base that can address the challenge of sustainability issues and avoid becoming part of the vulnerability cycle rather than a solution to it.

References

Adger, W.N., Eakin, H. and Winkels, A. (2009) 'Nested and teleconnected vulnerabilities to environmental change', *Frontiers in Ecology and the Environment*, Vol. 7, pp. 150–7.

Aggarwal, R.M. (2006) 'Globalization, local ecosystems and the rural poor', *World Development*, Vol. 34 No 8, pp. 1405–18.

Alasiewicz, J., Williams, M., Steffen, W. and Crutzen, P. (2010) 'The new world of the anthropocene', *Environmental Science Technology*, Vol. 44, pp. 2228–31.

Arntzen, J.W. (2003) 'An economic view on wildlife management areas in Botswana', CBNRM Support Programme, Occasional paper No 10. IUCN–The World Conservation Union.

Bosetti, V., Carraro, C. and Tavoni, M. (2008) 'Climate change mitigation strategies in fast-growing countries: The benefits of early action', *Energy Economics*, Vol. 31, pp. S144–51.

Dube, O.P. (2003) 'Impacts of climate change, vulnerability and adaptation options: Exploring the case for Botswana through Southern Africa. A review', *Botswana Notes and Records*, Vol. 35, pp. 47–168.

Dube, O.P. (2005) 'A collaborative effort towards developing capacity for operational fire monitoring and management systems in southern Africa', SAFNet AIACC working paper No 11. AIACC Project No AF42. Retrieved 2 April 2012 from http://www.aiaccproject.org/working_papers/working_papers.html

Dube, O.P. (2007) 'Fire weather and land degradation', in M.V.K. Sivakumar and N. Ndiang'ui (Eds), *Climate and Land Degradation*. Dordrecht: Springer, pp. 223–51.

Dube, O.P. and Sekhwela, M.B.M. (2007) 'Community coping strategies in semiarid Limpopo Basin part of Botswana', *Adaptation Capacity to Climate Change*. AIACC working paper No 47.

Dube, O.P. and Mafoko, J.G. (2009) 'Botswana', in SAFNet (Ed.), *Africa Environment Outlook Case Studies, Impacts of Fire on the Environment*. Nairobi: UNEP and SARDC, pp. 7–18. Retrieved 2 May 2012 from http://www.sardc.net/imercsa/env_outlook/index.html

Folke, C., Carpenter, S.R., Walker, B., Scheffer, M., Chapin, T. and Rockström, J. (2010) 'Resilience thinking: Integrating resilience, adaptability and transformability', *Ecology and Society*, Vol. 15 No 4, p. 20. Retrieved 2 April 2012 from http://www.ecologyandsociety.org/vol15/iss4/art20/

Freeman III, A.M. (2003) *The Measurement of Environmental and Resource Values: Theory and Methods*, second edition. Washington, DC: Resources for the Future.

Goldberg, S., Ma, J. and O'Donohue, J. (2003) 'Mass extinction', *The Traprock*, Vol. 2, pp. 15–18.

Holden, E., Linnerud, K. (2007) 'The sustainable development area: Satisfying basic needs and safeguarding ecological sustainability', *Sustainable Development*, Vol. 15 No 3, pp. 174–87.

Holm, J.D. (2010) 'When family ties bind African universities', *The Chronicle of Higher Education*, 19 August 2010.

ICSU (2010) *Regional Environmental Change: Human Action and Adaptation*. Paris: International Council for Science.

Kaplinsky, R. (2000) 'Globalisation and unequalisation: What can be learned from value chain analysis?' *Journal of Development Studies,* Vol. 37 No 2, pp. 117–46.

Kgathi, D.L., Mmopelwa, G. and Mosepele, K. (2005) 'Natural resources assessment in the Okavango Delta, Botswana: Case studies of some key resources', *Natural Resources Forum*, Vol. 29, pp. 70–81.

Le Billon, P. (2001) 'The political ecology of war: Natural resources and armed conflicts', *Political Geography*, Vol. 20, pp. 561–84.

Lutz, W. and Samir, K.C. (2010) 'Dimensions of global population projections: What do we know about future population trends and structures?' *Philosophical Transactions of The Royal Society*, Vol. 365, pp. 2779–91.

Martens, P. and Raza, M. (2010) 'Is globalisation sustainable?' *Sustainability 2010*, Vol. 2 No 1, pp. 280–93.

Mbaiwa, J. E. (2004) 'Prospects of basket production in promoting sustainable rural livelihoods in the Okavango Delta, Botswana', *International Journal of Tourism Research*, Vol. 6, pp. 221–35.

Mbaiwa, J.E. (2005) 'The problems and prospects of sustainable tourism development in the Okavango Delta, Botswana', *Journal of Sustainable Tourism*, Vol. 13, No 3, pp. 203–27.

Moswete, N.N. and Dube, P.O. (2011) 'Wildlife-based tourism and climate: Potential opportunities and challenges for Botswana'. Paper presented at fifth IIPT African Conference, 'Meeting the challenges of climate change to tourism: Case studies of best practice', Lusaka, May.

Musumali, M.M., Larsen T.S. and Kaltenborn, B.P. (2007) 'An impasse in community based natural resource management implementation: The case of Zambia and Botswana', *Oryx*, Vol. 41, No 3.

Nyamnjoh, F.B. (2008) 'From publish or perish to publish and perish: What Africa's 100 best books tell us about publishing in Africa', *Journal of African and Asian Studies*, Vol. 39 No 5, pp. 331–5.

Omolewa, M.R. (2002) 'The practice of lifelong learning in indigenous Africa', in C. Medel-Añonuevo (Ed.), *Integrating Lifelong Learning Perspectives*. Hamburg: UNESCO Institute for Education, pp. 13–17.

Owuor, J.A. (2007) 'Integrating African indigenous knowledge in Kenya's formal education system: The potential for sustainable development', *Journal of Contemporary Issues in Education*, Vol. 2 No 2, pp. 21–37.

Potts, D. (2007) 'The state and the informal in sub-Saharan African urban economies: Revisiting debates on dualism'. Working paper No 18: *Cities and Fragile States*. London: Crisis States Research Centre, LSE.

Reid, W.V., Chen, D., Goldfarb, L., Hackmann, H., Lee, Y.T., Mokhele, K., Ostrom, E., Raivio, K., Rockström, J., Schellnhuber, H.J. and Whyte, A. (2010) 'Earth system science for global sustainability: Grand challenges', Science, Vol. 330 No 6006, pp. 916–17.

Ross, M.L. (2004) 'What do we know about natural resources and civil war?' *Journal of Peace Research*, Vol. 41 No 3, pp. 337–56.

Rozemeijer, N. (2003) 'CBNRM in Botswana: Revisiting the assumptions after 10 years of implementation'. Retrieved 2 April 2012 from http://www.cbnrm.net/pdf/rozemeijer_n_005_cbnrminbotswana.pdf

Scandrett, E. (2002) 'Lifelong learning for ecological sustainability and environmental justice'. Thematic paper on sustainable development for *Inquiry into the Future for Lifelong Learning*. Retrieved 16 April 2012 from http://www.niace.org.uk/lifelonglearninginquiry/themes/sustainabililty/default.htm

Scott, P. (2000) 'Globalisation and higher education: Challenges for the 21st century', *Journal of Studies in International Education*, Vol. 4 No 1, pp. 3–10.

Semali, L. (1999) 'Community as classroom: Dilemmas of valuing African indigenous literacy in education', *International Review of Education*, Vol. 45 No 3–4, pp. 305–19.

Smith, A. and Stirling, A. (2010) 'The politics of social-ecological resilience and sustainable socio-technical transitions', *Ecology and Society*, Vol. 15 No 1, p. 11.

Steffen, W., Crutzen, P.J. and McNeill, J.R. (2007) 'The anthropocene: Are humans now overwhelming the great forces of nature?' *Ambio: A Journal of the Human Environment*, Vol. 36 No 8, pp. 614–21.

Stephens, J.C., Hernandez, M.E., Román, M., Graham, A.C. and Scholz, R.W. (2008) 'Higher education as a change agent for sustainability in different cultures and contexts', *International Journal of Sustainability in Higher Education*, Vol. 9 No 3, pp. 317–38.

Tautona Times, Vol. 9 No 17 (25 July 2011) The Electronic Press. Circular of the Office of the President retrieved 23 August 2012 from www.gov.bw/ Global/OP%20Ministry/TAUTONA%20TIMES%20vol_%209%20no_%20 17.pdf

Terry, M.E. and Cunningham, A.B. (1993) 'The impact of commercial marketing on the basketry of southern Africa', *Journal of Museum Ethnography*, Vol. 4, pp. 25–48.

UB Council (2008) *A Strategy for Excellence: The University of Botswana Strategic Plan to 2016 and Beyond*. Gaborone: University of Botswana.

UNDP (2007) *Fighting Climate Change: Human Solidarity in a Divided World*. Human Development Report 2007–2008. New York: United Nations Development Programme.

West, P., Igoe, J. and Brockington, D. (2009) 'Parks and peoples: The social impact of protected areas', *Annual Review of Anthropology*, Vol. 35, pp. 251– 77.

Williams, C. and Millington, A.C. (2004) 'The diverse and contested meanings of sustainable development', *The Geographical Journal*, Vol. 170 No 2, pp. 99–104.

Winkler, R. (2006) 'Valuation of ecosystem goods and services part 1: An integrated dynamic approach', *Ecological Economics*, Vol. 59, pp. 82–93.

6

Scaling up the African universities' capacity for learning cities and regions: Challenges and opportunities in Tanzania and East Africa

Mpoki John Mwaikokesya

Introduction

With the ubiquity of the information economy, in the past few decades there has been an ever-increasing policy focus on the necessity for learning. One key observation is that, in recent years, there has been a shift in the mode of generating new knowledge, ideas and innovation processes from the dominant individually constructed learning into more socially constructed processes (Engeström, 2001; Lave, 1991; Lave and Wenger, 1991; Osborne *et al.*, 2007). These allow shared efforts, resources and organisations in a particular geographical location, hence the notion of learning regions, learning villages, cities or municipalities.

As part of this trend, universities in particular are expected to play a significant role in generating new ideas and developing lifelong learning attitudes for socio-economic transformation, innovations and competitive advantage. Universities are also viewed as essential agents for enhancing a variety of economic outcomes including graduates' purchasing powers to create a competitive advantage in local labour markets (Gal, 2010). As Gal further comments, when universities are integrated into local and international knowledge networks they can serve as knowledge bases and sources of innovation for industries, businesses and other actors in society (*ibid.*, p. 94). Conversely, when universities are disengaged from the larger society in which they operate or when their objectives or missions contradict the societal expectations, they turn into 'ivory towers'.

African countries and their municipalities are at different stages of transforming their traditional learning systems to become robust learning avenues. These avenues will enhance learning opportunities, develop critical learning communities and allow effective knowledge sharing, thereby increasing the number of actors within a region, and their potential (Ford, 2002). However, although the concept of learning cities has become more popular, developing a learning city has remained a lengthy and complex process. Drawing on Tanzania's experiences, this chapter explores efforts in developing countries to establish learning cities and regions. The chapter assesses the role of universities and examines key opportunities and challenges facing African countries.

Conceptual issues underlying this chapter

Addressing such a complex issue as 'learning cities' requires an exposition of fundamental concepts. The concept of learning cities or regions was explored in an Organisation for Economic Co-operation and Development (OECD) study (OECD, 2007) which explored the contributions made to economic development by higher education institutions in 12 OECD countries. However, it was during the 1980s that the term first gained popularity (Morgan-Klein and Osborne, 2007). In economic geography, the concept claims its origin in studies of 'regional innovation systems' (Cooke and Morgan, 1998, p. 70) and is attributed to Richard Florida (1995), who coined the term to mean necessary factors for regional competitiveness, particularly research and development, knowledge creation and innovations.

Although the term has recently been at the forefront of much educational literature and discourse, surprisingly there has been no universally accepted definition of the concept (Doloreux and Parto, 2004; Jutte, 2010; Stenvall *et al.*, 2010). Salient features within a learning city are generally perceived to include: the existence of high-quality links between different regional stakeholders such as local businesses, community groups and education providers, 'such that the sharing of information and exchange of information that are important for economic success becomes much easier and cheaper within a region than it is within a national context' (Toland and Yoong, 2005, p. 54).

Boshier offers one of the useful definitions of a learning city or a region as:

> *... a form of community development in which local people from every sector act together to enhance the social, cultural, economic and environmental conditions of their communities. It is a pragmatic approach to mobilize resources and expertise from all sectors of community: local government, economic (private or cooperative enterprises, public (library, museum, recreation, etc.), education (from kindergarten to university).* (Boshier (2006, p. 36)

Other related terminologies are 'innovative milieu', 'new industrial district' and 'local productive system' (Doloreux and Parto, 2004, p. 7). The learning city or region refers to 'a society of people and organisations where an effective environment for studying is designed, with emphasis put on the aim of studying through partnership, and where the constant learning and innovative activity of every citizen is assured' (Bagdonas, 2010, p. 71). From this point of view, Bagdonas suggests that the essence of learning cities is to achieve, among other things, competencies necessary for modern employment, and organisations that are able to compete internationally. In a learning city there are deliberate attempts to promote all forms of learning for all ages in various contexts (Boshier, 2006). The dimensions of learning cities therefore may include:

- Creation of vibrant national, local and international networks
- Creation of an environment where different forms of learning – formal, non-formal and informal – exist such that individual and collective learning is possible.

Thus, the creation of learning cities and regions is not an easy task. It requires commitment not only of resources, but also of political will, and the strong networking of many different actors, including civil society, business, sports, local authorities and municipalities, academic institutions, the media and the public at large.

Why learning cities or regions?

Learning cities are significant for many reasons. They are critical avenues for gathering and promoting lifelong learning, and they act as a focal point for innovations and learning that take advantage of local communities (Doukas, 2010). As Piazza (2010, pp. 211–12) suggests, a learning city is critical since 'it assumes the role of a catalyst and a hub for learning' as well as being 'a unique place for the development of a culture of lifelong learning'. Learning cities play a significant role in regional development. They also suggest the importance of the spatial and regional contexts of a knowledge economy. The prevailing socio-economic challenges in different nations require an approach where the local and regional actors mutually act towards achieving the national goals (Longworth and Osborne, 2010). A strong regional knowledge base and cooperation between industry and research institutions is also a basis for meaningful development within countries (Gal, 2010).

Lifelong learning

Lifelong learning is another essential concept in the learning cities discourses, as is reflected in the works of international organisations such as the OECD and the United Nations Educational, Scientific and Cultural Organization (UNESCO) (Field, 2006; Istance *et al.*, 2002; Osborne and Morgan-Klein, 2007). Though it is beyond the focus of this chapter to provide a detailed discussion of the concept of lifelong learning, the term is related to learning that is 'life-wide' and 'life-deep' in nature (Maclachlan and Osborne, 2009, p. 575), signifying a paradigm shift from a traditional focus on 'front-loaded' formal education and educational institutions into 'learning' (Schuetze and Casey, 2006, p. 279).

In Africa, the origin of lifelong learning is linked to traditional African indigenous education offered to adults to ensure the development of skills, integration, social cohesion and values, and acceptable behaviour (Avoseh, 2001; Omolewa, 2002).

Lifelong learning is used to stress the importance of learning both within and beyond formal educational provision (Torres, 2003). Given its premium importance in recent years, countries across the globe are occupied with developing institutional capacities to transform, adapt and lay appropriate foundations for lifelong learning (Chapman and Aspin, 1997). However, while several countries in Western Europe, for example, are embracing lifelong learning as a strategy to support their national policies for successful society, only a few countries in Africa are doing so (Maratuona, 2006; Torres, 2009). It is for this reason that Coffield (2000) suggests that the national adoption of lifelong learning evolves through three overlapping stages, namely 'romance', 'evidence' and 'implementation' – with most of the efforts remaining at the romantic stage (Walters and Watters, 2001). Critics such as Torres (2003; 2009) note a similar trend when they observe that lifelong learning in the global south continues to be used interchangeably with basic education. The challenge therefore is to disentangle rhetoric from reality in achieving lifelong learning. This will include transforming culture and practices in educational institutions so that the focus is not simply on increasing participation and completion rates but on equipping students with a range of learning strategies to be used in life beyond school (Chapman and Aspin, 1997; Hosseini, 2006).

Longworth and Davies (1996) suggest there are some key global issues that necessitate an acceptance of the principle of lifelong learning. These include: changes in the nature of work; restructuring of industries; the influence of science and technology; the shift of educational focus onto individuals rather than groups; youth unemployment; and changes in birth rates. A meaningful lifelong learning accomplishment can hardly be achieved if it is restricted to an elite group rather than strategically and substantively involving a whole community (Chapman and Aspin, 1997). This suggests there is a primacy for establishing new forms of alliance and collaboration between educational institutions and other actors in society.

Learning cities in the political north

In response to the above challenges, most countries in the political north are at an advanced stage in setting up learning cities (Longworth, 2001). In Western Europe, for instance, universities and regional bodies such as the OECD and the European Commision have developed tools such as Towards a European Learning Society (TELS) to facilitate the development of learning cities. Networks such as the PASCAL Observatory have been established and play a significant leadership role. As Longworth and Osborne (2010) note, since 2002 more than 50 cities in the UK have been identified as learning cities, along with Kaunas (in Lithuania), Limerick (in Ireland) and Rotterdam (in the Netherlands) and more than 70 in Germany. Such a trend is also noted in other European countries such as Finland, where a network of 20 learning municipalities was established.

Contexts, realities and learning cities in Africa, with a focus on Tanzania

It is a daunting task to discuss or generalise issues in Africa. The region is complex because of its size as a continent and because of the tremendous diversity within its constituent countries. Notwithstanding these complexities, several realities are shared by a majority of African countries.

Economically, the majority of African countries suffer from serious poverty (with the exception of a few countries such as South Africa, Botswana, Libya and Egypt, where economic progress is relatively better). African education structures and patterns are characterised by historical, political and socio-economic hardships; colonial exploitative processes; neo-liberal hegemonic restructuring; privatisation policies; and globalisation processes. Since the African countries gained independence, their economic, political and social structures have remained weak and stagnant. The majority are still struggling with widespread illiteracy, unemployment, poverty and rapid population growth. They have remained generators of raw materials for the developed countries, but often fail to meet their own basic needs. Their weak and underdeveloped economic systems have impacted adversely on other sectors, including education and health.

The concept and practice of learning cities or regions seem to be relatively new and probably not vibrant in Tanzania or in East Africa at large. The origin and practice, however, can be traced to the early 1960s when Julius Nyerere (the influential African adult educator and one of the early intellectuals in East Africa) urged universities to avoid being intellectually isolated from the larger society and strive for promotion of partnership, the public service and lifelong learning:

> *For let us be quite clear; the University has not been established purely for prestige purposes. It has a very definite role to play in development in this area, and to do this effectively it must be in, and of, the community it has been established to serve. The University of East Africa has to draw upon experience and ideas from East Africa as well as from the rest of the world. And it must direct its energies particularly towards the needs of East Africa ... It is in this manner that the University will contribute to our development ... In this fight the University must take an active part, outside as well as inside the walls.* (Nyerere, 1963, pp. 218–19)

For universities to implement their core mission thoroughly, therefore, there should be efforts to promote learning cities or regions through which actors from different levels work together to promote and use learning and scientific knowledge effectively. Regarding lifelong learning, Nyerere insisted on the necessity to focus on all forms of education – formal, non-formal and informal learning – and underlined the need for lifelong learning, both for an individual's development and for national transformation:

Education is something that all of us should continue to acquire from the time we are born until the time we die. This is important both for individuals and for our country as a whole. A country whose people do not learn and make use of their knowledge will stay very poor and very backward ... we can all learn more ... there is much more that everyone can learn about our work and about areas of knowledge that were not taught at school. (Nyerere, 1973, pp. 137–41)

Developing a culture of lifelong learning is therefore an essential concern, suggesting that in the African context the challenge is not only to provide education for all citizens but also to create a culture of learning (Longworth and Osborne, 2010). In Tanzania, despite several efforts to provide basic education for all, the current situation suggests the need to do more in terms of developing a learning society and a culture of learning (Bhalalusesa, 2005).

Continent-wide attempts at promoting learning networks include the New Partnership for Africa's Development (NEPAD). This is a regional initiative aimed at challenging African leaders to develop a new vision that can guarantee Africa's renewal and capacity for addressing growing levels of poverty, under-development and inequality. NEPAD's principal aims include the strengthening of partnerships between Africans in order to deliver the Millennium Development Goals. Priorities include bridging the education gap by promoting networks of specialised research for Africa's development. NEPAD also supports the establishment of higher education institutions, regional centres of excellence, and inter-institutional collaboration (FARA/NEPAD/CTA/INWENT, 2009).

As one of the critical actors in a region or city, universities can provide quality research, training and community services aimed at addressing myriad socio-economic problems. Universities' efforts to establish networks within and outside the country are identified as essential for the motivation to partner with national governments and other actors in bringing about development (*ibid.*). Universities can uniquely play three specific roles, namely 'to combine knowledge and expertise, to think and plan together; to develop strategic alliances and frameworks; and to facilitate practical ways of working together with other stakeholders in support of those strategies' (Cook, 2010, p. 34). Universities can also act as catalysts to mobilise other actors to achieve different goals in society. They can disseminate scientific information for regional development. The university's third mission, community engagement, dictates that they are in a strategic position to promote learning cities and regions.

In Tanzania, the number of universities has significantly increased from two in 1990 to 40 public and private universities and university colleges in 2011 (Tanzania Commission for Universities, 2011). The increased number of institutions by itself, however, does not necessarily mean successful learning cities or regions. Universities need to collaborate among themselves and to partner with other stakeholders in the community if they are to become a driving force for national and regional development and thus regional competitiveness (Newlands, 2003). A meaningful impact of universities is a function of networking with actors such as businesses, municipalities and non-governmental organisations (NGOs). A notable increase of these potential actors in recent years in Tanzania offers an essential avenue and potential for developing interesting learning cities or regions.

The contribution of universities in Africa can be enhanced even further when a strong network for innovations among different actors is assured (Jutte, 2010).

Most Tanzanian universities appear to be at an early stage of developing regional inter-university networks. One pan-African initiative is the Zain Africa Challenge. This is a televised, academic fast-paced quiz competition programme that brings together more than 100 public and private universities to compete for the Zain Scholars Trophy, with over US$1,000,000 in grants and prizes. The competition is sponsored by the Zain mobile-phone company and covers a wide range of topics including: history, science, African culture, geography, literature, music and current events. The Zain challenge involves ministries of education in each of the participating countries (Zain Africa Challenge, 2010) and is one of the exemplary ways in which the business–university network can promote learning regions.

Second, the Inter-University Council for East Africa (IUCEA) is a regional intergovernmental organisation established by Kenya, Tanzania and Uganda in 1980. It serves as a platform for East African universities to discuss academic and non-academic issues related to higher education, and help to maintain high and comparable academic standards. IUCEA also aims to promote sustainable and competitive development of universities in the region by responding to the challenges facing higher education and helping universities to contribute to national and regional development needs, including strengthening cultural and professional ties among partner states (MOEVT, 2010). In partnership with European institutions, IUCEA works on projects aimed at creating, developing and strengthening social science and humanities research networks through which scholars and institutions can collaborate (IUCEA, 2010).

Is Dar es Salaam a learning city?

Many milestones need to be passed before a city becomes a learning city. As mentioned earlier, until recently, there have been few studies of learning cities in the African context. In one of his studies, Longworth cautions that cities should not label themselves as learning cities without transforming their traditions and basic learning infrastructure. Drawing on the European Lifelong Learning Initiative conceptual framework, Longworth suggests that a city can only become a learning city when it:

> ... *goes beyond its statutory duty to provide education and training for those who require it and instead creates a vibrant, participative, culturally aware and economically buoyant human environment through the provision, justification and active promotion of learning opportunities to enhance the potential of all its citizens.* (Longworth, 2001, p. 602)

Some of the indicators that a city is developing into a learning city include: partnership and resources; learning events and family involvement; innovative ways of using information and communication technology for learning; and networks of people and organisations.

Dar es Salaam is one of the capital cities in East Africa, and is not only Tanzania's capital but also the country's economic and political centre. Dar es Salaam can be singled out as the most developed city in Tanzania in terms of educational facilities and the availability of higher education institutions. The frequently cited institutions in Dar es Salaam include the University of Dar es Salaam (UDSM, the oldest university in the country), Ardhi University (AU), Open University of Tanzania (OUT), Hulbert Kairuki Memorial University (HKMU), International Medical Technological University (IMTU), Tumaini University and Muhimbili University. Despite the growing number of private universities in Tanzania since 1995, most of these are very small and lack strong research and training capacity (IUCEA, 2005, cited in Oketch, 2009).

In addition, the increasing number of higher learning institutions in Dar es Salaam has not motivated a robust inter-institutional collaboration and there seems to be a missing link between the different learning and education actors such as municipalities, universities and NGOs. Despite the growing number of NGOs in Dar es Salaam, only a few have formal collaboration with the universities in terms of utilising expertise and research outputs. Deficiencies in the existing education system include growing concerns that most of the formal education provided is still bureaucratic. Teachers are still viewed as authoritative figures and education involves the unidirectional role of transferring knowledge and skills to the learner (UDSM, 2005). In extreme instances, it has also been reported that a number of students are leaving primary school before achieving basic literacy levels (Minnis, 2006).

The adoption of learning cities and the positioning of universities to promote such a venture for most countries in the south, including Tanzania, is therefore still characterised by many challenges. One such challenge is the conceptualisation of lifelong learning. Torres (2003, p. 20) noted that lifelong learning is conceptualised and emphasised as a principle for learning systems in most countries in the global north but is still prescribed and implemented narrowly as mainly basic education in developing countries such as Tanzania. Similarly, non-formal education is largely associated with remedial education for those who missed it, rather than being recognised as lifelong learning for all (Preece, 2009).

Other challenges include inadequate or non-use of universities as sources of scientific knowledge and innovation. Although universities are identified as the most valuable resources for generating scientific knowledge and producing specialised personnel, the capacity inherent in universities is hardly utilised for policy development and implementation (NEPAD, 2009). A related problem is the need to transform the culture in universities to promote engagement, as 'many universities are ignorant of the objectives and activities of regional bodies and communities' (*ibid.*, p. 3). Most of the current efforts are simply directed towards expanding participation.

Limitations within universities include shortage of funds and resources arising from their failure to cope with numbers of students that far exceed the capacity of campuses; shortage of highly qualified faculty staff, particularly with the newly introduced private universities; poor quality of teaching and learning; an ineffective ICT environment; negligible output of research; outmoded methods of institutional governance; and poor links with the productive sectors of the economy (Altabach, 1987). Most university libraries have insufficient librarians, are poorly stocked and have outdated and dilapidated reference books, journals and other teaching and learning resources (Ilomo, 1985; Lujara *et al.*, 2007).

Given these limitations, most of the efforts in universities themselves run contrary to the perspectives pertaining to a learning city and lifelong learning.

At the University of Dar es Salaam, for instance, despite a relatively recent curriculum review in 1994, there are concerns that teaching and learning are still based on traditional teacher-centred lecturing models, as reflected in the University of Dar es Salaam external academic audit report (UDSM, 2005). Although the university had been committed to the use of seminars and tutorials in teaching, 'students were still treated as mere recipients of knowledge; they were not given adequate opportunity to participate fully in the teaching/learning through asking questions and making comments' (UDSM, 2005, p. 10).

The way forward

A framework suggested by Boshier (2006, pp. 36–7) is a potential way forward for universities and other actors in Tanzania towards developing vibrant learning cities and regions. The steps could include the sensitisation of policy makers, academicians and the community at large on the centrality of promoting learning rather than education: 'Learning has to be a preoccupation of every agency and setting' (Boshier, 2006, p. 37).

Since the lack of resources seems to be a major limitation in executing lifelong learning, there is a need to take stock and locate all potential resources for learning, both human and non-human. This needs to be done at institutional, city or regional levels.

At present, there is a loose set of links and networks between universities and other actors. There is a need to bring together academicians, practitioners, NGOs and experts from different sectors to explore possible areas for networking and ways in which each sector can mutually promote lifelong learning. For example, the Tanzanian National Library might find ways to collaborate with the universities in providing more learning resources and opportunities to the public. Similarly, ICT resources and connectivity have consistently been cited as a backbone for lifelong learning, so there is a need to take deliberate measures to improve student, staff and public access to ICT facilities and open resources. This may include providing free access to internet and other resources in public libraries since the current arrangement of charging a user fee may deter some users.

Deliberate measures should also be taken to transform traditional authoritarian teaching methods into a more collaborative process. This can be facilitated by activities such as learning festivals, competitions and so on.

Conclusion

This chapter has explored the contextual challenges facing universities in Tanzania and the opportunities available for them to promote learning cities and regions. While it is clear that universities by themselves cannot promote learning cities, we have highlighted their critical role in promoting them and mobilising other actors. This chapter has also drawn attention to the differing rates of progress towards establishing learning cities between countries in the global north and those in the global south. Despite the challenges facing them, universities in the global south need to develop more vibrant learning networks and broader partnerships with other actors in society in order to promote learning regions and, eventually, a culture of lifelong learning. We suggest, therefore, that whereas the concept of learning cities and learning regions seems to be new and less developed in Tanzania, there is potential for learning regions to thrive.

References

Altbach, P. (1987) *Higher Education in the Third World: Themes and Variations*. New Delhi: Sangam Books.

Avoseh, M.B. (2001) 'Learning to be an active citizen: Lessons from traditional African lifelong learning', *International Journal of Lifelong Learning*, Vol. 20 No 6, pp. 476–86.

Bagdonas, A. (2010) 'The educational interests of citizens and actions to satisfy them in the learning city of Kaunas', in N. Longworth and M. Osborne (Eds), *Perspectives on Learning Cities and Regions: Policy, Practice and Participation*. Leicester: NIACE, pp. 70–83.

Bhalalusesa, E.P. (2005) 'Education for all in Tanzania: Rhetoric or reality?' *Adult Basic Education: An Interdisciplinary Journal for Adult Literacy Educational Planning*, Vol. 15 No 2, pp. 67–83.

Boshier, R. (2006) 'Widening access by bringing education home', in A. Oduaran and H.S. Bhola (Eds), *Widening Access to Education as Social Justice: Essays in Honor of Michael Omolewa*. Dordrecht: Springer, pp. 23–43.

Chapman, J. and Aspin, D. (1997) *The School, the Community and Lifelong Learning*. London: Cassell.

Coffield, F. (2000) 'Introduction: A critical analysis of the concept of learning society', in F. Coffield (Ed.), *Differing Visions of a Learning Society: Research Findings*. Bristol: The Policy Press, pp. 1–38.

Cook, R. (2010) 'The pan-northern collaboration project between the HE sector and the cultural industries in the UK', in N. Longworth and M. Osborne (Eds), *Perspectives on Learning Cities and Regions: Policy, Practice and Participation*. Leicester: NIACE, pp. 29–42.

Cooke, P. and Morgan, K. (1998) *The Associational Economy: Firms, Regions and Innovation*. Oxford: Oxford University Press.

Doloreux, D. and Parto, S. (2004) 'Regional innovation systems: A critical synthesis', United Nations University: Institute for New Technologies, discussion paper series, No 2004–17. Retrieved 20 April 2012 from http://www.intech.unu.edu/publications/discussion-papers/2004-17.pdf

Doukas, C. (2010) 'Space and time dimensions of lifelong learning: The approach of learning cities', in N. Longworth and M. Osborne (Eds), *Perspectives on Learning Cities and Regions: Policy, Practice and Participation*. Leicester: NIACE, pp. 181–197.

Engeström, Y. (2001) *Expansive Learning at Work: Towards an Activity-theoretical Reconceptualisation*. London: University of London.

Field, J. (2006) *Lifelong Learning and the New Educational Order*, second edition. Stoke on Trent: Trentham Books.

Florida, R. (1995) 'Toward the learning region', *Futures*, Vol. 25 No 5, pp. 527–36.

Ford, B. (2002) 'Learning in post industrial organisations: Experiences of reflective practitioners in Australia', in D. Istance, H. Schuetze and T. Schuller (Eds), *International Perspectives on Lifelong Learning: From Recurrent Education to the Knowledge Society*. Buckingham: Open University, pp. 115–26.

Gal, Z. (2010) 'The role of research universities in regional innovation: The case of southern Transdabubia, Hungary', in N. Longworth and M. Osborne (Eds), *Perspectives on Learning Cities and Regions: Policy, Practice and Participation*. Leicester: NIACE, pp. 84–105.

Hosseini, N.D. (2006) 'Lifelong learning and the knowledge society: Challenges for developing countries', *Journal of College Teaching and Learning*, Vol. 12 No 3, pp. 79–84.

Ilomo, C.S. (1985) 'Towards more effective school library programmes in Tanzania'. Occasional paper No 23. Dar es Salaam: Tanzania Library Services.

Istance, D., Schuetze, H. and Schuller, T. (2002) 'From recurrent education to knowledge society', in D. Istance, H. Schuetze and T. Schuller (Eds), *International Perspectives on Lifelong Learning: From Recurrent Education to Knowledge Society*. Maidenhead, Open University Press, pp. 1–21.

IUCEA (2010) 'Overview of the IUCEA'. Inter-University Council for East Africa. Retrieved 10 May 2010 from http://www.iucea.org/index. php?option=com_contentandview=articleandid=1andItemid=109

Jutte, W. (2010) 'The art of managing networks and shaping constructive partnerships', in N.O. Longworth and M. Osborne (Eds), *Perspectives on Learning Cities and Regions: Policy, Practice and Participation*. Leicester: NIACE, pp. 252–67.

Lave, J. (1991) 'Situating learning in communities of practice', in L. Resnick, J. Levine and S. Teasley (Eds), *Perspectives on Socially Shared Cognition*. Washington, DC: American Psychological Association.

Lave, J. and Wenger, E. (1991) *Situated Learning*. Cambridge: Cambridge University Press.

Longworth, N. (2001) 'Learning communities for a learning century', in D. Aspin, J. Chapman, M. Hatton and Y. Sawano (Eds), *International Handbook of Lifelong Learning*. London: Kluwer Academic Publisher.

Longworth, N. and Davies, W.K. (1996). *Lifelong Learning*. London: Kogan Page.

Longworth, N. and Osborne, M. (2010) 'Introduction', in N. Longworth and M. Osborne (Eds), *Perspectives on Learning Cities and Regions: Policy, Practice and Participation*. Leicester: NIACE, pp. 1–28.

Lujara, S.K., Kissaka, M., Trojer, L. and Mvungi, N.H. (2007) 'Introduction of open-source e-learning environment and resources: A novel approach for secondary schools in Tanzania' *World Academy of Science, Engineering and Technology*, Vol. 26, pp. 331–5.

Maclachlan, K., and Osborne, M. (2009) 'Lifelong learning, development, knowledge and identity', *Compare*, Vol. 39 No 5, pp. 575–83.

Maratuona, T. (2006) 'Lifelong learning for facilitating democratic participation in Africa', *International Journal of Lifelong Learning*, Vol. 25 No 6, pp. 547–56.

Minnis, J. (2006) 'Nonformal education and informal economies in sub-Saharan Africa: Finding the right match', *Adult Education Quarterly*, Vol. 56, pp. 119–33.

MOEVT (2010) *Higher Education Handbook*. Ministry of Education and Vocational Training. Dar es Salaam: Government Printer.

Morgan-Klein, B. and Osborne, M. (2007) *The Concepts and Practices of Lifelong Learning*. New York: Routledge.

NEPAD/FARA/CTA/INWENT (2009) NEPAD tertiary education dialogue, 'Engaging tertiary institutions in the CAADP process', held at the FARA Secretariat offices, 28–30 July. Retrieved 12 April 2009 from http://www.hubrural.org/IMG/pdf/Nepad-Tertiary-Institutions-Dialogue-Accra-Report.pdf

Newlands, D. (2003) 'The role of universities in learning regions'. Paper presented at ERSA, August 2003 Congress, Jyvaskyla, Finland.

Nyerere, J. (1963) 'Inauguration of the University of East Africa', in J.K. Nyerere (Ed.), *Freedom and Unity [UhurunaUmoja]: A Selection from Writings and Speeches*, 1959–65. Dar es Salaam: Oxford University Press, pp. 218–21.

Nyerere, J. (1973) 'Adult education year', in J.K. Nyerere (Ed.), *Freedom and Development [Uhuru na Maendeleo]: A Selection from Writings and Speeches*, 1968–1973. Dar es Salaam: Oxford University Press, pp. 137–41.

OECD (2007) 'Regional engagement: The future for higher education?' Retrieved 10 October 2009 from www.oecd.org/edu/imhe

Oketch, M. (2009) 'Public–private mix in the provision of higher education in East Africa: Stakeholders' perceptions', *Compare*, Vol. 39 No 1, pp. 21–33.

Omolewa, M. (2002) 'The practice of lifelong learning in indigenous Africa', in C. Medel-Anonuevo (Ed.), *Integrating Perspectives of Lifelong learning in the South*. Hamburg: UNESCO UIE, pp. 13–17.

Osborne, M. and Morgan-Klein, B. (2007) *The Concepts and Practices of Lifelong Learning*. London: Routledge.

Osborne, M., Sankey, K. and Wilson, B. (Eds) (2007) *Social Capital, Lifelong Learning and the Management of Place: An International Perspective*. London: Routledge.

Piazza, R. (2010) 'From permanent education to the learning region: Elements of analysis and comparison of pedagogic models', in N. Longworth and M. Osborne (Eds), *Perspectives on Learning Cities and Regions: Policy, Practice and Participation*. Leicester: NIACE, pp. 198–228.

Preece, J. (2009) *Lifelong Learning and Development: A Southern Perspective*. London: Continuum.

Schuetze, H. and Casey, C. (2006) 'Models and meanings of lifelong learning: Progress and barriers on the road to a learning society', *Compare*, Vol. 36 No 3, pp. 279–87.

Stenvall, J., Syvajarvi, A., Vakkala, H. and Harisalo, R. (2010) 'Trust capital and change management in successful organization mergers', in N. Longworth and M. Osborne (Eds), *Perspectives on Learning Cities and Regions: Policy, Practice and Participation*. Leicester: NIACE, pp. 141–67.

Tanzania Commission for Universities (2011) *The Universities and University Colleges of Tanzania*. Dar es Salaam: TCU.

Toland, J. and Yoong, P. (2005) 'Learning regions in New Zealand: The role of ICT', *International Journal of Education and Development using ICT*, Vol. 1 No 4, pp. 54–68.

Torres, M. (2003) 'Lifelong learning: A new momentum and a new opportunity for adult basic learning and education (ABLE) in the south', *Adult Education and Development, Supplement*, Vol. 60, pp. 1–240.

Torres, M. (2009) *From Literacy to Lifelong Learning: Trends, Issues and Challenges in Youth and Adult Education in Latin America and the Caribbean.* Paris: UNESCO UIL.

UDSM (2005) *Report on the 2004 UDSM Academic Audit Report.* Dar es Salaam: University of Dar es Salaam.

Walters, S. and Watters, K. (2001) 'Lifelong learning, higher education and active citizenship: From rhetoric to action', *International Journal of Lifelong Education*, Vol. 20 No 6, pp. 471–8.

Zain Africa Challenge (2010) 'Zain Africa challenge'. Retrieved 20 February 2010 from http://www.zainafricachallenge.com/ZAC/info.html

Prospects for learning cities in Africa: Lessons from the PIE experience

Peter Kearns and Abel Ishumi

Introduction

Chapter 1 highlighted that formal agreements between universities and their cities are only just beginning to emerge on the African continent. While Gaborone in Botswana and Durban in South Africa can demonstrate recently formulated partnerships, prospects for the rest of the continent are usually still at the speculation stage.

But, as the Botswana chapters have already identified, partnerships require culturally sensitive innovation and sharing of insights and lessons from international experiences, which can be adapted to the distinctive contexts and needs of African cities and their universities.

Experience elsewhere suggests that partnerships between universities and learning cities can offer much to address a range of social, cultural and economic issues in a strategic way that harnesses the power of learning in diverse community contexts.

This chapter places the university engagement and learning cities debate in a historical, global context, using the PASCAL International Exchanges (PIE) project as one example of an electronic resource that enables African universities and other stakeholders to exchange ideas and experiences around the world. PIE was inaugurated by PASCAL in January 2011 to share information experience between universities and cities. At present, 11 universities and cities are participating in PIE across five continents, with two of their cities (Dar es Salaam and Dakar) located in

Africa. A third African city, Kampala, has recently been added to the PIE exchanges.

In this context, this chapter provides an overview of some aspects of the development of PIE to date with a focus on themes raised by university academics in Dar es Salaam and Dakar. It suggests some directions for the role of universities in the development of learning cities in Africa if the potential of this approach to social, cultural and economic development in cities is to be realised. The emphasis is on developing an African model that is responsive to the distinctive needs and conditions of African cities and their higher education institutions.

The learning city concept

The learning city (community/region) concept emerged from the work of the Organisation for Economic Co-operation and Development (OECD) on lifelong learning, drawing attention to the opportunities to harness learning in many contexts through partnership and a shared strategic vision. Projects funded by the European Commission have explored strategies for building sustainable learning communities and a significant information base now exists through the EUROlocal project and other sources.

An early manifestation of the concept of a learning city was in an OECD report, *City Strategies for Lifelong Learning*, prepared in 1992 for the second Congress of Educating Cities in Gothenburg. This conference led to the formation of the International Association of Educating Cities (IAEC, 2012).

The European Union envisaged lifelong learning as an organising principle for promoting all forms of education so that the European Year of Lifelong Learning in 1996 gave a considerable boost to the development of learning cities in countries such as the UK. This led to the establishment of the UK Learning Cities Network in that year (Hamilton and Jordan 2011, p. 196). By this time it was well recognised that learning occurs in many contexts so that informal learning was important in a learning city.

This flavour was caught up in a statement by Kearns *et al.*, as follows:

> *Cities are not simply places where people live and work, they are also places where people experience leisure, culture, enter-*

*prise and education ... A learning city unites all the diverse
providers of learning to meet the needs and aspirations of its
citizens. Through the range of local resources they bring
together, learning cities can provide local solutions to local
challenges* (Kearns *et al.* (1999), p. 6)

As chapter 1 has already indicated, universities are recognised as major
providers of learning, particularly in the context of lifelong learning. This
broad concept of a learning city uniting with learning providers to produce
'local solutions to local challenges' remains relevant to university–learning
city partnerships in Africa and is discussed below.

The research and writings of Norman Longworth on learning cities (communi-
ties/regions) have been influential and have reflected a number of initiatives
supported with European Commission funding (Longworth, 1999; 2006).

Longworth drew on his work with the European Lifelong Learning Initiative
to articulate a broad humanistic definition of a learning city:

*A learning community is a city, town or region which mobilises all
its resources in every sector to develop and enrich all its human
potential for the fostering of personal growth, the maintenance
of social cohesion, and the creation of prosperity.* (Longworth
(1999, p. 109))

At the same time he expressed the important role of local government in
fostering such a community:

*A learning community is a city, town or region which goes
beyond its statutory duty to provide education and training for
those who require it, and instead creates a vibrant, participa-
tive, culturally aware and economically buoyant human environment through the provision, justification and active promotion of
learning opportunities to enhance the potential of all its citizens.*
(*ibid.*, p. 112)

While these 1999 statements articulated this humanistic concept of a learning
city, Longworth's later work builds on a number of projects funded by the
European Commission to elaborate various aspects of the learning city
concept. The engagement challenge for African universities is to develop

a distinctive role with the numerous stakeholders in cities in a way that promotes mutuality and partnership.

The Botswana experience, outlined in detail in this book, offers further insights into the university role as a collaborator. Much useful information and knowledge has also been gained from the experience of European countries over more than two decades in developing learning partnerships of various kinds (cities and regions). In the light of the experience of PIE, this chapter asks: what adaptations should be made in developing the concept of a learning city relevant to the needs and conditions of African contexts?

PASCAL international exchanges (PIE)

While PIE is broadly concerned with strategies for building sustainable learning cities, not all participating contributors are formally involved in university–learning city partnerships, and a flexible approach has been adopted. Two initial subjects were identified for PIE of experience: strategies to build inclusive learning cities; and cultural institutions as arenas for lifelong learning.

It was expected that the PIE agenda would evolve with experience, and this has indeed happened. PIE is frankly experimental in testing the potential of the internet to foster online exchanges of information and experience, and to serve as a forum to generate new ideas and approaches. After a year of experience, it is reasonable to say that the jury is still out, although much valuable information and experience has been collected and shared on the PIE website (PASCAL Observatory, 2010–11).

The PIE methodology involves two principle actions. Each contributor provides a short stimulus paper of about two or three pages with a set of questions. These papers are posted on the PIE website to encourage blog responses to the issues raised from participating universities and cities, and the PASCAL community generally. PIE stimulus papers are intended to provide a general profile of the city, summarise a few key developments, and include a set of four or five questions for discussion. The Dar es Salaam, Dakar and Bielefeld papers provide typical examples. They can be sourced from the PIE website at http://pie.pascalobservatory.org/pie-themes.

In addition, the managers of the PIE projects (Kearns and Wilson) post briefing and discussion papers from time to time to draw attention to key areas of

PIE and city development. Papers on 'Culture, learning and development' and 'Making learning city devclopment creative and innovative' are available on the PIE website and illustrate this aspect of PIE development.

PIE has now progressed to a second stage of development, based on five major themes: cultural policy; responding to social change; preserving the environment; information and communications technology and media; and mobilising civil society. As with the city stimulus papers, each theme is launched with a paper which is intended to open up the subject for subsequent blogging.

Heritage and cultural policy

A core theme in PIE development throughout 2011 was the role of heritage and cultural institutions as arenas for lifelong learning and building communities. This has taken a number of forms throughout the year and is relevant to the wider university engagement agenda as reflected in the UNESCO (1998) statement cited in chapter 1. Some examples in PIE exchanges include:

- The inaugural PIE subject of cultural institutions as arenas for lifelong learning
- The publication during 2011 of the report, *Heritage, Regional Development, and Social Cohesion*, based on papers delivered at the June 2010 PASCAL international conference in Östersund, Sweden (Kearns *et al.*, 2011)
- PIE briefing and discussion papers on culture, learning and development; and making learning-city development creative and innovative
- The PIE major themes on cultural policy.

The intrinsic interest of PIE in heritage and culture reflects a belief that they provide important resources for lifelong learning and building communities, and that culture is central to sustainable learning cities. This is also emphasised in Ntseane's chapter in this book as an area of learning where the university could contribute. The important role of cultural institutions as arenas for lifelong learning and advancing social inclusion is brought out in the Glasgow stimulus paper and in papers by O'Neill (2011) and Sani (2011). O'Neill demonstrates how museums and galleries in Glasgow have progressed between elitist, welfare and social justice phases in their development. Sani illustrates the role of museums in 'the learning age' through a number of projects funded by the European Commission.

The material in the heritage and cultural strand of PIE development is relevant to fostering lifelong learning and building learning cities with universities in Africa. It points to the significance of drawing on traditional approaches to learning in strategies that recognise the centrality of a sense of identity and belonging in building sustainable learning cities.

This need exists as much in Europe as in Africa, as Zipsane pointed out in a challenging blog (Zipsane, 2011) titled 'We are more! The overlooked potential of learning through cultural engagement'. One of the early insights from the PIE experience is to ensure that partnerships linking learning cities include cultural providers so that the great potential of cultural institutions and contexts for lifelong learning is fully exploited.

Dar es Salaam

The Dar es Salaam stimulus paper for PIE was written by Professor Abel Ishumi and Mpoki Mwaikokesya (2011) with a focus on the problems caused by rapid urbanisation in a city that has experienced exponential growth. The paper pointed out that Dar es Salaam had grown from a mere 5,000 people in 1895 to some three to four million at present.[6] This rapid growth has confronted the city with a broad spectrum of challenges, and it is 'in a seeming state of unpreparedness and inadequate anticipatory planning [which] could have a choking effect on the present and an even greater implication for future development'.

In this focus on the effects of unchecked urbanisation resulting from the migration of large numbers of people from rural areas into cities such as Dar es Salaam, the paper illustrates one of the great challenges to be addressed across much of Africa. There is a broad spectrum of issues affecting the quality of life of people in burgeoning cities. Africa is not alone in being confronted by the challenge of rapid urbanisation, and a similar situation exists in much of Asia and elsewhere. These are critical issues where international exchanges of ideas and experience could have much value and where universities have a role to play.

The Dar es Salaam stimulus paper develops the problem of urbanisation in Dar es Salaam in terms of six key challenges:
- Unemployment, which is estimated at 46 per cent of the population of the city, and particularly affects young people

- Poverty, which is extensive and severe, claiming 51 per cent of the population who live on less than the equivalent of US$1 a day
- A widening income disparity between the poor and affluent
- Poor housing
- Poor urban transportation, with much traffic congestion
- The 'invasion' of public open spaces.

The main point made about these issues in the stimulus paper hinges on the reality that their scale and complexity means they cannot be successfully addressed by the city council alone. There is a critical need for broad partnership and collaboration – involving central government, private citizens and a range of public and private institutions, including universities. What has been termed in the PIE exchanges 'mobilising civil society' is a necessary part of this partnership building.

While the stimulus paper does not go into detail about possible action, it suggests several projects that fit well with the concept of a Dar es Salaam learning city acting in a collaborative way with universities and other education providers to address the problems of rapid urbanisation. These include decongesting the city with the support of central government, investors, and property developers to encourage the development of planned satellite towns; action to encourage urban slum dwellers to relocate to satellite towns; preparing user-friendly information materials to foster understanding of a range of threats, including ill- health, in congested urban contexts; and encouraging many more projects across broad areas of public education, welfare, harnessing community resources, and job creation. There is a strong case in the stimulus paper for the view that the critical issue for Dar es Salaam is how to work towards broad structures for collaboration and partnership that foster a shared vision of the future and encourage enterprising initiatives to address the spectrum of challenges confronting the city. Through research and collaboration, university departments have potential to play a strong role in addressing these challenges.

A further issue to emerge is whether the learning city concept can contribute to progress. The Dar es Salaam experience has posed a challenge of a different order and magnitude from the other city experiences posted on the PIE website, and it is not surprising that blog responses have addressed selected aspects of the overall situation, rather than the central question.

Up to now, there have been 16 blog responses to the Dar es Salaam paper. A useful contribution to the stimulus paper was that ongoing exchanges of experience through twinning cities and other partnership arrangements can have value. A partnership example was given of Glasgow, where a collaborative agreement exists between universities in the city. It was suggested that such agreements between stakeholder groups could extend in a kind of 'ripple effect' as a practical way of building partnership and collaboration. The twinning idea was taken up with experience from the PALLACE project (Longlearn, 2007) which linked schools in a number of countries during 2002–5. The value of this strategy for a 'trickle down' effect was recognised, although establishing a mutual learning process was seen as an issue.

Blog responses perceived re-engaging marginalised young people as a priority. This question has been taken up elsewhere on the PIE website with the role of social enterprises as one of the strategies suggested.[7] This strategy gives young people practical experience in running a business and fosters the acquisition of relevant knowledge and skills through this experience. Other contributions took up the university role, arguing that universities had to be active players in addressing the issues identified, not just observers. Overall, the exchanges supported the view in the stimulus paper that the growing problems of urbanisation and poor planning were some of the critical issues confronting cities in developing countries such as Tanzania.

Environment as a major theme

Chapter 5 by Dube highlights a range of environmental issues that connect with universities and the concept of lifelong learning. A lead paper by an eminent Tanzanian environmentalist, Godfrey Kamukala (2011), opened up the new environment theme of PIE. His paper elaborated some of the issues raised in the Dar es Salaam stimulus paper with a focus on air pollution; solid waste generation and disposal; water pollution; sand mining; and environmental management.

The questions he posed for PIE exchanges included whether the issues discussed were present in other African cities; the immediate steps that could be taken in moving towards a 'sustainable green economy and city' and what should be the long-term structural objectives in progressing global sustainability.

There are obviously long-term issues where strategic responses are needed over time to achieve sustainable development. Two of the suggestions made in the blog exchanges were:

- Dar es Salaam City Council should establish a multidisciplinary think tank of planners, ecologist-environmentalists, sociologists, anthropologists, economists and technologists to bring forward integrated responses
- A cadre of urban social anthropologists should be created within the employment of the city council.

The first of these proposals related to an action team set up in Vancouver and bodies established in cities such as Lusaka, Kitwe, Ndola, Luanshya, Mongu and Kabwe.

The PIE exchanges on environment reinforced the view emerging from the discussion of the Dar es Salaam stimulus paper that considerable innovation and leadership are required in addressing the challenges thrown up by rapid urbanisation. Universities hold a potential source of contributors to such think tanks from different disciplines. We comment below on some of the steps that appear to be needed.

The Kampala contribution

The need for partnership in addressing the major challenge of rapid urbanisation has been taken up in a new addition to the PIE exchanges for Kampala. The stimulus paper by Dr Joseph Oonyu and Dr Josephine Esaete examines the issues resulting from rapid population growth in Kampala, and recognises that partnership between the Kampala City Authority and Makerere University's College of Education and External Studies could contribute much (Oonyu and Esaete, 2012, p. 3).

Their paper further contains the argument that broad partnership and ongoing interaction of this nature could serve to transform Kampala City Authority into a learning organisation, as defined by Peter Senge:

> *Learning organisations ... where people continually expand their capacity to create the results they truly desire, where new and expansive patterns of thinking are nurtured, where collective aspiration is set free, and where people are continually learning how to learn together.* (Senge, 1990, p. 3)

Linking the alliances between city authorities and education institutions to a development process in which city administrations evolve as learning organisations, 'where new and expansive patterns of thinking are nurtured … and where people are continually learning how to learn together' (*ibid.*), adds a further dimension to the case for partnership enunciated in the Dar es Salaam stimulus paper. It points to ways in which African cities and universities working together can enhance capacity to address the major challenges confronting them.

The Kampala City stimulus paper also has considerable value in suggesting very practical ways in which a university/city administration partnership can contribute to addressing the big issues confronting city entities (Oonyu and Esaete, 2012, p. 3).

Dakar

The Dakar stimulus paper written by Lamine Kane brought different perspectives to a consideration of how community learning strategies might be applied in supporting socio-economic and cultural development in African cities. This paper is notable for its recognition of the significance of heritage and cultural values:

> *Among all these influences, culture seems to me the most determinant factor that finally models and gives to education systems their souls and their life. Education and culture are then closely linked to one another.* (Kane, 2011, p. 1)

We agree fully with this perspective and would join Amartya Sen in asserting that cultural issues can be critically important for development if seen as supporting the freedom and well-being of people (Sen, 2001, p. 6).

Kane points out that the Senegalese cultural heritage is made up of a mixture of three distinct influences:
- The Negro-African civilisation, which is characterised by an endogenous culture and a diversity of national languages spoken alongside French, which is the sole official language
- The Arabo-Islamic civilisation, which dates from the ninth century and is characterised by the presence and influence of the Arabic language, the Islamic religion and the Holy Koran

- The European influence (from a French colonial presence lasting over three centuries) which brought the French language, Christianity and the Bible, and also the current administrative, juridical and political policies and practices.

While such a diverse heritage can bring problems, as the South African experience demonstrates (Hamilton *et al.*, 2011), it can also be a source of richness and strength, and a stimulus to learning and community building:

> *It is in these diverse and dynamic social groupings that now constitute well organised civil society organisations where citizens meet, discuss, exchange and find solutions to their problems. In these groupings people learn from one another, individuals are teaching groups and vice versa.* (Kane, 2011, p. 1)

This notion of the importance of heritage and culture leads easily to recognition of the significance of informal learning in a wide range of socio-cultural settings. Hence, it also leads to understanding of an approach to learning communities in Africa that mobilises civil society organisations and traditional ways of learning.

Kane develops this line of analysis by discussing the Senegalese experience of the Empowerment Adult Education programmes that were organised and launched by various civil society organisations. Participants learnt a wide range of things relevant to daily living, such as human rights, critical thinking, hygiene and health, and problem-solving methods. The methodology was generally based on traditional oral methods such as dialogue, theatre, poetry, songs and dance. These activities have led to initiatives in many Senegalese communities, such as community clean-ups, women's savings groups for economic improvement, health associations and various movements against gender discriminatory practices. The social movements resulting from adult education programmes demonstrate the power of informal and group learning strategies, especially when drawing on African communal and tribal life (Kane, 2011, p. 2).

Heritage and culture as vehicles for lifelong learning

The Senegalese experience outlined in Kane's stimulus paper demonstrates the important role that heritage can play in providing lifelong learning opportunities and in contributing to an organic approach to a learning community that draws on a living heritage from communal and tribal life. His paper offers a response to the question he poses: 'Are we to lose our own cultural and civilisation values as we deeply enter in the global world?' (Kane, 2011, p. 4).

A recent study by Walters *et al.* (2012, p. 46) about promoting lifelong learning in selected African countries also recognised the importance of linking strategies for learning communities with African traditions and practices of community-based learning. It concluded that these traditions and practices align well with the concept of a learning society. Consultations undertaken in Ethiopia and Kenya as part of the study pointed to the reality that a new vision for education could be reached only if 'it is embedded in the structure and life of local communities'. This understanding was carried over to one of the recommendations of the study:

> *Recommendation 4: Adopt the approach of building a learning society family by family, community by community, district by district through tapping into the long existing traditions of community learning and convert national policy guidelines into sustainable action at local levels.* (Walters *et al.* 2012, p. 46)

This reflects the sentiments articulated in chapter 1 about the Africanisation of universities as partners in development. While this approach is compelling in rural areas, it remains to be seen how it might be applied in the rapid growth cities, such as Dar es Salaam. The fate of traditional tribal and community bonds in the cauldron of rapid urban growth requires close examination to identify strategies that would progress the spirit of this recommendation in urban contexts. We envisage this as the task of a new generation of African learning cities.

The broad concept of culture implicit in the Dakar stimulus paper reflects the concept of culture adopted by the 1982 Mexico City Declaration on Cultural Policies:

> *In its widest sense, culture may be said to be the whole complex of distinctive spiritual, material, intellectual and emotional features that characterise a society or social group. It includes not only the arts and letters, but also modes of life, the fundamental rights of the human being, value systems, traditions and beliefs.* (Commonwealth Foundation, 2008, p. 12)

This broad concept of culture should be seen as an essential underpinning of an African approach to building sustainable learning cities that are able to draw on the strengths of heritage while also addressing the challenges of the twenty-first century global society. Building such an amalgam is a key development task for African cities.

The key role of cultural and heritage issues was recognised in the report of the 2010 PASCAL Östersund conference:

> *Cultural and heritage issues are increasingly significant in a world of mass migration and rampant urbanisation leading to increased diversity in many communities. In this context, intercultural understanding, tolerance, and cultural competence are necessary attributes of sustainable and cohesive learning communities in building a sense of community and shared identity.* (Kearns *et al.*, 2011, p. 11)

Lessons from Dar es Salaam, Kampala and Dakar PIE contributions

There are two key insights that emerge from the Dar es Salaam, Kampala and Dakar contributions to PIE. First, there is the need for partnership, collaboration and a shared vision in addressing the problems of rapid urbanisation in African cities. Second, there is the importance of heritage and culture in harnessing the living traditions of an African community to provide learning opportunities throughout life and build a sense of identity and community.

The first insight emerges from the scale and magnitude of the urban development problems confronting cities such as Dar es Salaam and Kampala, which go beyond the capacity of city councils alone to resolve. Broad partnerships are required that mobilise key stakeholders, including civil society organisations, central government and universities. A learning city initiative can provide a framework and vision for such partnership development. The city council role is centrally important in ensuring that an appropriate framework for partnership is put in place.

The Dakar experience of drawing on heritage and fostering informal learning in many contexts demonstrates key dimensions of an African learning city model that builds on a living heritage to foster a sense of identity and community. The local initiatives engendered by this strategy exemplify the multiplier effects that can result.

A good deal has been done to promote cultural development in cities and local government through initiatives such as Agenda 21 for Culture (Institute of Culture, 2004), the work of the Arterial Network (2011) to advance cultural policies and Africa's creative sector, and the Commonwealth Foundation's Putting Culture First initiative (Commonwealth Foundation, 2008). Much could be gained by ensuring that cultural and learning developments in cities are connected so that cultural institutions and policies become vehicles for advancing learning throughout life and for building community.

Towards a new generation of twenty-first-century learning cities

The experience of African cities and their universities, such as those in Dar es Salaam, Kampala and Dakar, adds to insights emerging from a number of cities in East Asia. Together, they suggest there is a need to work towards a new generation of learning cities that build on international experience in fostering lifelong learning and creating innovative learning cities. At the same time, there is a need to carry forward a living cultural heritage and sense of identity, and address the big issues confronting cities in an era of mass migration and rampant globalisation.

Such a generation of innovative learning cities will be both fundamentally local in their organic development, and richly global in their responsiveness to twenty-first-century issues and opportunities. While partnership and a shared vision will be at their core, they will be characterised by shared values, enterprise, and many forms of non-traditional partnership that mobilise civil society and draw on the many learning resources existing in communities.

There is currently much development of learning cities in the countries of East Asia such as China, South Korea, and Chinese Taiwan[8], which has thrown up the question of the characteristics of an East Asian approach to the learning city. A Korean educator, Han SoongHee, answered this question in the following terms:

> *In sum, the East Asian model of a learning city seems to focus more on cultural learning experiences and liberal adult educa-*

134

tion, especially for the elderly, the economically inactive, and the under educated. (SoongHee, 2011, p. 210)

Which learning-city model to adopt is still an open question in this period of dynamic development, driven by the efforts of organisations such as the UNESCO Institute for Lifelong Learning and PASCAL, as well as local initiatives. However, there is a strong case that African cities and their universities should not be left behind in harnessing the learning city model and adapting it to local conditions, as is happening in East Asia.

We accordingly conclude this chapter with three suggestions for action to carry forward development of an African approach to mobilising the great potential of the learning city model. This approach will build sustainable and liveable African cities that foster well-being, community and learning opportunities throughout life:

- There should be active recruitment of a diverse network of African cities and their universities to join Dar es Salaam, Kampala and Dakar in participating in the PASCAL International Exchanges (PIE) to share ideas and experience within this network and the PASCAL community[9]
- A coordinated campaign should be undertaken to communicate to city councils the value and benefits of a learning city approach to addressing major development issues such as health, environment, poverty, public safety and the response to large-scale migration
- Ways should be found to support conceptual development in clarifying the characteristics of an African model for learning city development, and strategies that progress this vision.

Europe has done much to foster ideas of lifelong learning and learning communities within its own cultural contexts. The African traditional philosophical heritage of learning as a collective endeavour is a potential resource for adaptation in the urban context. There is a need to generate approaches that are both responsive to the diverse local needs and conditions across the continent, while also contributing to societal well-being locally and globally.

Much could be gained if a network of collaborating African learning cities were to emerge with links to PASCAL and UNESCO, and through these organisations to similar networks of learning cities in other regions.

The idea of a global learning village has much to commend it.

References

Arterial Network (2011) *Adapting the Wheel: Cultural Policies for Africa.* Cape Town: Arterial Network.

Commonwealth Foundation (2008) *Putting Culture First: Commonwealth Perspective on Culture and Development.* London: Commonwealth Foundation.

Hamilton, C., Harris, V. and Hatang, S. (2011) 'Fashioning legacy in South Africa: Power, pasts and the promotion of social cohesion', in P. Kearns, S. Kling and C. Wistmann (Eds), *Heritage, Regional Development and Social Cohesion.* Östersund: Fornvårdaren 31, pp. 146–59.

Hamilton, R. and Jordan, L. (2011) 'Learning cities: The United Kingdom experience', in P. Kearns, S. Kling and C. Wistmann (Eds), *Heritage, Regional Development and Social Cohesion.* Östersund: Fornvårdaren 31, pp. 193–207.

Institute of Culture (2004) *Culture 21.* Barcelona: United Cities and Local Governments.

IAEC (2012) 'International association of educating cities'. Retrieved 12 April 2012 from http://www.bcn.es/edcities/

Ishumi, A. and Mwaikokesya, M. (2011) 'Dar es Salaam stimulus paper: The City of Dar es Salaam – a "haven of peace" in search of ideas and initiatives for renewal and change'. Retrieved 11 June 2011, from http://pie.pascalobservatory.org/pascalnow/blogentry/pie/dar-es-salaam-stimulus-paper

Kamukala, G. (2011) 'The city of Dar es Salaam striving to resolve environmental problems'. Retrieved 26 November 2011 from http://pie.pascalobservatory.org/pascalnow/blogentry/pie/city-dar-es-salaam-striving-resolve-environmental-problems

Kane, L. (2011) 'Dakar stimulus paper: Achievements of African learning cities – the Senegalese example'. Retrieved 11 June 2011 from http://pie.pascalobservatory.org/pascalnow/blogentry/pie/dakar-stimulus-paper

Kearns, P., Kling, S. and Wistmann, C. (Eds) (2011) *Heritage, Regional Development and Social Cohesion.* Östersund: Fornvårdaren 31.

Kearns, P., McDonald, R., Candy, P., Knights, S. and Papadopoulos, G. (1999) *VET in the Learning Age: The Challenge of Lifelong Learning for All*. Vol. 1. Adelaide: NCVER.

Keming, H. (2011) 'The development of an institutional framework of lifelong learning in China', in J. Yang and R. Valdés-Cotera (Eds), *Conceptual Evolution and Policy Developments in Lifelong Learning*. Hamburg: UNESCO Institute for Lifelong Learning, pp. 61–9.

Longlearn (2007) 'City rings and the PALLACE project'. Retrieved 15 January 2011 from http://www.longlearn.org.uk/pallace.html

Longworth, N. (1999) *Making Lifelong Learning Work: Learning Cities for a Learning Century*. London: Kogan Page.

Longworth, N. (2006) *Learning Cities, Learning Regions, Learning Communities: Lifelong Learning and Local Government*. London: Routledge.

O'Neill, M. (2011) 'Museum access: Welfare or social justice?' in P. Kearns, S. Kling and C. Wistmann (Eds), *Heritage, Regional Development and Social Cohesion*. Östersund: Fornvårdaren 31, pp. 14–27.

Oonyu, J. and Esaete, J. (2012) 'Kampala City stimulus paper'. Retrieved 27 February 2012 from http://pie.pascalobservatory.org/pascalnow/blogentry/pie/kampala-stimulus-paper

PASCAL Observatory (2010–11) 'Pascal international exchanges'. Retrieved 12 April 2012 from http://pie.pascalobservatory.org/

Sani, M. (2011) 'Museums in the learning age', in P. Kearns, S. Kling and C. Wistmann (Eds), *Heritage, Regional Development and Social Cohesion*. Östersund: Fornvårdaren 31, pp. 28–39.

Sen, A. (2001) 'Culture and development'. Keynote address at World Bank meeting in Tokyo, 13 December 2001. Retrieved 12 June 2011 from http://info.worldbank.org/et00ls/voddocs/351/688/sen-tokyo.pdf

Senge, P. (1990) *The Fifth Discipline: The Art and Practice of The Learning Organisation*. New York: Doubleday.

SoongHee, H. (2011) 'Introduction to building a learning city', in J. Yang and R. Valdés-Cotera (Eds), *Conceptual Evolution and Policy Developments in Lifelong Learning*. Hamburg: UNESCO Institute for Lifelong Learning, pp. 209–21.

The Economist, 13 December 2010

UNESCO UIE (1998) Report on the preparatory meeting for the world conference on higher education, Paris, October 1998, of the International Working Group on University-based Adult Education. Hamburg: UNESCO UIE.

Walters, S., Yang, J. and Roslander, P. (2012) *Study on Key Issues and Policy Considerations in Promoting Lifelong Learning in Selected African Countries: Ethiopia, Kenya, Namibia, Rwanda and Tanzania*. Tunis: Association for the Development of Education in Africa.

Zipsane, H. (2011) 'We are more! The overlooked potential of learning through cultural engagement'. Retrieved 27 January 2011 from http://pie. pascalobservatory.org/search/node/Zipsane?page=2

PART 2

COMMUNITY ENGAGEMENT
AND SERVICE LEARNING

Community engagement and service learning have evolved in response to imperatives to develop citizenship responsibility among students and develop the tradition of the university's third mission, community engagement. This third-mission role is slowly becoming more sophisticated in some universities, though the practice is uneven. In some cases it has become an extension of the extra-mural tradition that was introduced into West and East Africa in the mid-1940s. In other cases it is a response to changing political systems and efforts to nurture a greater sense of social responsibility. The chapters in this section of the book cover speculations and practical descriptions as well as empirically based findings about different practices across anglophone parts of the continent.

Chapter 8 by Preece *et al.* reports on an action research project between four universities that were participants in the PASCAL Universities for Regional Engagement (PURE) initiative. The universities were based respectively in Nigeria, Malawi, Botswana and Lesotho. The project is offered as a starting block for the more ambitious, formalised partnership concept of learning cities or regions. It shows how the traditional mission of community service can develop into a more collaborative, 'engagement' approach. This addresses some of the criticisms outlined in earlier chapters about the 'ivory tower' image of universities, lack of recognition of indigenous knowledge practices and the multidisciplinary nature of development problems.

The eight case studies explore collaborative, community needs-led activities, using a multidisciplinary approach with an effort to integrate indigenous knowledge practices in community training where relevant. The authors show that community service/engagement operates on a continuum of approaches which vary from staff-based initiatives to engagement with student service learning components. While the case studies demonstrate mutual learning gains, the short-term nature of the projects raises arguments about the need for a lifelong learning approach to partnerships in order to address sustainability issues. Furthermore, the absence of an institution-based policy framework for such work reveals the fragility of student and staff commitment without recognised reward systems and dedicated funding.

Chapter 9, by Openjuru and Ikoja-Odongo, reminds us that community engagement in the form of outreach and part-time course provision is not a new concept. Moreover, if there is a university-wide strategy, some of the coordination problems outlined in chapter 8 can be addressed. The authors describe the historical and contemporary context for extra-mural work at Makerere University in Uganda – one of the earliest universities to establish links with the wider public as a result of the British Commission intervention in the 1940s (see chapter 1). Like Modise and Mosweunyane (chapter 3), the authors position Makerere University within the neo-liberal discourse of knowledge transfer partnerships, thus linking community engagement with concepts of innovation and competitiveness.

The chapter explores the concept of community engagement in a slightly different way from chapter 8, showing the diversity and slipperiness of terms that all purport to have a relationship to engagement. Community engagement in this context is linked to decentralised delivery of knowledge transfer in the form of courses or research, all aimed at serving the lifelong learning needs of communities, organisations and businesses. But here again (as in chapter 1), the emphasis is on recognising that knowledge production is a two-way process and no longer the prerogative of universities. This is the only chapter that links to distance education as a feature of engagement, thus emphasising the relationship between curriculum development and consulting the wider community. While there is strong evidence of cross-university engagement, the authors tend to focus on staff, rather than student, involvement in the partnerships. Field attachments in the form of work experience are mentioned but the subsequent two chapters elaborate on the potential and the challenges of developing such attachments as service learning components for students.

Tagoe, in chapter 10, identifies community service learning as a strategy to break down the one-way relationship between universities and their communities by linking university students directly with community needs. This is intended to encourage the mutual learning benefits outlined in the action research project of chapter 8.

Tagoe, however, argues specifically for its introduction into the discipline of adult education – the traditional discipline that embraced extra-mural work. Like Openjuru and Ikoja-Odongo, Tagoe shows the historical evolution of adult education through extra-mural work (this time in Ghana, emanating from recommendations in the British Commission reports of the 1940s), arguing that 'adult education has always been about social transformation'. However, he shows that the origin of the service learning term emanated from the USA and is most commonly applied in South Africa (the subject of chapter 11). He positions service learning as a deliberate initiative to integrate 'community service with educational objectives [that] ensure equal focus to the provider and recipient'. Its pedagogical focus is experiential learning, rather than the traditional lecture mode of education – supporting the claim articulated by Mwaikokesya in chapter 6. In this respect, learning is linked directly to reflection and action, but the service learning element also includes the notion of reciprocity so that 'all parties help determine what is to be learned'.

Although Tagoe defends service learning strongly as an ideological aspect of community engagement that potentially empowers knowledge producers, O'Brien, in chapter 11, demonstrates the complexities of this ideology when it is put in practice. O'Brien's chapter reports on an extensive study of service learning within the South African contexts (36 service learning initiatives involving at least 96 communities, more than 800 higher education students and relevant academic staff at nine universities). She frames service learning within four discourses of engagement: scholarship, benevolent engagement, democratic engagement and professionalism. She reflects on the power relationship, development processes, identities and environmental issues related to service learning as engagement activities.

The chapter is a timely reminder of the definitional and context-specific complexity of community engagement and service learning. The practice also suffers from issues of curriculum coherence, competing priorities of service learning partners, problems of understanding boundaries, identities and the place of indigenous knowledge in the context of new knowledge. Thus these chapters collectively show that there is still much work to do in establishing productive engagement relations between higher education institutions and their surrounding environments.

Community engagement within African contexts: A comparative analysis

Julia Preece, Idowu Biao, Dorothy Nampota and
Wapula N. Raditloaneng

Introduction

The chapters in the first section of this book have discussed the role of universities in contributing to learning cities and regions on a political level. Many universities do not have such an integrated political relationship with their region or city. Indeed, as other publications on this topic have shown, such relationships may take several years to develop and university members may themselves remain unconvinced of the value of moving away from more traditional strategies for knowledge creation. It is therefore pertinent to look at other models of university engagement on a rather more localised scale. Such an approach serves to demonstrate concrete examples of what is possible in order to attract wider political interest, or it may simply provide the building blocks to nurture a stronger institutional commitment to engagement.

It is this latter perspective that influenced the ITMUA project. ITMUA stands for Implementing the Third Mission of Universities in Africa. It was a pan-African action research study funded by the Association of African Universities between 2010 and 2011, involving the University of Calabar in Nigeria, the Universities of Botswana and Malawi, and the National University of Lesotho. The aim was to explore the extent to which university community service missions were addressing, and could be developed to address, national priorities in relation to some of the eight Millennium Development Goals (MDGs[10]) that had been agreed in the year 2000 by most countries around the world as global targets to be reached by 2015.

This chapter briefly revisits the literature that informed the project's approach to community service and how this term has more recently evolved into the notion of community engagement. A short explanation of the methodology, its phases of institutional audit, stakeholder discussions and case studies, and a summary of the outcomes of phases 1 and 2 precede a brief description of the case studies, their findings and subsequent recommendations for institutional reform.

Concepts and policies

The conceptual relationship between community 'service' and 'engagement' has evolved considerably over a relatively short time. For instance, Lazarus *et al*. (2008) trace the shift in terminology across South African policy documents over a period of ten years from 'community service' to 'knowledge-based community service' to 'community engagement' and now to a 'scholarship of community engagement' (p. 61). Inman and Schuetze, as recently as 2010, highlight the changing perceptions of university–community–regional relationships. During the timescale of ITMUA itself, the distinctions between the concepts of community service and engagement became blurred.

Nevertheless, university mission statements and strategic goals across the partner universities tend to refer to 'service' rather than 'engagement' but often within wider policy contexts of commitment to national development.

So, for example, the Lesotho poverty reduction strategy paper (Government of Lesotho, 2004) and education sector strategic plan (Government of Lesotho, 2005) highlight priorities in line with the MDGs, including poverty reduction, food security, education and lifelong learning, improved health and reduction of HIV/AIDS. The National University of Lesotho's own vision statement provides a complementary platform for these policy documents, with the aim to 'be a leading African university responsive to national socio-economic needs, committed to high quality teaching, lifelong learning, research and community service' (National University of Lesotho, 2007, p. 4). Strategic goals embrace 'strengthening partnerships', addressing the MDGs and 'producing relevant and responsive programmes'.

The Malawi growth and development strategy (Government of Malawi, 2005) and national education sector plan (Government of Malawi, 2007) highlight priorities in line with the MDGs, including poverty reduction, food security, education and lifelong learning, improved health and reduction of HIV/AIDS. Malawi University's vision statement includes the phrase 'research and services for sustainable development of Malawi and the world' (University of Malawi, 2004, p. 12). Strategic goals address MDG issues such as HIV and AIDS and human rights (p. 39).

The Economic Community of West African States (ECOWAS) Vision 2020 (ECOWAS, 2009) and Nigeria's national policy on education (Government of Nigeria, 2004) highlight priorities of poverty reduction, food security, education and lifelong learning, and health and reduction of HIV/AIDS. Calabar University's vision statement and strategic goals also include the words 'community service' (University of Calabar, 2004, p. 36).

The Botswana poverty reduction strategy paper (Government of Botswana, 2004) and University of Botswana strategic plan (Government of Botswana, 2007) highlight concerns with poverty reduction, food security, education and lifelong learning, and reduction of HIV/AIDS. The university's strategic goals include the strengthening of engagement with different communities, access and participation.

During the start-up phase of attempting some common understandings of the terminology for the project, it became apparent that there is no universal definition of either 'community' or 'community service'. Hall (2010, p. 23) states that community:

> *... can be taken as a cluster of households or an entire region, as an organisation ranging from a provincial government department to an NGO, as a school, clinic, hospital, church or mosque or as part of the university itself ... communities are loosely defined as social organisations. But community also functions as an adjective, as a qualifier that indicates work that is socially beneficial.*

Although the University of Botswana has its own definition of community service, the following definition by Lulat (2005) was adopted for the purposes of auditing community service activities across the partners:

> *[An] extension of university expertise to the world outside the university, the community, in the service of improving the quality of life of the community and which is effected through a university*

> *model in which community service is integral to all aspects of the
> university: mission, structure and organisation, hiring and pro-
> motion, curriculum and teaching, research and publications etc.*
> (*ibid.*, p. 262)

In this definition, it is apparent that community service should be applied within a whole institutional strategy. It is also seen as closely aligned to the notion
of community work as 'a process of creating a shared vision among the community (especially the disadvantaged) and partners ... in society' (Hall, 2010,
p. 25). In general, it is associated with doing public good. Community service,
however, needs a process of participatory dialogue in all its activities. It is now
recognised as requiring a more collaborative, needs-led approach where learning is seen as a two-way process between higher education and community
(Keith, 2005). Furthermore, it has potential for much more integration with
the university's other core missions of teaching and research so that it can contribute to knowledge production as well as knowledge dissemination.

As a result of this more elaborate vision, 'community engagement' is now
the more popular term. With engagement, the notion of partnership with a
range of agencies within and around the community is implied. Schuetze, for
instance, states that:

> *Community engagement is defined broadly, namely as the colla-
> boration between institutions of higher education and their
> larger communities (local, regional/state, national, global) for
> the mutually beneficial exchange of knowledge and resources in
> a context of partnership and reciprocity.* (Schuetze (2010, p. 25)

The term community 'engagement' therefore takes us beyond simply addressing communities of need and encourages us to think of a wider resource of
partners within communities and regions. It encourages the notion of reciprocity and knowledge transfer in multiple directions. This was the approach that
the ITMUA project attempted to address throughout its research. The research
questions for each institution were:

- How is the university's third mission being developed and imple-
  mented?
- How do third-mission activities contribute to addressing the
  Millennium Development Goals?
- To what extent and in what ways can the university enhance
  and integrate its existing activities (research and teaching linked

to community service) to accommodate MDG priorities in its region?
- What works, in what context and what are the challenges for implementation?

Methodology

An action research, phased approach to the study was used. Action research is a recognised strategy in educational research where participation and dialogue are combined with a process of application and review (Stringer, 2004). There were four phases:
- Phase 1: an initial audit of relevant policy literature and existing activities that could be classified under the banner of community service
- Phase 2: a consultative phase with four stakeholder groups – academics, civil society, postgraduate students and government ministries – to examine how the university roles were perceived in relation to the MDGs and surrounding communities
- Phase 3: where two case studies per institution piloted a multi-disciplinary approach to community service/engagement along-side in-depth qualitative evaluation
- Phase 4: reporting back to the wider academic community and the consultative stakeholder groups. This included revised action plans and the production of policy briefings on how to improve the university's contribution to national and local development needs.

The studies were analysed country by country, then comparatively across countries (Nampota, 2011), drawing on qualitative data from interviews, observations and focus-group discussions, in order to identify patterns and context-specific issues for a better understanding of what works where, how and why.

Findings

Phase 1: Initial audit

An internal audit of existing activities was benchmarked against inter-national standards of community engagement. Examples of existing practice were collected from each university. Their community-service activities were then measured against a benchmarking tool (Charles and Benneworth, 2009) that was adapted from the global PASCAL Universities for Regional Engagement (PURE) project. Features of this benchmarking tool were selected and reworked to accommodate the MDG focus of the ITMUA project.

The benchmarking tool classified the universities' involvement in community service across five levels (*ibid.*, p. 4):
- Level 1 indicated that the main form of activity was through isolated individuals 'acting from a mixture of altruism and desire to access resources'
- Level 3 indicated 'some institutional commitment but tends to be restricted to key departments and focused around core research roles'
- Level 5 would indicate 'strong institutional commitment with wide-ranging involvement from across the university including students. University is a key stakeholder in the initiative and seeks to enrol other agencies and facilitate collaboration across traditional boundaries'.

The level of activity in each university ranged from level 1 to level 3. The ITMUA aspiration was to move towards level 5.

Phase 2: Consultation
Following this audit, each university carried out the consultation phase in the form of workshops with the four stakeholder cohorts. In total, 26 postgraduate students, 58 university academics, 21 representatives from civil society organisations and 11 people from government ministries took part. Although each country context demonstrated different degrees to which community engagement activities were operating, the overall findings were remarkably similar. In their analysis of current university activities, most people could cite examples of university responsiveness to, for example, MDG 1 (poverty reduction), MDG 2 (universal primary education), MDG 6 (HIV/AIDS prevention and awareness) and MDG 7 (environmental awareness).

Examples of university visibility in Lesotho included farming activities and services to local communities, collaboration with the Ministry of Education regarding monitoring of free primary education provision, the institution's own HIV/AIDS policy and 'know your status' campaigns by the Faculty of Health Sciences.

In Malawi, examples of curriculum innovation included the Fine and Performing Arts Department Theatre for Development course; a Faculty of Law practical legal studies course to help students deal with specific cases at the Zomba prison; and a Home Economics Department theory and practice course in early childhood care to enable students to appreciate issues of nutrition and health in local communities.

Examples of Calabar's activities included agricultural feasibility studies and advice on sustainable land management, building of toilets in five riverine communities to use urine and human faeces for crop production, and incorporation of indigenous knowledge in conservation processes.

Examples of the University of Botswana's activities included its contribution to ending the HIV/AIDs scourge through the Students Against Aids initiatives and the counselling services provided at the university clinic.

However, while the concept of community service was broadly understood, it was recognised that much more work was needed to integrate community service with teaching and research. Unlike the other three partners, the University of Botswana recognises community service in its promotion criteria for staff, and this became a stakeholder recommendation for all the partners. Other recommendations for improvement, articulated across the stakeholder groups, included the need for collaborative planning and implementation with communities and employers; the introduction of more intern programmes for students; more community-based research; and wider dissemination of research findings to improve service delivery and community livelihoods.

Phase 3: Case studies

Following these audits and discussions, each university selected two case studies for in-depth monitoring with a view to examining the challenges and practicalities of what worked where, how and why. The criteria for selecting projects included their potential for multidisciplinary involvement and their involvement in a collaborative needs analysis to ensure that the university was responding to community-identified needs, rather than initiatives that had been decided solely by the university. In each case, the following questions formed the focus for the monitoring and evaluation stage:

- What processes were involved in conducting the community service activity?
- What were the perceived benefits to community, university and other providers?

- What were the main challenges in terms of organisation, addressing the community problems, etc.?
- What were the recommendations for improving and sustaining the university's community engagement?

Lesotho identified one remote rural project and a second one closer to the main campus. The Mohoma Temeng project in a remote mountain area of Qacha's Nek caters for orphans and vulnerable children across 40 scattered villages. Members required skills in managing income-generation projects, looking after livestock and supporting the care needs of their surrounding villages. Meanwhile, the Roma pensioner project was a response to earlier studies into the ways in which pensioners use their monthly stipend of approximately US$38. A needs analysis revealed a range of education and health-care needs from nutrition to gardening, from managing abusive families to making pension funds stretch further. Pensioners wait for several hours during collection days, providing a window of opportunity for health and other interventions. Participating disciplines in both projects included the Faculties of Agriculture and Health Sciences, Adult Education and Business Management, along with students from a counselling course in the Department of Theology and external contributors such as the police and NedBank.

For Malawi, the Nyanya Group village headman project, located about four kilometres from Chancellor College (CC) and consisting of 18 villages, was the main case study. A needs analysis conducted in the community revealed a range of education, nutrition and health-care needs including irrigation farming in order to reduce hunger, skills for combating and mitigating HIV and AIDS and meeting other needs related to large population size, alcohol and drug abuse, and general poverty that impacted on schooling of children. Participating students included those involved in a Theatre for Development project to raise awareness of exploitation and decision-making issues in the community. The Muula community-based childcare (CBCC) project had originally been developed by one Master's-level student in the Home Economics Department in response to the community's nutrition and early childhood education needs. ITMUA evaluated this project and reviewed its current curriculum in order to identify issues for training the project caregivers.

Calabar identified two new projects. The sex workers project in the Atakpa area of Calabar addressed the needs of 12 female sex workers. The women required greater awareness of sexually transmitted diseases, training in vocational skills and skills in managing income-generation projects in order to abandon sex work ultimately. The Departments of Adult and Continuing Education and Nursing were involved in this project, in addition to two civil society organisations with the mission of reducing HIV/AIDS infection. The women farmers initiative in the Uwanse area of Calabar sought to make farming, particularly vegetable farming, a cheaper venture through training in compounding of organic fertiliser. The project taught basic principles of bookkeeping and sought to equip women farmers with marketing strategies appropriate both for their farm products and for the area of Calabar. The Departments of Crop Science and Adult and Continuing Education were involved in this project, as well as two civil society organisations with a mission that includes women's concerns. The needs analyses that preceded the establishment and running of the two projects revealed a range of education and health-care needs. The sex workers emphasised sewing as their preferred vocational skill while female farmers showed great appreciation for the ability to prepare their own fertiliser using local materials.

Botswana selected a remote project in the far west of the country and an established local community initiative that required an injection of skills support. For the remote rural location, a community-based planning programme called the 'zooming approach', based on the self-drive mindset of communities, was undertaken by Ba Isago University College in partnership with the W.W. Kellogg Foundation. The location was D'Kar and the surrounding resettlements in Ghanzi, which were occupied by a minority group, the San Tribe. Efforts to sustain projects once the donors had completed their term with these communities had previously failed. The aim of the zooming approach is to build local leadership capacity and empower communities at source to reduce poverty and improve their livelihood. It focuses on creating a favourable development environment, sustaining individual confidence and ensuring resources for communities to lead their own social and economic transformation. The participants needed skills in identifying income-generating projects, the basics of small business management, entrepreneurship, effective financial management, marketing cultural products, bookkeeping for small businesses, good leadership and governance.

The second project, Lentswe-La-Oodi Weavers, was a cooperative owned predominantly by women, which had operated since 1973. With little marketing exposure, their assorted artwork sat, unsold, in their store. There was no skills transfer or training, goods were sold only in Oodi, and there was a need to create an external market. The women needed business, management, entrepreneurial, marketing and accounting skills.

In almost all of the case studies, leadership came from academic staff, though students were often involved. In the Lentswe-La-Oodi Weavers project, leadership came almost entirely from a group of students who had established themselves as a voluntary business advisory clinic as part of their degree studies. In most cases student involvement was voluntary, though in the Malawi Nyanya group village headman project, students were also assessed on their involvement as part of their coursework.

The case studies were comparatively analysed in relation to the different ways in which the universities and communities engaged with each other; their ability to address the MDGs; the learning articulated by students, academics and community members; and some of the challenges associated with this kind of work.

The process of community engagement
The experiences of these projects reveal differing approaches to community engagement that can be plotted on a continuum from 'outreach' activities to 'community engagement with service learning'.

'Outreach' represents one extreme of the continuum, usually referring to a one-off activity conducted by the university to help address community needs. A slightly more progressive concept is 'community service', which is reflected in the mission statements of the four universities.

Both 'outreach' and 'community service' concepts are criticised for their one-dimensional relationship – universities providing knowledge and resources to address a community problem. Schuetze's (2010) concept of 'community engagement' departs from this understanding and emphasises collaboration between the university and the community for mutual exchange of knowledge and resources. Other researchers have added the concept of 'service learning to community engagement. 'Service learning' incorporates the notion that students should be assessed for the learning they undergo in the process of collaborating with the community (Bringle and Hatcher, 2007).

The community service continuum could thus appear as follows (Nampota, 2011, p. 110):

| Outreach community service | → | Community engagement | → | Community engagement with service learning |

One general observation from implementation of the case-study projects is that the partner institutions did not conduct their activities in isolation. Rather, different groups of people collaborated in the implementation of the projects in each case. In some projects, whole departments were involved while, in others, only a few individuals took an active part.

Two projects involved academic staff only. In other cases local and international stakeholders played a part, depending on the needs identified. In general, collaborations were necessary in the implementation of all the projects. While some of the collaborations increased funding opportunities, others enhanced the process of addressing varied but interconnected needs faced by the communities. It became evident, however, that a multidisciplinary approach to community service is a must if the development needs of communities are to be addressed meaningfully.

Addressing the MDGs
All the projects addressed MDG 1, reduction of poverty and hunger, linking to MDG 2, education, and MDG 6, HIV and AIDS. However, other MDGs were also addressed, arising largely from the needs of the communities in the different countries and reflecting the varied range of development challenges which the African continent faces (Oyewole, 2010).

In terms of poverty, in addition to income-generating skills, issues of freedom and capability for agency (Sen, 1999) were addressed. The latter feature includes knowledge or skills to act independently for productivity or personal welfare.

Phase 4: Reporting back
The stakeholder feedback phase consisted primarily of reporting back on project findings and discussing recommendations arising out of the comparative analysis.

Lessons from the project experiences

The projects demonstrated a range of different learning outcomes for the various participants.

Student learning
The findings showed that students and staff who took part in the projects benefited from the context-specific experience of putting theory into practice.

Community members acquired skills, knowledge and understanding that they were able to put to immediate use.

The Theatre for Development students in Malawi learnt more about the problems of their neighbouring communities and how Theatre for Development theories can be applied to real-life situations. In addition, the students learnt how to gain entry into the community and how to arrive at shared meanings with community members, which was particularly necessary:

> *We had a lot of problems to get village headmen understand our goals and give us the right people for our activities. Initially they just gave us their relatives because they thought that we are there to give presents to some people and these had to be their relatives.* (Focus group 1 with Theatre for Development students)

> *The community members thought that we had come to spy on them so they initially did not mention the challenges they face to enable us to work out possible solutions with them through theatre. It took several visits and talking to different groups of people for us to get the rapport that was necessary for us to work.* (Focus group 2 with Theatre for Development students)

Community learning

Community members in general mentioned the irrigation farming skills and techniques they had learnt and put into practice as their academic benefits.

One major benefit mentioned by all groups of respondents was greater understanding of their own problems. This is exemplified by the following from two groups of community members in Malawi:

> *The activities have helped us to understand our own problems ... sometimes you think they are not your problems, or indeed that they are not problems at all. But through theatre, we realised that some of the issues we experience are problems – if we fall sick after drinking water from the river, it is a problem.* (Community focus group)

> *That the poor yields result from our own practices, the money we get from selling land finishes quickly but the poverty that results from the selling of land lasts forever.* (Community focus group)

Botswana community members emphasised their appreciation of the consultation process:

> *We had a gathering of leaders and community members where there was consultation ... everything they did they consulted with us.* (Councillor)

They also mentioned learning a number of practical skills. The training programme in D'Kar, for example, included strategic planning forums, technical skills training workshops, demonstrations, look and learn tours, engagement with Government of Botswana departments in Ghanzi District and participation in practical development projects:

> *The project provided special leadership skills to the traditional and elected leaders running the Trusts, who needed to provide visionary leadership in future projects.* (Focus group)

> *I gained a lot from training on good governance ... as a Board member I was able to put the knowledge into practice and applied it in handling critical issues at board meetings ... it enlightened me a lot.* (Board member)

> *I learnt how to manage my profits, how to sustain my business so that it does not suffer ... how to market myself ... where I can go to seek assistance.* (Workshop participant)

Academic staff learning

It was not only workshop participants who learnt. The project director, for instance, had this to say:

> *As the director of the project I have benefited immensely from working with the community, Kellogg and D'Kar Trust. I had been told that in D'Kar things are impossible, I have seen that things are possible to do with the community ... there is need for persistence, and understanding and patience.* (Project director)

And this was echoed by university staff:

> *The college has benefited by engaging the services of many highly qualified consultants to run workshops, produce modules,*

> *which are now owned by the college and can be used to improve its curriculum.* (Ba Isago staff)

> *I have widened my knowledge on how communities differ in involvement of different projects.* (Training facilitator)

Challenges

There were also challenges, particularly in relation to how far the university was raising expectations for ongoing support against a concern to avoid setting up a dependency relationship between the community and university. The responses were similar across all the case studies. In Botswana, for instance, there were still indications that the dependency mindset had not disappeared completely. Some participants were finding it difficult to break old habits of waiting for things to happen for them:

> *We needed information, new knowledge about running a business ... we expected money to enhance our businesses or start one ... for the garden a lot of items are needed, such as electricity for pumping water, tractors and ploughs, forks for digging the ground ... we need farm implements.* (Community focus group)

In all the communities, there was evidence that the knowledge and understanding gained from the training had a direct effect and made a difference for some participants. Some, for instance felt able to start up small businesses. However, a change in mindset is a process that occurs over a period of time.

The reward systems for staff involved in community service work were not clearly stated in any of the four partner institutions. In addition, staff observed that community service work outlined in the strategic plans and policy of three of the partner institutions did not appear to be fully recognised in the organisational structure. In the University of Malawi, for example, the research mission benefits from the existence of the university research coordination office. However, this structure is not available for community service, resulting in limited inclusion of such work in the formal curriculum.

Concluding remarks

The case studies indicated that with focused coordination, community needs-led collaboration and effort by key players in each institution, academic staff from different disciplines, students and community members can work together for a common goal. This results in shared and mutual learning that contributes to the university knowledge base as well as enhancing wider teaching and learning skills. Furthermore, it was evident that such work has a positive impact on addressing the MDGs, thus contributing to a contemporary and relevant curriculum. However, the long-term nature of development requires sustained involvement that would stretch beyond the lifespan of the case studies. This needs ongoing funding and commitment which would be hard to sustain without an institutional infrastructure that both rewards and supports engagement activities.

Policy recommendations

These recommendations centred on ideas for institutional improvement. Wade and Demb (2009) highlight some baseline requirements for implementing an effective institutional engagement mission. They are summarised here as mission and leadership; staff involvement, promotion, tenure and reward systems; policy; budget allocation and organisational structure. Indeed, globally, there is growing interest in developing community engagement as a university strategy to meet national and regional development needs, as evidenced in the UNESCO 2009 world conference, 'Higher education: The new dynamics of higher education and research for societal change and development'.

However, the findings from these case studies indicated that the current university approach is usually *ad hoc*, poorly documented and uncoordinated, making it difficult to market, disseminate or promote institutional activities to the nation or funders.

A centralised coordination strategy for each institution is therefore recommended. In the process of institutionalising community engagement, the project partners also felt that it was important to emphasise how community engagement work enhances the teaching and research core missions of universities. University policy should therefore encourage staff to use community engagement as an integrating thread to university work.

Centralised coordination would require a dedicated management position for third-mission work. Associated activities would then include regular curriculum review to ensure relevance to national development priorities, and recognition of staff and student involvement through credit and promotion structures. Community engagement consultation strategies should ideally be built into policy frameworks to reflect initiatives such as needs analyses, university dissemination and marketing of their work, and regular consultations with external agencies and ministries to ensure a holistic and collaborative contribution to development.

One suggestion for ensuring institutional implementation of policy change was that universities should request that their government provide ring-fenced funding that is specifically targeted at the community service or engagement mission as an institutional policy.

These recommendations were summarised in policy briefing papers that were submitted to the partners' respective stakeholders.

References

Bringle, R.G. and Hatcher, J.A. (2007) 'Civic engagement and service learning: Implications for higher education in America and South Africa', *Education as Change*, Vol. 11 No 3, pp. 79–89.

Charles, D. and Benneworth, P. (2009) *Benchmarking the Regional Contribution of Universities*. Newcastle University: HEFCE.

ECOWAS (2009) 'Vision 2020'. Economic Community of West African States. Retrieved 11 January 2012 from http://ecowascdp.org/

Government of Botswana (2004) *Poverty Reduction Strategy*. Gaborone: Government Printer.

Government of Lesotho (2004) *Poverty Reduction Strategy 2004/5–2006/7*. Maseru: Government Printer.

Government of Lesotho (2005) *Education Sector Strategic Plan 2005–2015*. Maseru: Government Printer.

Government of Malawi (2005) *Growth and Development Strategy 2006–2011*. Lilongwe: Government Printer.

Government of Malawi (2007) *National Education Sector Plan 2007–2017*. Lilongwe: Government Printer.

Government of Nigeria (2004) *National Policy on Education*. Abuja: Federal Government of Nigeria Press.

Hall, M. (2010) 'Community engagement in South African higher education', in Council on Higher Education (Ed.), *Community Engagement in South African Higher Education. Kagisano No 6*. Auckland Park: Jacana Media, pp. 1–52.

Inman, P. and Schuetze, H.G. (2010) 'Introduction', in P. Inman and H.G. Schuetze (Eds), *The Community Engagement and Service Mission of Universities*. Leicester: NIACE, pp. 2–12.

Keith, N.Z. (2005) 'Community service learning in the face of globalization: Rethinking theory and practice', *Michigan Journal of Community Service Learning*, spring, pp. 5–24.

Lazarus, J., Erasmus, M., Hendricks, D., Nduna, J. and Slamat, J. (2008) 'Embedding community engagement in South African higher education', *Education, Citizenship and Social Justice*, Vol. 3, pp. 57–83.

Lulat, Y.G.M. (2005) *A History of African Higher Education from Antiquity to the Present*. Santa Barbara CA: Greenwood Publishing Group.

Nampota, D. (2011) 'Emerging issues on the "process" and "outcomes" of community service from the experiences of the eight country case studies', in J. Preece (Ed.), *Community Service and Community Engagement in Four African Universities*. Gaborone: Lentswe La Lesedi, pp. 107–20.

National University of Lesotho (2007) *Strategic Plan 2007–2012*. Roma: NUL.

Oyewole, O. (2010) 'Africa and the global knowledge domain', in D. Teferra and H. Greijn (Eds), *Higher Education and Globalisation: Challenges, Threats and Opportunities for Africa*. Maastricht: Maastricht University Centre for International Cooperation in Academic Development (MUNDO), pp. 19–32.

Schuetze, H.G. (2010) 'The third mission of universities: Community engagement and service', in P. Inman and H.G. Schuetze (Eds), *The Community Engagement and Service Mission of Universities*. Leicester: NIACE, pp. 13–32.

Sen, A. (1999) *Development as Freedom*. Oxford: Oxford University Press.

Stringer, E. (2004) *Action Research in Education*. Columbus, Ohio: Pearson/ Merrill Prentice Hall.

UNESCO (2009) 'World conference on higher education'. Retrieved 11 November 2011 from http://www.unesco.org/en/higher-education/

University of Botswana (2007) *Strategic Plan 2007–2012*. Gaborone: UB.

University of Calabar (2002) *Strategic Plan 2002–2007*. Calabar: UNICAL Press.

University of Malawi (2004) *Strategic Plan*. Zomba: University of Malawi.

Wade, A. and Demb, A. (2009) 'A conceptual model to explore faculty community engagement', *Michigan Journal of Community Service Learning*, spring, pp. 5–16.

9

From extra-mural to knowledge transfer partnerships and networking: The community engagement experience at Makerere University

George Ladaah Openjuru and John Robert Ikoja-Odongo

Introduction

Community engagement/services, outreach activities or extra-mural services are a core function of all universities. According to Atim (2004), the history of these services in Makerere University dates back to 1953 with the formation of the Department of Extra-Mural Studies to help prepare the country for independence. This combination of services remains a core function but is now one of the strategic goals and objectives of the university, based on its vision and mission (Makerere University, 2008a). Makerere University is unusual in that it can demonstrate some university-wide strategies and structures to promote this work.

The university's strategic goals and objectives for the next ten years are premised on its core functions of teaching and learning; research and innovation; and knowledge transfer partnership and networking. The latter discourse – originally known as 'outreach' (Makerere University, 2008a) – is shifting further to the concept of university–community engagement in place of the old extra-mural outreach paradigm. This shift was brought about by the realisation that just as knowledge, technology and skills reside in universities, so public and private sectors also command knowledge bases from which the university can learn and leverage its entrepreneurial and innovative capability. Knowledge production and transfer between universities and the broader public and private sector is a two-way traffic that calls for the development and fostering of a symbiotic relationship. Knowledge-transfer partnership is a tool that offers an edge to public- and private-sector relationships in this new global and competitive economy. The aim of this chapter is to provide information about what Makerere University is doing by way of community engagement under this new knowledge-transfer partnership paradigm.

The chapter provides examples of the existing structures used to deliver community programmes by the different academic units and the types of community engagement activities, approaches and methods being used to deliver the programmes. The chapter highlights how, in the new arrangement, the private sector and collaborating communities are seen as knowledge recipients as well as knowledge generators (Makerere University, 2009) and act as equal partners with the university. Major achievements in outreach/community activities and their challenges are also outlined. The chapter concludes with a call for a more innovative and comprehensive approach that cleverly integrates the three core focuses of the university in term of research, teaching and community engagement. There is also a need for diversification of university engagement activities to meet the most pressing learning and development needs of the communities served by the university.

Different understandings of university community engagement activities

University community engagement programmes are perceived in many different ways. Some universities call them extension services. The term 'outreach' is still popular among higher education institutions in the USA. For instance, according to Michigan University:

> *Outreach is a form of scholarship that cuts across teaching, research, and service. It involves generating, transmitting, applying, and preserving knowledge for the direct benefit of external audiences in ways that are consistent with university and unit missions.* (Provost Committee on University Outreach, 2009, p. 1)

This shows that the primary focus of all engagement activities is the deployment of university scholarly resources for the benefit of communities outside the university. These manifest themselves in a number of forms such as research projects, extra-mural training and educational programmes, online courses, innovative community development projects and action research projects.

The University of Washington applies community engagement to continuing education and professional development in its local communities by providing opportunities such as online learning for non-traditional students, most of whom are working adults. The service runs programmes and partnerships that include offering free course materials over the internet (such as class outlines, lecture notes and handouts) and evening undergraduate programmes (University of Washington, 2010).

The University of Oklahoma offers non-traditional learning through independent study or students attending concentrated weekend or evening classes. Its community engagement mission is, 'The University of Oklahoma is a lifelong learning organisation dedicated to helping individuals, businesses, groups and communities transform themselves through knowledge' (University of Oklahoma, 2010, last paragraph).

At the University of Tennessee, engagement and continuing education services and programmes address the various lifelong learning needs of its students (The University of Tennessee, Knoxville, 2010). As a development of these initiatives, community engagement programmes at the University of Nevada at Las Vegas include support of and partnership with communities, state regions and beyond. This serves learner needs and interests through innovative courses and comprehensive programmes and services to adults, senior and part-time students, military personnel, government employees, and learners who are unable to attend traditional campus-based credit courses and programmes (University of Nevada, Las Vegas, 2010).

Kentucky State University states that it offers educational community engagement programmes that strive to reach, teach and inspire members of its community in order to enhance knowledge and relationships between itself and the wider population (Kentucky State University, 2010).

One common factor in the definition of university community engagement is that it is about serving the communities outside the university through continuing education, research projects or other community intervention schemes. This brief review of universities in the USA gives a flavour of the variety of activities undertaken and will accordingly inform our discussion in this chapter.

Community engagement is an important function of a university, and universities engage on the understanding that they:

- Have no monopoly on knowledge and knowledge creation and use
- Acknowledge that a wealth of knowledge resides with communities
- Acknowledge that the ultimate beneficiary of what goes on in universities is actually the community
- Run the risk of becoming irrelevant in their society if they do not maintain the engagement arm of their institutions.

For that reason, there is need for a symbiotic relationship between universities and the communities they serve (Aguti, 2010).

The traditional engagement and extra-mural programmes at Makerere University

In 1953, the Department of Extra-Mural Studies at Makerere University was founded to serve the whole of the then three East African countries of Kenya, Uganda and Tanzania. Although the name has changed several times, the department continued with its traditional programmes that reflect 'Taking the university to the people and bringing the people to the university' (Sicherman, 2005, p. 298). Such programmes offered extended training opportunities to non-traditional learners through short courses. However, the department has evolved into the Department of Community Education and Extra-Mural Studies (CEEMS), and its traditional programmes are now primarily the mandate of the Centre for Lifelong Learning in the College of Education and External Studies.

The current short courses focus on training and capacity-building workshops throughout the country. These are conducted through a network of nine regional learning centres. The workshops are meant to improve performance in decentralised service delivery for local governments. For example, with support from development partners, the department organises workshops on new adult and community education methods for staff from non-governmental organisations (NGOs) and government departments that are promoting adult literacy education (Okech, 2004).

There is also now a Department of Open and Distance Learning in the School of Distance and Lifelong Learning which runs three degree programmes through distance education. These are Bachelor of Commerce, Bachelor of Education and Bachelor of Science. The department also runs the Commonwealth Diploma in Youth Development Work through which learners are able to access university education without the need for a full-time stay at the university.

In addition to these courses and programmes, however, community engagement is increasingly a feature of work across the university, as the next section outlines.

The current direction for community engagement at Makerere University

Makerere University's engagement approach is enshrined in its mission statement, which says that the university aims 'to provide innovative teaching, learning, research and services responsive to national and global needs' (Makerere University, 2008a, p. 2). This mission brings together all the university core functions in order to ensure that the university interacts with the community for mutual benefit.

The overarching direction in the university's *Strategic Plan 2008/09–2018/19* is to reposition 'Makerere University to meet emerging socio economic challenges.' And one of the strategic directions is 'knowledge transfer partnerships' (*ibid.*, p. 14). This is meant to enhance the capacity of the university to link with and service community, private and public sectors as well as other tertiary institutions (Makerere University, 2009). This strategy is based on two broad goals, namely: 'creating an enabling environment for the public and private sector to interface with the university in the promotion of education in a competitive setting' and 'providing a partnership framework for assessment and utilisation of university products in the value chain' (Makerere University, 2008a, p. 18). The first goal is serviced by the following objectives, strategies and key performance indicators (*ibid.*).

Objectives:
- To increase private-sector participation in university activities
- To promote increased joint research, technology innovation and transfer initiatives to address stakeholder needs
- To establish a partnership for the public and the private sector utilisation of university competencies.

Strategies to realise these objectives:
- Involve stakeholders in the development of the university policy agenda
- Establish collaborations and networking with public- and private-sector institutions
- Create research and technology innovation and incubation business centres and model villages.

Key performance indicators to measure success:
- Number of joint projects established with the private sector
- Number of operational business and technology innovations incubation centres established
- Number of study scholarships provided by the private sector.

Strategies to establish a partnership for the public and private sector to utilise university competencies:
- Involve the public and private sectors in the development of the university curriculum
- Involve stakeholders in planning supervision and evaluation of the students on field attachments
- Create a resource pool of university expertise for the public and private sector to utilise.

Community engagement in university schools and colleges

In line with the strategic plan, Makerere University's various colleges, schools and institutes are part of its community engagement activities.

From 2005, many faculties and colleges started running short courses for the public on campus. For example, the Faculty of Computing and Information Technology (FCIT) conducts a number of computer training programmes aimed at equipping non-university students with computing and ICT skills. These include training military and police personnel and out-of-school youths. FCIT runs a 24-hour study programme which has significantly increased access by non-traditional learners. As a follow-up, it is establishing several IT academies for schoolchildren. So far, 15 primary and secondary schools have been set up to cater for the training needs of universal primary and secondary education (Makerere University, 2010). Other faculties are running evening and weekend training programmes for both university and non-university students.

All community engagement activities since 2008 have been guided by research, innovations, the knowledge-transfer partnerships and networking strategic focus. Some of these activities form a tripartite relationship between Makerere University, international development partners and the communities (Okech, 2004). Under this arrangement, the university raises winning grant proposals that are supported by development partners. In the years 2008–10, for instance, the university received research-grant support from the governments of Sweden and Norway, Japan International Cooperation Agency, Carnegie Corporation of New York, World Bank, Danish International Development Agency and United States Agency for International Development/Collaborative Research Support Programmes. These were all for funded research projects in the College of Health Science and the Faculty of Technology in which the tripartite partnership between Makerere University, international development partners and the local communities is visible.

The Faculty of Technology is working with different communities in Uganda to come up with alternative fuel-efficient and environmentally friendly energy sources for rural communities (Makerere University, 2009).

The College of Health Science has focused research on areas such as improving newborn health and survival through community-based intervention linked to health facilities in Mayuge and Iganga Districts. Mayuge and Iganga are located in the eastern part of Uganda, are largely rural and are made up of poor peasant farmers growing maize, millet, sorghum and other food crops. Education to prevent infant mortality is a key concern for such impoverished communities. The College of Health Science is also active in the fight against malaria by providing the anti-malaria drug, Coartem, and contributes to the fight against HIV/AIDS through the provision of free antiretroviral drugs, and HIV and AIDS test kits.

There are several ways in which other parts of the university contribute to the university mission by working in partnership with communities, NGOs and the private sector.

Under the knowledge-transfer concept, faculties are working in districts and sites around the country to develop new methods of production and technologies to improve the productivity of the Uganda farming communities. The Faculty of Agriculture, for instance, is working with farmer groups to demonstrate and extend appropriate pig-production strategies as an avenue for alleviating poverty among resource-poor farming households. The faculty also carries out research in Ankole cattle to develop appropriate technology for intensive goat and cattle meat production with a view to producing quality meat for local and export markets.

Another good example of a partnership is the collaboration between the faculty and Kakira Sugar Works, Dairy Development Authority and Kakira Outgrowers Rural Development Fund. This has focused on development of molasses urea blocks with local feedstuff for improved cattle productivity in the dairy farming communities in Busoga Region and Mukono District. Through this project, the dairy farmers have been linked to the agro-processing industries to improve the nutrition of their dairy livestock (Makerere University, 2009).

Other examples since 2008 include the improvement of energy efficiency and environmental conservation at Mpanga Growers Tea Factory, promotion of food security and livelihoods in Pader and Gulu Districts (all in the northern part of Uganda), and animal and human trypanosomes in four districts in northern Uganda through treatment and follow-up surveillance.

The Faculty of Social Science, in collaboration with Wakiso District Local Council in central Uganda, near Kampala, has formulated a community-based wetland management plan under the Wetlands Inspection Division. Faculty staff participate in a number of committees that formulate government policy. The Department of Women and Gender Studies uses telecentres in Iganga and Mbale Districts in eastern Uganda and Kanungu District in western Uganda to train people in networking (Makerere University, 2009).

The Margaret Trowel School of Industrial and Fine Arts is involved with women with HIV/AIDs from three up-country stations and imparts new skills through arts and crafts. The women's works of art are exhibited both locally and internationally. The school organises workshops to revitalise bark-cloth making in rural communities of Buganda.

The Faculty of Forestry and Nature Conservation is working with communities near forests to raise alternative crops that are not eaten by monkeys and that also provide fast-maturing seeds which farmers grow and sell in order to alleviate poverty. Training farmers in deterring monkeys is another feature of this project. The faculty is also active in forestry regeneration, which entails planting seedlings, researching the best areas for tropical rainforests, wildlife conservation, the study of primates and their effects on people, and fighting the effects of logging on wildlife. It is doing this in Budongo forest in Masindi District in mid-western Uganda.

The Faculty of Veterinary Medicine provides consultancy and support to the community through:

- A small animal clinic, for both teaching and patient care
- A large animal mobile clinic that serves a 40 km radius
- An artificial insemination sub-centre and breeding consultancy
- Short courses and seminars for animal farmers and extension workers.

An example from the East African School of Library and Information Science includes training both professionals and non-professionals in various areas of new knowledge in libraries and information management.

Staff from the Main Library Services Department go out to train school librarians in their settings and help them to organise their libraries. The libraries also develop databases that are shared with other institutions.

The Faculty of Law operates a refugee law project which seeks to ensure fundamental human rights for all asylum seekers, refugees and internally displaced persons within Uganda. It envisions a country that treats all people within its borders with the same standards of respect and social justice. It works to see that all people living in Uganda, as specified under national and international law, are treated with the fairness and consideration due to fellow human beings. This project has a fully operational office outside the campus, complete with its own management structure (Refugee Law Project, 2010). Through this organisation, the faculty provides support to a number of refugees coming across the borders of Uganda. For example, it provides language education and helps to resettle refugees in the country.

At the School of Distance and Lifelong Learning, a number of action research projects with communities are operating in addition to the traditional provision. One of these outstanding projects addresses the problem of youth employability and entrepreneurship. It aims to train young people in applying successfully for a job or going into self-employment by establishing an enterprise. Other projects focus on improving the participation of parents and communities in the performance of their children in universal primary education programmes (Makerere University, 2010).

University-wide structures for partnership and networking

The university has interpreted its engagement mission to interface with its wider community and region in a very proactive way. This section provides examples of a number of structures that have been established specifically to facilitate the growth of university partnerships and networking opportunities at university-wide level.

The Innovation at Makerere project

The Innovation at Makerere project (codenamed I@mak) was established to develop local long courses (undergraduate and full-time Master's); an internship programme; short courses; support for research on decentralisation; and curriculum development (Ogeda and Nakabugo, 2006, p. ii).

Following these objectives, a number of projects were implemented by different faculties, schools and institutes at Makerere University. It was therefore a university-wide project. According to the assessment report (Ogeda and Nakabugo, 2006), the specific objective of the programme was to improve decentralised service delivery to contribute to poverty reduction through the improvement of agriculture, health, education, governance and financial management.

The university has produced a number of publications for use by both academics and practitioners involved in service delivery in a decentralised system. These include: *Frequently Asked Questions on Decentralisation in Uganda*; *Handbook on Decentralisation in Uganda*; *Decentralisation and Transformation in Uganda*; *Psychiatry for Primary Health Care in Uganda*; *Teaching Mental Health in the Districts*; and *Agro Forestry Approach to Land Use: A Training Manual for Extension Agents*. This was a university-wide multidisciplinary project managed by the university's Institute of Social Research. Different schools and faculties collaborated to run community engagement projects under the common theme of I@mak.

Higher education institutions are well placed to offer sustainable capacity building and provide a continuum of activities including research, skill building, career development and curriculum reviews that are likely to outlive external-driven capacity-building interventions. The programme was mutually beneficial to both government and higher education institutions (*ibid.*, p. ii).

Model village

As part of the I@mak initiative, two model villages were created – one located in Nsumba Village in Rakai District and the other in Obayia Village in Terego District in West Nile. The project produced new ideas for communities of practice meetings with the partnering local governments. Regular meetings are held to share experiences and practices in service delivery (Makerere University, 2007b; Makerere University, 2008b). This model village project, complete with a village resource centre, was implemented by a university-wide project committee known as the I@mak.com (Innovation at Makerere Committee) in collaboration with the local government district leadership.

The model village idea is one of the most unusual examples of community engagement activity by Makerere University and is based on community needs. In addition to motivating the provision of services by local government, it includes setting up agricultural sites through which local communities can be equipped with skills for self-sustainability. These skills come through agriculture, establishment of resource centres, provision of inter-locking soil-stabilising brick-making machines, alternative energy technologies, provision of soil kits, training of extension staff and peer farmers on the use and supply of improved seeds, and training village members on improved sanitation options.

The model village concept mobilises local communities into productive working groups. To explain some of the above skills in more detail, agricultural demonstration sites are set up, for instance, and appropriate plant varieties are introduced. With technologies developed from the university, the communities are trained in constructing water-harvesting tanks, and alternative energy technologies. Through the village, local people are trained in the skills of constructing latrines and as a result the majority of surrounding homesteads have developed further sanitation facilities following the model village examples (Makerere University, 2009). The idea of a model village is an effective way of bringing about change in the lives of rural people.

Makerere University private sector forum

The objective of the global Smart Partnership movement is to promote socio-economic transformation. The university-wide Makerere University Private Sector Forum (MUPSF) was set up in response to the Africa-wide Smart Partnership Dialogue to work as a cross-sector forum that brings together the public and private sectors and the university to address issues of mutual concern. Within the university, the Academia Network Committee provides the university-wide committee structure that works with MUPSF. Through this arrangement, the private sector is brought into close collaboration with the university (Ministry of Foreign Affairs, 2009).

Through MUPSF, the university is stimulating the private sector's active participation in university activities and policy agendas, and the promotion of education and access of the private/public sector to university services. A Smart Partnership Dialogue Think Tank, established in July 2009, is charged with identifying the type of knowledge that can be transferred between the university and the community (Makerere University, 2010).

Research management and coordination system

In an effort to make research accessible to the wider community in Uganda and internationally, the university has developed a Research Management and Coordination System (RMACS). Through this endeavour, stakeholders, the general public and the international community are rapidly informed about the research activities and outputs from Makerere University.

The Triple Helix Intervention

Makerere University's Triple Helix Intervention brings together actors from government, academia and the private sector to find innovative solutions to problems faced by businesses in order to improve performance and profitability and make business more competitive locally and globally. To date, 22 cluster initiatives have been launched in the areas of agriculture and food value additions, manufacturing, management consultancy, ICT and education. The Uganda Gatsby Trust (UGT), based in the Faculty of Technology, is a good example of such an initiative and has established the first industrial parks in Jinja and Mbarara. These parks are aimed at improving the performance of small and medium enterprises. The government is now working with UGT to execute its industrial programme. The Department of Food Science also contributes to the Triple Helix Intervention by training entrepreneurs in food processing.

Gender mainstreaming

The university has established two schemes to support women and girls, who are statistically underrepresented at secondary and tertiary levels of education.

The first is a Female Scholarship Initiative (FSI) run through the gender mainstreaming division. The aim is to provide financial support for girls from poor families so that they can access higher education at Makerere University. This scheme has proved successful in increasing access, and more than 690 girls have benefited. In addition to the scholarship support, all the FSI beneficiaries undergo mentoring in building self-esteem, gender, leadership, entrepreneurship and job-seeking skills. This mentoring has contributed to the quality of the FSI graduates.

The second scheme relates to a national policy to enhance female education opportunities. In the 1990–1 academic year, the university introduced a strategy of adding 1.5 points to the entry grades for every girl aspiring to higher education at Makerere University. This strategy has been adopted by the government and has enabled an increase in the number of girls entering all institutions of higher learning across the country.

Field attachments

A field attachment system was approved by Senate in July 2006 to provide students with hands-on work experience in their discipline. This is now a major component in many academic programmes at Makerere University. The university has written guidelines for field attachment, with a useful feedback loop to improve the curriculum. There are several models of implementation, such as school practice for teachers and internship for medical students. The importance of field attachments in university training and as an engagement function cannot be disputed (see Northern Illinois University, 2005) but the arrangements do not necessarily reflect the more formalised service learning approach such as that described in chapter 11. In service learning students are assessed, as part of their course work, on their own identified learning from the experience. Nevertheless, all stakeholders in university education recognise the valuable contribution that field attachments make to the quality of training and the immediate support they provide to the communities outside the university. As a result, many programmes include compulsory field attachments.

Field attachments at Makerere University have been known by different names in different faculties, such as internship, school practice, community-based education and services (COBES), and industrial training. After several consultations with various stakeholders, the university adopted 'field attachment' as the official name for this educational practice.

One of the primary objectives of field attachment is to enhance and strengthen links between the university and stakeholders. Through this arrangement, partners have an opportunity to be involved in the training and review of programmes at the university while the university is better able to appreciate client demands and the quality of graduate required to fulfil these demands (Makerere University, 2007a). Empirical studies into the outcomes and effectiveness of these programmes are limited since the schemes are relatively new. Nevertheless, the following section highlights some of the anecdotal and informal observations that will need to inform future studies.

Challenges of university engagement programmes

While Makerere University has taken some unusually positive steps to embed community engagement within its infrastructure, there are a number of challenges when it comes to implementation. The greatest of all these challenges is lack of funding. The bulk of the funding for university engagement has been from the government but this support is slowly disappearing (Atim, 2004). The university now depends almost exclusively on donor support from development partners and locally generated funds.

Another challenge is that there are no clear objectives for encouraging engagement and no comprehensive guidelines for operating the wide range of activities outlined above. This can result in duplication, wasted efforts and lack of coordination. For example, the provision of short courses is duplicated by different faculties that offer the same course under the name of the same university.

Furthermore, not enough is being done to increase access to university credit-based education even though this is what the engaged agencies and communities most desire. People want access to standard university courses and to be able to obtain credit towards degrees on a part-time and distance education basis without having to leave their work or home responsibilities.

An additional issue is the unevenness with which community engagement operates across the university. Most of the research-related activities, for instance, operate from science-based faculties and largely from the Faculty of Agriculture. This means that equally crucial issues such as good governance and management are not being addressed by the university through community engagement.

Finally, the charging of fees for some of the non-credit courses for non-university students tends to exclude many people who could benefit from these engagement activities.

Conclusion

This review of examples of university engagement activities indicates that engagement is a very important function of Makerere University, which it executes in a number of ways: collaborative research projects; direct community intervention services; field attachments; continuing education; and flexible programmes such as distance-learning evening and weekend programmes both on and off-campus. It is through community engagement that the university can improve its teaching and learning in terms of curricula that are immediately relevant to the needs of the community.

However, there is not enough public or private support for the implementation of the important community engagement functions of the university. Even within traditional university community engagement units, it is treated as a secondary role in spite of being listed as a core function.

This position will need to be changed by more direct policy interventions at senior management level. One of the changes that can be made is through a curricular integration of community engagement functions into the normal or regular teaching and learning functions of the university. Curriculum delivery should be that which naturally utilises and promotes community/university coexistence whereas current practice is that the two are separate. A positive trend has started, however, in the form of compulsory field attachment for all university programmes.

References

Aguti, J. (2010) 'Outreach in Makerere University'. Unpublished presentation to National Council of Higher Education, Kampala, April.

Atim, D.K. (2004) 'Fifty years of growth and learning: A historical overview', in D.K. Atim, Y.N. Nsamba and A. Okech (Eds), *Fifty Years of Makerere University Based Adult Education in Uganda 1953–2003: A Publication to Commemorate Five Decades of Taking the University to the People and Bringing People to the University*. Kampala: Institute of Adult and Continuing Education, pp. 1–42.

Kentucky State University (2010) 'Land grant educational outreach'. Retrieved 27 September 2010 from http://www.kysu.edu/landGrant/educationaloutreach/

Makerere University (2007a) *Guidelines for Field Attachment*. Kampala: Makerere University.

Makerere University (2007b) *I@Mak.com Bulletin*. Kampala: Makerere University.

Makerere University (2008a) *Makerere University Strategic Plan 2008/09–2018/19*. Kampala: Makerere University.

Makerere University (2008b) *I@Mak.com Bulletin*. Kampala: Makerere University.

Makerere University (2009) *Makerere University Annual Report 2008*. Kampala: Makerere University.

Makerere University (2010) *Makerere University Annual Report 2009*. Kampala: Makerere University.

Ministry of Foreign Affairs (2009) *Report of the Global 2009 SMART Partnership Think Tanking Dialogue, Held in Munyonyo Uganda*. Kampala: Government of Uganda.

Northern Illinois University (2005) *The Role of Higher Education in Economic Development*. Illinois: Higher Education Alliance.

Ogeda, M.C. and Nakabugo, M.G. (2006) *Decentralised Service Delivery: A Makerere University Training Pilot, Outcome Assessment Study*. Kampala: Makerere University.

Okech, A. (2004) 'International partnership and cooperation in adult education', in A. Okech (Ed.), *Adult Education in Uganda: Growth, Development, Prospects and Challenges*. Kampala: Fountain Publishers, pp. 247–66.

Provost Committee on University Outreach (2009) *University Outreach at Michigan State University: Extending Knowledge to Serve Community*. Michigan: Michigan University Board of Trustees.

Refugee Law Project (2010) 'Refugee law project: Faculty of Law'. Retrieved 27 October 2010 from http://www.refugeelawproject.org/

Sicherman, C. (2005) *Becoming an African University: Makerere University 1922–2000*. Kampala: Fountain Publishers.

The University of Oklahoma (2010) 'OU intersession University of Oklahoma outreach'. Retrieved 27 October 2010 from http://www.ou.edu/outreachceap/intersession_home.html

The University of Tennessee, Knoxville (2010) 'University outreach and continuing education'. Retrieved 27 September 2010 from http://www.outreach.utk.edu/aboutoutreach.html

University of Nevada, Las Vegas (2010) 'Division of educational outreach at the University of Nevada, Las Vegas'. Retrieved 27 September 2010 from http://edoutreach.unlv.edu

University of Washington (2010) 'UW educational outreach'. Retrieved 27 September 2010 from http://www.outreach.washington.edu/uweo/about/

10

Incorporating community service learning into university-based adult education in Ghana

Michael Tagoe

Introduction

Within the last decade, higher education institutions have been going through flux as their method of working shifts towards the concept of community engagement. This transformation is in response to the previously poor attention given to extension work as contributing to the 'third mission'. Extension work is the original term adopted by many universities for working outside the university with communities who would otherwise not have engaged with the institution.

While universities in Ghana have practised community involvement since their establishment, they have often treated communities as 'pockets of need, laboratories for experimentation, or passive recipients of expertise' (Bringle and Hatcher, 2002, p. 504). Changing the dynamics of the relationship between universities and communities has led to an emphasis on the incorporation of community service learning into mission statements and courses in order to reconfigure teaching and learning and empower students to apply their knowledge to addressing real-life problems. Boyer (1996, pp. 19–20) has also challenged universities to bring new dignity to community engagement by connecting its rich resources 'to our most pressing social, civic, and political and ethical problems, to our children, to our schools, to our teachers, to our cities.'

Most of the studies on community service learning have focused on universities in South Africa, the USA, Australia, Asia and the UK, and on courses such as political science, social work, journalism, psychology and business administration at undergraduate and postgraduate levels. However, the community service learning movement has had very little effect on adult education (Kiely *et al.*, 2006). In this chapter, we examine how community service learning could be integrated into university-based adult education courses to transform teaching and learning for the faculty and for students. Specifically, we argue that although adult education as a discipline has contributed significantly to models used in community service learning, the interface between adult education and community service learning has been weak. It is within this context that we discuss the benefits that could be derived if community service learning were integrated into adult education as a discipline.

Community engagement and universities

Universities all over the world have fostered a relationship with society. Apart from teaching and learning, which often takes place on the campuses, links with society are facilitated through research and extension service. Extension service, the 'third mission' of most universities, has undergone reforms recently as universities try to redefine their role in dealing with societal challenges. The massive support for this university–community engagement is rooted in Boyer's notion of the scholarship of engagement. Since the 1990s, the call by Boyer (1990, 1996) for universities to rediscover their roots and to address societal problems has brought engagement to the forefront of university activities, especially in developed and some developing countries.

Various definitions have been offered to describe this university–community partnership. Ramaley (2003, p. 18) defines engagement as 'an educational or research initiative conducted through some form of partnership and characterised by shared goals, a shared agenda, agreed upon definitions of success that are meaningful both to the university and the community participants … The resulting collaboration or partnership is mutually beneficial and is likely to build the capacity and competence of all parties.' In its report on the engaged institution, the Kellogg Commission on The Future of State and Land-Grant Universities (1999, p. 1) defines engagement as the 'redesign of teaching, research and extension and service functions to become more systematically and productively involved with community concerns and needs.' Wallis (2006) sees community engagement as a two-way relationship that leads to productive partnerships that yield mutually beneficial outcomes. According to Wallis (*ibid.*) and Wallis *et al.* (2005), community engagement is much more than community participation, consultation, development or service.

Bell *et al*. (2007) offer examples of community engagement activities, which include:

- Community-based learning: students learn academic content in community settings through partnership-designed activities that provide specific knowledge benefits to a particular community. This type of learning is credit bearing and curriculum based, and it is fully integrated into a student's course of study
- Community-based research: involves collaborative research in which university staff, students and the community work together to design, conduct and report on research undertaken. The research is of both intellectual and community importance and the products of engaged research are of demonstrable benefit to the academy and the community
- Partnerships between university and external organisations: are focused on a mutually designed agenda to address specific community needs or opportunities through collaborative work in which each partner contributes essential expertise. External organisations include business, industry, government, community-based/non-profit enterprises and education.

Fourie (2006) shares the same view as Bell *et al*., (2007). However, he argues that engagement in teaching and learning ought to reflect local and African history, context, circumstances and problems, as well as opportunities for life-long learning, professional development and civic development.

Community service learning

Since Robert Sigmon and William Ramsey coined the term in 1967 at the Southern Regional Education Board in the USA, service learning has attracted much attention but little consensus over a universally accepted definition (Giles and Eyler, 1994). Two important definitions (Jacoby, 1999; Bringle and Hatcher, 1995) are critical to our understanding of what service learning is. Jacoby defines service learning:

> *... as a form of experiential education in which students engage in activities that address human and community needs together*

with structured opportunities intentionally designed to promote
student learning and development. Reflection and reciprocity are
key concepts of service learning. (Jacoby, 1999, p. 20)

Bringle and Hatcher define service learning as a:

... course-based, credit-bearing educational experience in which
students (a) participate in an organised service activity that meets
identified community needs and (b) reflect on the service activity
in such a way as to gain further understanding of course content,
a broader appreciation of the discipline, and an enhanced sense
of civic responsibility. (Bringle and Hatcher, 1995, p. 112)

In South Africa, the Joint Education Trust (JET, 2001) has adapted Bringle and Hatcher's definition in programme documents by stating that service learning is a 'thoughtful, organised and reflective service-oriented pedagogy', adding that it is 'focused on the development priorities of communities through the interaction between and application of knowledge, skills and experience in partnership between community, academics, students, and service providers within the community for the benefit of all participants' (Joint Education Trust, 2001, cited in Hatcher and Erasmus, 2008, p. 50). Again in South Africa, Fourie (2006, p. 44), quoting the definition of community service learning at the University of the Free State, argues that it is:

... curriculum-based, credit bearing educational experiences, in
which students (a) participate in contextualised, well-structured
and organised service-learning activities aimed at meeting iden-
tified development and service needs in a community, and (b)
reflect on the service activities in order to gain a deeper under-
standing of curriculum content and community life as well as
achieve personal growth and a sense of social responsibility.
(Fourie, 2006, p. 44)

Essentially, what these definitions reveal is that service learning is primarily an academic enterprise (Bringle and Hatcher, 1999). While other forms of service programmes such as volunteerism, community service, internships and field education may have some educational benefits, service learning deliberately integrates community service activities with educational objectives and ensures equal focus to the provider and the recipient (Furco, 2007; Berle, 2006; Bringle and Hatcher, 2009). According to Jacoby (1996, p. 20), the term 'community' refers to 'local neighbourhoods, the state, the nation, and the global community'. The human and community needs that service learning addresses are those needs that are defined by the community.

A community service learning model

The theoretical roots of community service learning have been traced to John Dewey's works, *How We Think and Experience Education* (cited in Giles and Eyler, 1994) and *Democracy and Education* (Dewey, 1916). Although Dewey never mentioned service learning in his works, his experimentalism with an emphasis on the principles of experience, enquiry and reflection have been identified as the key elements of a theory of service learning (Giles and Eyler, 1994). Dewey's legacy to service learning is about how learning takes place, what learning is, and the relation of learning to action (Giles and Eyler, 1994). Experiential learning as a philosophy of education is based on what Dewey (1938, cited in Kolb and Kolb, 2005, p. 193) called a 'theory of experience.'

Dewey believed that experiences contribute to learning, but cautioned that not all experiences were educative. Experience becomes educative when critical reflective thought creates new meaning and leads to growth and the ability to take informed actions (Bringle and Hatcher, 1999). For experience to be truly educative, Dewey suggests the use of projects as a means to produce learning from experience and (cited in Giles and Eyler 1994, p. 80) sets forth four situations that are necessary for 'projects to be truly educative'. First, they must generate interest in the learner; second, they must be intrinsically worthwhile to the learner; third, they must present problems that awaken new curiosity and create a demand for information; and fourth, they must cover a considerable time span and be capable of fostering development over time.

Freire (1972), a critical adult educator, reflects Dewey's position in supporting the need for experience to be incorporated in teaching and learning. He argues that when experience is not embedded in teaching, students are filled with a stockpile of deposited knowledge which often leaves them disengaged from the learning process and alienated from their social world. For Freire, apart from this type of education stifling critical reflection and critical thinking, students are unable to truly become human. It is true knowledge – that comes through invention and reinvention through the restless, impatient, continuing, hopeful inquiry – that results in creativity and transformation. Situating experience in learning gives students the opportunity to put theory into practice. It allows them to reflect on the educational content and its relevance to the wider society.

To Dewey, thinking and action are inextricably linked. As cited in Bringle and Hatcher (1999), Dewey provides the foundation for the role that reflection assumes in the learning process and the bridge it provides between experience and theory. According to Dewey, reflection is an 'active, persistent, and careful consideration of any belief or supposed form of knowledge in the light of the grounds that support it' (cited in Bringle and Hatcher, 1999, p. 112). Kolb (1984) and Kolb and Kolb have built on the propositions of Dewey and Freire in their experiential learning theory, which is founded on six propositions (Kolb and Kolb 2005, p. 194):

1. Learning is ... a process and not [just an] outcome. To improve learning in higher education, students ... [need to engage in the process and provide feedback on their experiences].
2. All learning is relearning. Learning is best facilitated by a process that draws out students' beliefs and ideas about a topic so that they can be examined, tested, and integrated with new, more refined ideas.
3. Learning requires the resolution of conflicts between dialectically opposed modes of adaptation to the world. Conflicts, differences, and disagreement are what drive the learning process. [Students] move back and forth between opposing modes of reflection and action and feeling and thinking.
4. Learning is a holistic process of adaptation to the world ...learning [goes beyond cognition to include the affective, spiritual and behavioural aspects of personality development].
5. Learning results from synergetic transactions between the person and the environment.
6. Learning is the process of creating knowledge.

Apart from reflection, one other important element in service learning is reciprocity. In an attempt to distinguish service learning from other forms of volunteerism, writers have consistently emphasised the relevance of reciprocity (Henry and Breyfogle, 2006). If reflection is seen as the foremost factor that distinguishes service learning from community service and volunteerism, Kendall (1990, cited in Henry and Breyfogle, 2006, p. 27) describes reciprocity as the second vital factor to defining an activity as a service learning experience. Reciprocity is the exchange of both giving and receiving between the 'server' and the person or group 'being served.' All parties in service learning are learners and help determine what is to be learned. Reciprocity in service learning overcomes the traditional paternalistic, one-way approach to service in which one group provides the service and the other group becomes the recipient. Lamsam (1999) has explained that reciprocity in service learning allows both university and community to be teachers and learners. Each has something to offer and to learn from the other. The community teaches students, while they also learn from the students. Hoxmeier and Lenk (2003) have argued that reciprocity is a 'win–win' aspect of the service learning contract. Each participating party experiences net benefits from their involvement.

University-based adult education at the University of Ghana

University extension, according to Lamble and Thompson (2000), began in Oxford and Cambridge in England in the mid-nineteenth century. Later, university extension, known as 'extra-mural' work, became part of the university colleges established in British-colonised African countries. The transfer of models of university extension and university-based adult education in Africa could be traced to three bodies established in the 1940s, namely: the Asquith Commission on Higher Education in the Colonial Territories, the Elliot Commission and the Bradley Committee – all of which urged that extra-mural departments be established as part of the university colleges in British West Africa to develop adult education (Raybould, 1956; Amedzro, 2004).

The Asquith Commission Report which, together with other reports, laid the theoretical foundation for higher education in the colonies, explained that universities could only bring about development if, apart from teaching undergraduates and sponsoring research, they undertook a 'leading part in the development of adult education' (cited in Agbodeka, 1998, p. 73). Indeed, the Bradley Report stressed the need for an extra-mural department, which would integrate the life of the university with that of society (Amedzro, 2004). The idea of extension (that is, adult education) becoming the third role of universities after teaching and research was gradually accepted in the UK during the 1940s (Agbodeka, 1998). Of the universities in Britain in the 1940s, Oxford University had an elaborate adult education programme for the working class, and the Bradley Report therefore suggested emulating this practice by initiating extra-mural studies in the Gold Coast (Amedzro, 2004).

In Ghana, as part of the preparations for establishing the University College of the Gold Coast, the authorities came to accept the important role of extension and therefore decided to include extra-mural studies as one of the early departments. It was a decision that was designed to help to build the intellectual capacity of the nation. It was argued that teaching undergraduates and sponsoring research might increase physical resources but could not match the role of extension in raising the intellectual standards of the nation at large (Agbodeka, 1998). To promote the university's role in community affairs, a Department of Extra-Mural Studies was established in 1948 to focus more on extension services than teaching (Fordham, 2000). The department became the Institute of Extra-Mural Studies when it was incorporated into the University College of the Gold Coast in 1949 as the extension wing of the university college. It had two major objectives for its establishment. Firstly, it was to provide opportunities that would arouse the people's interest in and consciousness of education. This would then lead to the foundation of an adult education organisation and help members to participate in their political and social lives more meaningfully. Secondly, the experiment was to illustrate the type of link that could be established between a university college or university and the larger community (Hagan, cited in Amedzro, 2004, p. 50).

The whole idea of extension was service to society. From 1949 to the time of independence, the department provided opportunities to ordinary people who could not participate in the regular programmes of the university colleges in Africa. It provided liberal studies in politics and government, history, economics, public affairs and international relations to provide opportunities for individual improvement (Jones-Quartey, 1975). It also provided opportunities for the university college to have a presence in the communities through community development programmes. This was done in Ghana through the People's Educational Association (PEA), a voluntary association similar to the Workers' Educational Association (WEA) in Britain (Skinner, 2007).

In the 1950s, several monumental events happened in the Gold Coast, starting with independence, which was attained in 1957, and the formation of the first civilian government.

Independence set the stage for structural transformation of all sectors of the economy. In the area of university education, the Convention People's Party (CPP) under Dr Kwame Nkrumah changed the status of the University College of the Gold Coast to a fully fledged university. It became the University of Ghana in 1961. The Department of Extra-Mural Studies became the Institute of Extra-Mural Studies in 1957 and then the Institute of Public Education in 1962. According to Dr Nkrumah, 'True academic freedom – the intellectual freedom of the university – is everywhere fully compatible with service to the community; for the university is, and must always remain, a living, thinking and serving part of the community to which it belongs' (*Daily Graphic*, 1974, p. 17). Armed with this truth about the role of the university for the community, Dr Nkrumah initiated far-reaching reforms in the university to achieve his objectives. These changes reflected a new outlook in the services provided by the university-based adult education institution. The provision of non-certificated programmes gave way to certificated courses as demanded by ordinary Ghanaians through the workers' colleges in Accra, Sekondi-Takoradi, Tamale and Kumasi, established by the CPP Government. The overthrow of the CPP Government in 1966 also marked some changes in the provision of university-based adult education.

After 1966, the Institute of Public Education was renamed the Institute of Adult Education. It redeemed its academic orientation when it established a research and teaching unit to teach its own discipline. A Diploma in Adult Education programme and an MA/MPhil programme were then introduced in 1987 to train middle-level adult educators. During this period, teaching and research were added to the core function of extension service. As part of its extension services, the institute continues to offer community-based programmes in areas such as environmental management, population and family life education, including HIV/AIDS, as well as income-generation skills training for various interest groups all over the country. In the 1990s, the institute finally severed all links with remedial courses for students and focused more on degree programmes. Today, the Institute of 'Adult' Education has become the Institute of 'Continuing and Distance' Education, offering undergraduate and postgraduate programmes in adult education.

Why community service learning in adult education?

Of all the disciplines, adult education lends itself most readily to community service learning, because it is about community development and people. Adult education has always been about social transformation. It has been identified as vital for fostering ecologically sustainable development, for promoting democracy, justice and gender equity, and supporting scientific, social and economic development. It helps to build a world in which violent conflict is replaced by dialogue and a culture of peace based on justice (UNESCO, 1997). At the CONFINTEA V conference, adult education was defined as:

... the entire body of ongoing learning processes, formal or otherwise, whereby people regarded as adults by the society to which they belong develop their abilities, enrich their knowledge, and improve their technical or professional qualifications or turn them in a new direction to meet their own needs and those of their society. (UNESCO, 1997, p. 29)

Learning is the bedrock of adult education and therefore the teaching of courses needs to promote learning between students and communities. Additionally, adult education focuses on solving societal problems and therefore has always promoted social change. The objectives of adult education and community service learning are thus interrelated. Kiely *et al.* (2006) have argued that, as a pedagogy, service learning goes beyond the classroom into the community and provides adult learners with innovative experiential approaches to teaching and learning. They further posit that community problems, rather than predetermined textbooks and syllabuses, emerge as living texts driving theory and practice in service learning courses. As adult learners reflect and engage with many stakeholders, they make contributions to the pedagogy of service learning (Kiely, 2004).

Since service learning programmes place participants directly in potentially unfamiliar local and global community contexts, there are some courses offered that could have a substantial impact on community service learning and around which community-based programmes could be developed. These include contemporary issues in adult education; methodology of educational research; programme planning and evaluation; community education and development; human resource management and development; and gender and development. There would be several benefits to be derived if the Institute of Continuing and Distance Education promoted service learning courses. For faculty members, Bringle and Hatcher (1995) have argued that service learning brings new life to the classroom by invigorating their teaching. The typical 'banking education' is replaced with 'problem-posing education' (Freire, 1972). Furco (2001) has argued that faculty members benefit significantly when service learning is incorporated into their research.

In the twenty-first century, more attention is being paid to community-based participatory forms of research as an alternative to the dominant approach to research (Ahmed *et al.*, 2004; Minkler, 2004; Hall, 2009). Community-based, participatory research is a collaborative enterprise between academics and community members. Since successful service learning experiences are founded upon university–community partnerships, this type of research allows local people to influence the design and shape the scope of the research agenda.

For students, service learning has a positive effect on intellectual skills, personal development, personal confidence, leadership skills, team work, sense of ethics, moral development and increased social awareness (Jacoby, 1999; Stukas *et al.*, 1999; Colby *et al.*, 2009; Butin, 2006; Smith, 2008; Deeley, 2010). Service learning affords students a vision of career development, and a glimpse of what kind of work they can expect to do after graduation (Tan and Philips, 2005). Deeley (2010) has also indicated that service learning contributes to writing and oral skills.

Although the benefits that accrue to communities have been under-researched (Mitchell and Humphries, 2007), it is quite obvious that apart from providing the ambience for research by faculty members and learning sites for students, communities may benefit from service learning as owners and carriers of local knowledge. In many developing countries where indigenous knowledge has been sidelined by the university, the promotion of service learning would empower owners of knowledge to participate in finding solutions to their own problems (Semali *et al.*, 2006; Semali and Maretzki, 2004).

What needs to be done to integrate community service learning?

The Institute of Continuing and Distance Education perceives extension services as its core mandate, in addition to teaching and research, and has offered community service since its establishment. However, its strategic plan does not mention community engagement and community service learning. Nor are there communities collaborating with university departments for the mutual beneficial exchange of knowledge and resources in a context of partnership and reciprocity (Oaks *et al.*, 2009). Various strategies have been offered to help universities and institutions promote course-related, community service learning projects. For community service learning to serve as an effective tool that would survive the test of time, it needs careful planning and commitment (Cone and Harris, 1996). One strategy to achieve this is the comprehensive action plan for service learning (CAPSL) developed by Bringle and Hatcher (1996, 2000).

CAPSL 'provides a heuristic for guiding the development of a service learning programme in higher education' (Bringle and Hatcher, 1996, p. 236). It does so by focusing attention on four constituencies (institution, faculty, students and community) that must be considered and that provide a framework for institutions to develop their strategic plans. Bringle and Hatcher (1996) call for a self-assessment at the planning stage to find out: where the institution is, and where it is going; the institutional, student and faculty culture, climate and values; the resources and obstacles for developing service learning in the institution. At institution level, there needs to be a small group of key individuals or champions with the appropriate interest, motivation and skills. Once we have key individuals, there is need for a strategic action plan to implement service learning. The strategic plans of institutions should have community engagement and community service learning embedded in their mission statements.

Holland (1997) has argued that the association between an institution's mission and service learning is the most significant factor in successful introduction of service learning. Holland further posits that 'each institution must develop its own understanding of the degree to which service is an integral component of the academic mission' (Holland, 1997, p. 30). Young *et al.* (2007) have noted that both CAPSL and Holland's advice can be useful in assessing an institution's initial engagement in service learning and how that institution could later move from one level of commitment to another. Such tracking of activities could shed light on how service learning is initiated and institutionalised.

Although the recent study by Vogel *et al.* (2010) focuses on factors that influence the long-term sustainability of service learning, it identifies three factors that have emerged as key to the institutionalisation of service learning. The first of these relates to the institution's characteristics and policies, including the centrality of service to the institution's mission and the recognition given to service learning, teaching in general, and community-engaged research in faculty promotion, tenure and hiring policies. Second is the creation of resources and infrastructure to support service learning, including professional development opportunities and incentives to support faculty participation, dedicated institutional funding, a coordinating centre for service learning that is centrally placed within the academic structure of the institution, and the integration of service learning into the curriculum. Third are strategic activities, including strategic planning for institutionalisation of service learning, articulating how service learning helps advance broader institutional initiatives and priorities, and vocal support for service learning among high-level administrators and faculty members.

Conclusion

This chapter reveals the position of the Institute of Continuing and Distance Education in Ghana and the potential for incorporating a community service learning component into its activities. The institute regards extension service as its core mandate, and yet this third mission has seen little transformation. There is no strategic action plan for community engagement and there are virtually no courses that are related to community service learning.

Nevertheless, the literature review reveals that there are several benefits that might accrue to faculty and students. This is why the institute needs to clearly define a creative partnership with the community to address complex needs in communities through the application of knowledge. This partnership must be backed by effective institutional policy, and champions to sell the idea and make sure that the necessary curricular changes to incorporate community service learning into courses are introduced.

References

Agbodeka, F. (1998) *A History of University of Ghana: Half a Century of Higher Education* (1948–1998). Accra: Woeli Publishing Services.

Ahmed, S., Beck, B., Maurana, C. and Newton, G. (2004) 'Overcoming barriers to effective community-based participatory research in US medical schools', *Education for Health*, Vol. 17 No 2, pp. 141–51.

Amedzro, A. (2004) 'University-based adult education in Ghana 1948–2000', in K. Asiedu, K. Adoo-Adeku and A. Amedzro (Eds), *The Practice of Adult Education in Ghana*. Accra: Ghana Universities Press.

Bell, S., Scott, G., Jackson, J. and Holland, B. (2007) 'Towards a quality management and development framework for community engagement in the Australian higher education sector'. Paper presented at AUQF Conference, Hobart, July. Retrieved 18 September 2010 from www.auqa.edu.au/auqf/2007/program/papers/e21.pdf

Berle, D. (2006) 'Incremental integration: A successful service-learning strategy', *International Journal of Teaching and Learning in Higher Education*, Vol. 18 No 1, pp. 43–8.

Boyer, E. (1990) *Scholarship Reconsidered: Priorities of the Professoriate.* Princeton, NJ: Carnegie Foundation for the Advancement of Teaching.

Boyer, E. (1996) 'The scholarship of engagement', *Journal of Public Services and Outreach*, Vol. 1 No 1, pp. 11–20.

Bringle, R. and Hatcher, J. (1995) 'A service-learning curriculum for faculty', *Michigan Journal of Community Service Learning*, Vol. 2, pp. 112–22.

Bringle, R. and Hatcher, J. (1996) 'Implementing service learning in higher education', *Journal of Higher Education*, Vol. 67, pp. 221–39.

Bringle, R and Hatcher, J. (1999) 'Reflection in service learning: Making meaning of experience', *Educational Horizons*, Vol. 77 No 4, pp. 179–85.

Bringle, R. and Hatcher, J. (2000) 'Institutionalisation of service learning in higher education', *The Journal of Higher Education*, Vol. 71 No 3, pp. 273–90.

Bringle, R. and Hatcher, J. (2002) 'Campus-community partnerships: The terms of engagement', *Journal of Social Issues*, Vol. 58 No 3, pp. 503–16.

Bringle, R. and Hatcher, J. (2009) 'Innovative practices in service-learning and curricular engagement', *New Directions for Higher Education*, Vol. 17, fall, pp. 37–46.

Butin, D. (2006) 'The limits of service-learning in higher education', *The Review of Higher Education*, Vol. 29 No 4, pp. 473–98.

Colby, S., Bercaw, L., Clark, A. and Galiardi, S. (2009) 'From community service to service-learning leadership: A program perspective', *New Horizons in Education*, Vol. 57 No 3, pp. 20–31.

Cone, D. and Harris, S. (1996) 'Service-learning practice: developing a theoretical framework', *Michigan Journal of Community Service Learning*, Vol. 3, pp. 31–43.

Daily Graphic, February 1974.

Deeley, S. (2010) 'Service-learning: Thinking outside the box', *Active Learning in Higher Education*, Vol. 11 No 1, pp. 43–53.

Dewey, J. (1916) *Democracy and Education*. New York: MacMillan.

Fordham, P. (2000) 'Re-defining adult education in Africa', in S. Indabawa, A. Oduaran, T. Afrik and S. Walters (Eds), *The State of Adult and Continuing Education in Africa*. Windhoek: John Meinert Printing, pp. 197–205.

Fourie, F. (2006) 'Towards a South African scholarship of engagement: Core and supplementary tasks of a university?' Paper presented at the conference on community engagement in higher education, Cape Town, South Africa, September.

Freire, P. (1972) *Pedagogy of the Oppressed*. Middlesex: Penguin.

Furco, A. (2001) 'Advancing service-learning at research universities', *New Directions for Higher Education*, Vol. 114, summer, pp. 67–79.

Furco, A. (2007) 'Institutionalising service-learning in higher education', in L. McIlrath and I. Mac Labhrainn (Eds), *Higher Education and Civic Engagement: International Perspectives*. Aldershot: Ashgate, pp. 65–82.

Giles, D. and Eyler, J. (1994) 'The theoretical roots of service-learning in John Dewey: Towards a theory of service-learning', *Michigan Journal of Community Service Learning*, Vol. 1, pp. 77–85.

Hall, B. (2009) 'Higher education, community engagement, and the public good: Building the future of continuing education in Canada', *Canadian Journal of University Continuing Education*, Vol. 35 No 1, pp. 11–23.

Hatcher, J. and Erasmus, M. (2008) 'Service-learning in the United States and South Africa: A comparative analysis informed by John Dewey and Julius Nyerere', *Michigan Journal of Community Service Learning*, Vol. 15 No 1, pp. 49–61.

Henry, S. and Breyfogle, M. (2006) 'Toward a new framework of "server" and "served": De (and re) constructing reciprocity in service-learning pedagogy', *International Journal of Teaching and Learning in Higher Education*, Vol. 18 No 1, pp. 27–35.

Holland, B. (1997) 'Analyzing institutional commitment to service: A model of key organizational factors', *Michigan Journal of Community Service Learning*, Vol. 4, pp. 30–41.

Hoxmeier, J. and Lenk, M. (2003) 'Service-learning in information systems courses: Community projects that make a difference', *Journal of Information Systems Education*, Vol. 14 No 1, pp. 91–100.

Jacoby, B. (1999) 'Partnership for service learning', *New Directions for Student Services*, Vol. 87, fall, pp. 19–35.

Joint Education Trust (2001) 'Community higher education service partnership implementation grant strategy'. Retrieved 12 June 2010 from http://www. chesp.org.za

Jones-Quartey, K. (1975) *The Ghana Institute of Adult Education: 1948–1973. The Twenty-Fifth Annual 'New Year School' of the Institute of Adult Education, University of Ghana (1948/49–1973/74)*. Legon: Institute of Adult Education, University of Ghana.

Kellogg Commission on the Future of State and Land-Grant Universities (1999) *Returning to Our Roots: The Engaged Institution*. Washington, DC: National Association of State Universities and Land-Grant Colleges.

Kiely, R. (2004) 'A chameleon with a complex: Searching for transformation in international service-learning', *Michigan Journal of Community Service Learning*, Vol. 10, pp. 5–20.

Kiely, R., Sandmann, L. and Bracken, S. (2006) 'Overcoming marginalization and disengagement in adult education: Adult educators' contributions to the scholarship of engagement'. Paper presentation at the adult education research conference, University of Minnesota in Minneapolis, June.

Kolb, D. (1984) *Experiential Learning: Experience as the Source of Learning and Development*. Englewood Cliffs, NJ: Prentice-Hall.

Kolb, A. and Kolb, D. (2005) 'Learning styles and learning spaces: Enhancing experiential learning in higher education', *Academy of Management Learning and Education*, Vol. 4 No 2, pp. 193–212.

Lamble, W. and Thompson, G. (2000) 'Reconceptualising university extension and public service: A response to Lauzon', *Canadian Journal of University Continuing Education*, Vol. 26 No 2, pp. 111–21.

Lamsam, G. (1999) 'Development of a service-learning program', *American Journal of Pharmaceutical Education*, Vol. 63, spring, pp. 41–5.

Minkler, M. (2004) 'Ethical challenges for the "outside" researcher in community-based participatory research', *Health Education and Behaviour*, Vol. 31 No 6, pp. 684–97.

Mitchell, C. and Humphries, H. (2007) 'From notions of charity to social justice in service-learning: The complex experience of communities', *Education as Change*, Vol. 11 No 3, pp. 47–58.

Oaks, M., Franklin, N. and Bargerstock, B. (2009) 'Situating outreach and engagement in the university: Concepts, challenges, and opportunities', *Continuing Higher Education Review*, Vol. 73, pp. 224–33.

Ramaley, J. (2003) 'Seizing the moment: Creating a changed society and university through outreach', *Journal of Higher Education Outreach and Engagement*, Vol. 8 No 1, pp. 13–24.

Raybould, S. (1956) 'Adult Education in Nigeria', *International Review of Education*, Vol. 2, pp. 250–3.

Semali, L., Grim, B. and Maretzki, A. (2006) 'Barriers to the inclusion of indigenous knowledge concepts in teaching, research, and outreach', *Journal of Higher Education Outreach and Engagement*, Vol. 11 No 2, pp. 73–88.

Semali, L. and Maretzki, A. (2004) 'Valuing indigenous knowledges: Strategies for engaging communities and transforming the academy', *Journal of Higher Education Outreach and Engagement*, Vol. 10 No 1, pp. 91–106.

Skinner, K. (2007) 'Agency and analogy in African history: The contribution of extra-mural studies in Ghana', *History in Africa*, Vol. 34, pp. 273–96.

Smith, M. (2008) 'Does service learning promote adult development? Theoretical perspectives and directions for research', *New Directions for Adult and Continuing Education*, Vol. 118, pp. 5–15.

Stukas, A., Clary, E. and Snyder, M. (1999) 'Service-learning: Who benefits and why', *Social Policy Report, Society for Research in Child Development*, Vol. 13 No 4, pp. 1–14.

Tan, J. and Philips, J. (2005) Incorporating service learning into computer science courses, *Journal of Computing Sciences in Colleges*, Vol. 20 No 4, pp. 57–62.

UNESCO (1997) 'Adult learning: A key for the 21st century', CONFINTEA V background papers, Hamburg, July.

Vogel, A., Seifer, S. and Gelmon, S. (2010) 'What influences the long-term sustainability of service-learning in higher education? Lessons from a study of early adopters', *Michigan Journal of Community Service Learning*, Vol. 17, pp. 59–74.

Wallis, R. (2006) 'What do we mean by "community engagement"?' Paper presented at the knowledge transfer and engagement forum, Sydney, June.

Wallis, R., Wallis, A. and Harris, C. (2005) 'How universities can enhance sustainable development through successful engagement with their regional communities'. Retrieved 12 December 2010 from http://www.engagingcommunities2005.org/abstracts/Wallis-Robert-final.pdf

Young, C., Shinnar, R., Ackerman, R., Carruthers, C. and Young, D. (2007) 'Implementing and sustaining service-learning at the institutional level', *Journal of Experiential Education*, Vol. 289 No 3, pp. 344–65.

11

Constructing service learning in South Africa: Discourses of engagement

Frances O'Brien

Introduction

The concept and practice of service learning was imported into South Africa in the turbulent first decade of the country's new democracy. Since then, it has taken root in South African higher education institutions, with the growth of interest and expertise constituting 'a quiet revolution' (Higher Education Quality Committee, 2006, p. xxi). Service learning's increased popularity can be attributed to its potential, as a pedagogical tool and an educational approach, to offer much in an era when higher education faces sharply conflicting demands to 'carv[e] out niche areas of innovation within the competitive global arena while meeting the basic development needs of the majority of [its country's] increasingly marginalised and impoverished populations' (Netshandama and Mahlomaholo, 2010, p. 5).

In spite of its growing popularity, service learning has engendered confusion and scepticism (Council on Higher Education, 2010). Muller and Subotzky (2001, p. 172) have suggested that claims of the benefits of service learning are 'sometimes extravagant'. There are also deep concerns about its practicality, its legitimacy as a method of teaching and learning, the various forms of knowledge emerging from it (McMillan, 2002) and, particularly in South Africa, its impact on the communities, off-campus organisations and higher education institutions involved in its implementation (Mitchell and Rautenbach, 2002). Power inequalities constitute a primary concern in relation to its local implementation (Mahlomaholo and Matobako, 2006; Grossman, 2007; Osman and Attwood, 2007).

Driven by these challenges, a framework of engagement Discourses has been constructed and is presented in this chapter. It is intended to offer an understanding broad enough to incorporate multiple facets of service learning, but specific enough to describe and guide the local approach and practice. The Discourses are grounded in a study of South African literature, policies and dialogues, as well as the experiences of 36 service learning initiatives involving at least 96 communities, over 800 higher education students and the academic staff in multiple disciplines at nine universities. The study used grounded theory research methods (Glaser and Strauss, 1967; Strauss and Corbin, 1994) for reasons expounded in an earlier publication (O'Brien, 2005), with analysis characterised by a 'constructivist stance' (Charmaz, 2006).

The notion of Discourse needs some preliminary comment. The concept lends itself to utilisation of the diversity that characterises the local practices and understandings of service learning. In this chapter, Gee's (1990) understanding of Discourse is adopted – namely, a confluence or pattern of language and social practices that, together, shape how we interpret events and indicate what is normal and desirable. Gee suggests that a Discourse indicates which areas of interest are seen as legitimate, how we may write and speak about those interests, how we relate to those within and outside the Discourse, and our social identity, which he defines as 'being recognized as a certain "kind of person", in a given context' (Gee, 2000, p. 99). Discourse is, in short, a 'way of being' (Gee, 1999, p. 22), doing, relating, thinking, talking and writing. In this chapter, I take up Gee's (1999) practice of writing 'Discourse' with a capital 'D' so as to emphasise that it means not just language but also the 'other stuff' (Gee, 1999, p. 17), such as societal norms and power relations. An important caveat to the engagement Discourses is that they are not direct reflections of actual service learning initiatives. Rather, they are idealised images that highlight specific characteristics of service learning.

In the framework, engagement is the key concept or lens through which service learning is viewed and interpreted. Engagement is understood to mean interaction, be that practical and physical, as in the case of meetings, or conceptual, such as engagement with ideas, curriculum and the like. In the remainder of this chapter, four Discourses of engagement are outlined, namely those of 'scholarship', 'benevolence', 'democracy' and 'professionalism', in terms of their concerns, environments, identities, development processes and products, curricula and power issues. The chapter concludes with suggestions as to possible significance of the Discourses for current service learning and other endeavours that have engagement as a primary activity.

Discourse 1: Service learning as scholarly engagement

Service learning is:
- 'Engagement [to] produc[e] "knowledges"' (Bawa, 2003, p. 58)
- 'A component of the curriculum' (Henning, 1998, p. 44)
- 'An alternative tool in the suite of pedagogical approaches used in teaching, as well as a means to generate new knowledge about learning' (van Rensburg, 2004, p. 136)

In this Discourse, we find ourselves in a scholarly place which has knowledge generation, dissemination, integration and application as its primary concerns. Theoretical and specialised knowledge are held in high esteem. The primary identity of all involved in this Discourse of service learning is a scholarly one that sees academics, students, service providers and communities assume roles as teachers and curriculum developers, learners, knowledge enhancers, mentors, assessors, supervisors and researchers. Academics and students are dominant in this Discourse, and, for them at least, some of these roles are the norm. Other participants find that their scholarly contributions in service learning require a paradigm shift or offer new opportunities. A community member reflects: 'It was a shock to me – hearing [university] people saying they have come to learn from us' (Bruzas and O'Brien, 2001, p. 24), while others note that their involvement in student assessment 'is a sign of recognition of the mentor's importance in the student's learning process ... It is also a way of influencing the academic institution' (O'Brien, 2001, p. 4).

The Discourse adopts a modernisation notion of development as progress that diffuses outwards from the centre – that centre being the body of knowledge that lies at the core of a discipline. Thus service learning initiatives address development needs by means of diffusing knowledge, with development being synonymous with learning. On an individual level, intellectual development is sought, with critical thinking being highly prized. Change in people is initiated through reflection and critical questioning, with artefacts such as journals, portfolios and publications supporting and evidencing scholarly advancement. At an institutional level, development is deemed to have occurred when service learning is mainstreamed into academic programmes. It is then that service learning commands legitimacy in the scholarly world.

As a curricular activity in this Discourse, service learning prioritises specific (disciplinary) learning outcomes over the critical cross-field outcomes. Structured critical reflection is deemed important in this Discourse because it is the reflection that turns the service into learning. Reflection is also the key to meta-learning, that is, learning about learning processes. In this Discourse, assessment invariably focuses on students' learning rather than their services or practical, off-campus activities. Integrated assessment is aspired to. Characteristically, assessment comprises written texts in the form of examinations, portfolios, journals and take-home examinations.

Service is a pedagogical strategy that involves students in active engagement with communities. 'Students' texts are their experiences as they work in the real-world' (O'Brien, 2009, p. 31). Service comprises the application of learning, expertise and research, often in ways that loosen disciplinary boundaries. Services are often rendered in off-campus places referred to as 'learning sites'. Theoretical focuses are influential determinants in the choice of community-based learning sites and students' service activities.

Engagement within this Discourse of 'scholarship' takes the form of bringing together existing and new knowledge, indigenous and Western knowledges, and knowledge from different disciplines, theory and skills and different ways of knowing. It is where 'science meets the public' (Erasmus, 2007, p. 35) and the fundamentally interdisciplinary nature of knowledge comes to the fore. Not all knowledges and ways of acquiring them are held in equal esteem, however, and the differing status of knowledge sources highlights issues of power in scholarly engagement. Power presents as the dominant Discourse (von Kotze and Cooper, 2000). To be legitimate in the academy, knowledge must be presented in prescribed ways, usually written, and individually appropriated to meet institutional assessment practices – in other words 'when it is brought into the routines inside the academy, separated from the engagement and service' (Grossman, 2007, p. 311). Knowledge from people with high prestige in social circles of scholars is considered legitimate and wields more power than knowledge from those lower in the academic hierarchy. There is thus a drive to involve academics with high academic qualifications and research output in service learning so as to increase its legitimacy within academia. This Discourse typically witnesses changes in the power dynamics between academic staff and their students as they engage through service learning, with the traditional distance between them being reduced as each comes to recognise the value of the knowledge of the other.

Discourse 2: Service learning as benevolent engagement

Service learning:
• Means that you will apply your knowledge and skills in the service of a community or organisation (O'Brien, 2010, p. 258)

As 'benevolent' engagement, service learning is about doing good for the benefit of others. The Discourse is primarily concerned with 'good citizenship', promoted in the guise of voluntary service. Such a philanthropic orientation is congruent with perceptions of an environment that is deficient and needs-driven, and in which voluntarism, altruism and civic mindedness are promoted in national policies. Engagement in this Discourse typically takes the form of consultations, needs surveys, planning, service provision and evaluation.

The predominant role in this Discourse is that of server. The lead role player is the service provider, likely to be a government department or not-for-profit organisation (NPO). The higher education institution may provide services directly to communities or may complement the organisations that have service delivery as their primary mandate. A particular category of server is that of the organisations that provide financial resources for service learning initiatives. Whether an organisation, government department or higher education institution, however, service providers are usually perceived as 'outsiders' coming to help the 'poor insiders' (*ibid.*, p. 259).

Communities typically comprise 'historically disadvantaged' residents and, in the service learning encounter, they are service beneficiaries. During the course of a service learning initiative, however, community members are also likely to be good citizens as they fulfil the roles of volunteers, safe-keepers and celebrants in the implementation of service learning initiatives. Students electing to participate in service learning are likely to be those with altruistic intentions or a belief that their relative good fortune, in a country with widespread economic poverty, makes community service incumbent on them. One student explained thus: 'As an economist, I firmly believe that one's income is somebody else's expenditure. By that I mean I need to plough back to the community' (*ibid.*, p. 161). The staff from higher education institutions who become involved in service learning are those seeking to operationalise institutional policies on 'outreach'. Their provision of service through service learning typically sees them playing the role of project coordinator.

Development in this Discourse is deemed to be the progressive fulfilment of needs that leads in the long term to empowerment of the needy and vulnerable. Evidence of development is typically a physical product, facility or service. In addition, people are judged to have developed when they can achieve their goals independently of the service provider. The Discourse puts heavy emphasis on planning and reporting, usually by the service provider or higher education role players to the funders. On the individual development side, increasing self-awareness is valued, with skills rather than just intellectual understanding being recognised as important in the learning process.

As a curriculum strategy, service learning is employed for the development of students' skills. With practical ways of knowing being prioritised, assessment is more likely to be in the form of observation of students' performance of services than through the written assignments favoured in the Discourse of 'scholarly' engagement. In addition to practical skills, however, students are expected to demonstrate compassion and altruism.

This link with community upliftment may well see the curriculum being referred to as a project, with orientation, implementation and evaluation phases. A service is perceived as something that is provided or delivered and is decided on the basis of needs assessments or surveys. Through service learning, students intervene with the aim of instituting or extending a service, typically at 'key delivery sites' (Fourie, 2006, p. 46), with the guidance of 'site coordinators'.

Power in this Discourse lies with the service provider, which utilises its history, experience and other resources to rectify shortcomings in the service recipient. The nature of the service is determined by the service provider, and service beneficiaries have to fulfil criteria set down by the service provider for access. Because the services are delivered in an environment of scarcity, service beneficiaries are in a disempowered position by virtue of the limited options they have from which to choose the services they require. Empowerment is believed to be the way of conferring power on those without it, and both students and communities perceive the provision of services to be a means of empowerment, a notion contested by those outside this Discourse, particularly those in the Discourse of 'democratic' engagement.

Discourse 3: Service learning as democratic engagement

Service learning is:
- A radical response to the problems of building a new South Africa (O'Brien, 2010, p. 266)
- A social practice deeply shaped by relationships, power and roles (McMillan, 2002, p. 59)

The typical context of this Discourse is a political one, with issues of social justice and diversity being of primary concern. The main focus or *raison d'être* for service learning is enhancement of the public or common good. Needing to operate in a context of 'competing interests and power relations', however (von Kotze and Cooper, 2000, p. 217), public good is deemed to exist when there is a climate of *ubuntu*, 'affirm[ing] commonality and unity, while … validat[ing] diversity and individuality among human beings' (Goduka, 1999, p. 37). The Discourse defines engagement as dialogue, with the emphasis on understanding the other's life space rather than necessarily converting that space to mirror one's own. Engagement is characterised by mutuality and the flattening of the hierarchies prominent in the previous two Discourses.

Those participating in service learning in this Discourse share with those in the previous Discourse a primary identity as citizens. However, in contrast to the strong altruistic brief of the citizens in the 'benevolent' engagement Discourse, the democratically engaged citizens exhibit strong commitment to social action or societal change. The citizen strives to be 'free' rather than good, as in the previous Discourse. And if academic staff and students dominated the Discourse of 'scholarly' engagement, and service providers that of 'benevolent' engagement, in this Discourse communities are prominent. Their members are likely to be initiators, organisers and networkers in service learning endeavours, getting involved in order to connect with and share resources. Community members are typically defined in terms of their residence in a specific area or institution, or their membership of a work or social facility, rather than in terms of their deficits.

Students aspire to being change agents at best, or supporters, at least, of those encountering structural disadvantages. Along with service providers, higher education staff recognise opportunities and strengths in others, and emphasise their roles as advocate, supporter and sustainer of service learning relationships. Service providers are predominantly NPOs or community-controlled structures. They identify themselves as brokers and mediators between communities and the service learning participants from higher education.

'A genuine partnership can develop by having to seek direction with potential partners rather than guiding them on a track known to (one party) in advance' (personal communication with staff member at University of KwaZulu-Natal, 18 October 1999). This observation typifies the social, political or people-centred development germane to this Discourse. Development aims for 'inter-dependence between' sectors, as opposed to 'dependence upon' or 'independence from' others, a characteristic of development in the 'scholarship' and 'development' Discourses respectively. Service learning aspires to a greater cohesion among different sectors in society through partnership, collaboration and the like in our policies.

The Discourse mandates that a curriculum reflects the negotiation of many voices not traditionally heard in the development of academic or service delivery programmes. The content of the curriculum is strongly, though not exclusively, driven by community interests. Of importance in developing the curriculum are the assets that each sector can contribute to the collaboration between them. This is in contrast with the priority given to community needs and service availability which drive academic curricula in the previous Discourses.

In this 'democratic' engagement Discourse, feelings and common sense, or intuitive knowledge, are seen as being on a par with the conceptualisation valued in the 'scholarly' engagement Discourse. Personal experience is held in high esteem, based on the assumption that deep knowing emerges from being. Knowledge is seen as culturally defined and co-created, relative and multilayered. Learning outcomes for students typically include increased awareness of issues such as social justice, stereotyping and diversity and the development of civic and analytical skills. Interpersonal skills, insight, sensitivity to difference, tolerance and empathy take precedence as learning outcomes over the intellectual and practical skills emphasised by the 'scholarly' and 'benevolent' engagement Discourses respectively. The primary purpose of student involvement in communities' activities is to show solidarity with them. All in all, services in this Discourse are seen as bringing 'new life' to those involved and a shared identity. Such learning outcomes under 'democratic' engagement are reflected by this student, quoted in a study by van Rensburg:

I was a responsible tourist in the Community Service-Learning project. As a white English-speaking female in South Africa, I have developed through active participation to satisfy the needs of the community, a community I now realize was a foreign country to me. ... It developed a strong sense of caring for others in me. All tourists, however, must at some point, leave the foreign country. I left with a sense of 'being there'. It wasn't a 'been there, done that, bought the T-shirt' experience though. I was questioning my status as a tourist in my own country for the first time. I was beginning to see what the old system [of apartheid] did to people like me. The Community Service-Learning project was in the end, like applying for asylum, fleeing from the past, and applying for citizenship in a new country. (van Rensburg 2004, pp. 138–9)

The value placed in this Discourse on equity, reciprocity, goal alignment and co-created knowledge indicates a deep concern with power. There is a sensitivity, possibly heightened in South Africa, to historical power inequities, which saw service delivery and research endeavours, in particular, characterised by a lack of mutual accountability. Power appears as a direct focus and content of the academic curriculum. It is something to be studied.

In addition to studying power, the underlying goal of service learning in this Discourse is to alter power relations. The relationships and associations that constitute the primary vehicles for service learning are also critiqued in this respect. Participants 'draw attention to the ways in which power relations might be concealed within [their service learning practices], ultimately subjecting them to the very same forces they [those involved] claim to be resisting' (Osman and Attwood, 2007, p. 19). Engagement that prioritises power sharing utilises strategies such as joint ownership, negotiation, mutual accountability, participatory research techniques and dialogue, aiming for close alignment between the goals and concerns of all participants: 'successful negotiation of power issues [being] ... probably the single biggest challenge facing' relationship building and nurturing (O'Brien, 2010, p. 271).

Discourse 4: Service learning as professional engagement

Service learning:
- Is ... a sound investment towards the delivery of a more socially responsible student 'product' (Erasmus, 2007, p. 28)
- Facilitates the development of ... future leaders who are not only knowledgeable and competent, but also socially conscious and ethical professionals (O'Brien, 2010, p. 275)

A society committed to economic growth but challenged by insufficient high-level, relevant skills, inadequate funds and poor infrastructure is the environment constructed by this Discourse. It is primarily concerned with the procurement and maintenance of resources, particularly human resources, in contrast to the previous Discourses' interests in knowledge, service and social justice. Here, the engagement that is service learning is perceived as a transaction, replete with references to quality management and national accreditation.

Engagement between the academic, community and service provider sectors takes place at formal occasions convened for the purpose of discussion and planning. The engagement typically yields artefacts such as budgets, timetables, deadlines, contracts, and quality and logical frameworks, all of which enable service learning to be planned, implemented and evaluated. Time and high workloads are significant constraints for all, while higher education staff, in particular, worry about the sustainability of resources and the opportunity costs incurred when they buy into service learning.

The language of the marketplace dominates this Discourse. References to 'client', 'products' and 'management' are commonplace, and there is interest in seeking 'buy-in' for service learning – that is, commitment and participation by strategic stakeholders from different sectors. In addition, service learning becomes part of job descriptions and a criterion for staff selection and promotion, particularly in academic institutions. Such preoccupation with human and organisational development is congruent with many understandings of professionalism (Evans, 2008; Webster-Wright, 2009).

If those pursuing service learning in this Discourse have a common identity, it may be conceptualised as a stakeholder. That identity conveys the idea of an '"interest group" with some stake in a policy or a project ...' (Nefjees, 2000, p. 102). As in the 'benevolent' engagement Discourse, the service provider is dominant in this 'professional' engagement Discourse. However, the service provider coming to the fore here is the professional or occupational association or the professional-in-practice who assumes the roles of employer, supervisor and modeller for the student. Community members are the clients, learners, patients or users of the professional service rendered by students under the supervision of the service provider. Higher education staff highlight their roles as administrators, monitors, accreditors and managers in the service learning process. They may also assume the role of direct service provider. In such instances, academic staff also become employer, manager, supervisor, skills trainer and provider of material resources. Students typically fulfil roles of professional-in-training, employee and mentee, but may also see themselves as owner of interventions and creator of new products. Their stake in service learning is typically expressed as furthering their future professional prospects.

In this Discourse, development is primarily predicated on a neo-liberal ideology and comprises growth in human and economic 'capital'. In relation to service learning, such capital will manifest as the trained worker or professional, the productive community member and the academic with access to research and project funding. Communities and service providers are appreciated for the value they add to the curriculum. At an institutional level, the development of service learning is likely to be managed by the upper echelons, grounded in institutional policies, subject to quality promotion procedures and geared to attract scarce physical resources to facilitate it.

Curriculum in this Discourse prioritises the application of knowledge, with both practical and experiential knowledge put in the foreground. The attention given to skills development is akin to the pedagogy in the 'benevolent' engagement Discourse. In contrast with that Discourse, however, the choice of skills to be included in the curriculum is dictated by the profession for which the students are being groomed. Experiential knowledge is of equal importance in this Discourse, and service learning is admitted into the curriculum primarily for the opportunities it offers to expose students to the experience of an authentic work context in which they begin to take on the identity of the professional that they aspire to be.

Power in this Discourse is held by those with the resources to undertake service learning and those with accredited expertise. While higher education institutions may accredit students' learning, thereby enabling them to exit the institution with a formal qualification, only professional bodies can accredit those graduates to practise the profession for which they were educated. Power imbalances reveal themselves in all intersectoral relationships – in particular, between service providers and community members (those in receipt of their services), higher education and community, and between service providers and students – with the latter in each duo being in relatively disempowered positions.

Power between stakeholders in this Discourse is mediated structurally. One structure is the partnership, which comes into being through:

> *A formal written contract outlining the community selection cri-*
> *teria used, objectives for service learning, expected duties from*
> *both partners, the content/process to carry out service learning,*
> *and time commitments, and which is signed by both partners*
> *prior to the implementation of service learning.* (University of
> Natal, 2002, p. 21)

Table 1: Matrix of service learning Discourses

Engagement	Scholarly	Benevolent	Democratic	Professional
Primary focus	Knowledge	Good citizenship	Social change	Resource development
Predominant context	Research dominated	Poverty	Political and diverse	Under-resourced
Primary identity of participants	Scholar	Service provider, recipient	Activist	Stakeholder
Principal purpose of service learning	To increase knowledge	To do good	To promote equitable participation	To increase efficiency
Development: individual level	Intellectual	Practical	Interpersonal	Skills/ethical
Development: societal level	Curriculum	Infrastructural	Democracy	Human resources
Curriculum orientation	Research	Service	Experience	Practice
Power holder	Academic	Service provider	Community	Service provider
Engagement via	Inter-disciplinarity	Consultation	Dialogue	Transactions

Partnership is a means to an end – unlike its role in the 'democratic' engagement Discourse in which an equitable partnership is the desired goal. Partners favour meetings as a means of communicating effectively, in contrast to the debates, group discussions and dialogues that characterise the 'scholarly', 'benevolent' and 'democratic' engagement Discourses.

To provide an overview of each Discourse, the primary ideas and concepts are listed in a matrix in table 1.

Conclusion

In an effort to enhance our understanding of service learning, theorise it and increase its potential to benefit rather than harm those involved, the Discourses of 'scholarly', 'benevolent', 'democratic' and 'professional' engagement were constructed. They were grounded in the experiences, dialogues and scholarship around service learning in South Africa. Charmaz (2006, p. 185) has argued that taking the 'constructivist position to its logical extension' means that 'knowledge (should) transform practice and social processes', and 'grounded theory studies (should) contribute to a better world'. Cognisant of these directives, this chapter ends with the following recommendations.

Definitional flexibility
The framework makes explicit that considerable variation may be anticipated in different service learning initiatives. While some service learning endeavours may have similar features, each practice is likely to be unique in important respects. We should thus be cautious and critical in response to any attempt to develop a single definition of service learning. 'Definitional certainty' (Butin, 2003, p. 1687) will see service learning being defined so broadly that it offers little meaningful information, encourages scepticism and invites failure in at least some ways. It may be more helpful to use the Discourse elements (context, identity, development, curriculum, power and engagement) to structure dialogue and discussions in planning a service learning initiative collaboratively. In this way, each initiative will have a 'situated identity' (Gee, 1999) that allows evolvement of a definition of service learning that is shared, explicit and utilitarian. At the same time, the very process of its development will promote deeper understanding between those implementing the initiative and offer a transparent, authentic and realistic statement of their undertaking.

Curriculum coherence

The framework underlines the existence of points of diversion and collision between the Discourses. We are thus alerted to the importance of coherence within a curriculum. Unnecessary confusion for students and damage to intersectoral relationships are likely to result when the practical requirements for running the module and assessing the students' progress undermine the goals and articulated philosophies behind the module.

Flexibility in implementation

The varied contexts and identities that became apparent when looking across the Discourses indicate the need for flexibility in implementing service learning and in evaluating its impact. This flexibility is to take into account the different timetables and priorities of the participating sectors and their different states of readiness to engage with each other, to learn, serve and evaluate their participation. It may thus be necessary to adjust the initial plans in consultation with those involved. One may anticipate tensions between flexible implementation of and research around service learning and the current managerial ethos in which measurement, rigid plans and adherence to these are valued by our higher education sector. What it means, in the current higher education context, to pursue service learning within a 'democratic' Discourse, in particular, may indeed be a worthwhile topic for further research.

Questioning intersectoral boundaries

The focusing of the framework on engagement raises questions about the nature of the boundaries through and across which interaction occurs. The crossing of boundaries is a familiar notion in service learning and is particularly important in South Africa, with its history of enforced and often impermeable divisions between people and places. Do the thin lines we use in diagrams of interaction accurately represent the differences between the knowledges, the service and learning sites, and the people and sectors that service learning strives to traverse? Or would it be more realistic to depict 'chasms' (Bruzas, 2004, p. 57)? Future research into service learning would be usefully employed in problematising the differences that it encounters.

Use of framework outside service learning

The framework lends itself to use as an analytic tool for exploration of practices other than service learning, but that are in essence 'engaged'. Leadership, research and intersectoral projects, such as health promotion, are examples of such practices. The composite parts of the Discourse – namely, its context, the identity and roles of those involved, the development, learning and serving taking place and the prevalent power dynamics – may serve as 'theoretical codes' (Charmaz, 2006) with which to analyse other engaged practices. Higher education institutions may also develop indicators for each 'code' in order to assess the quality of engagement in their curricula and other practices.

The framework as an evolving process

Finally, it must be remembered that, by its very nature, a Discourse can be split, melded or elaborated. It evolves as other Discourses in society change and as new knowledge is constructed. The use of information and mobile technologies in service learning initiatives, and the place of indigenous knowledges in that work, are two issues that appeared only on the periphery of the service learning experiences that grounded the Discourses. One may anticipate that such issues will become more prominent and may well impact on the Discourses to a greater or lesser degree in the future. Thus the Discourses as presented in this chapter should be seen as springboards for further research and critical consideration. Indeed, continued analysis of local initiatives may well reveal other Discourses or a collapsing of two or more of the ones presented here. In this respect, the theoretical framework typifies what the originators of grounded theory called 'an ever-developing entity' rather than 'a perfected product', frozen in a particular time and context (Glaser and Strauss, 1967, p. 32).

References

Bawa, A. (2003) 'Rethinking community-based learning in the context of globalisation', in H. Perold, S. Stroud and M. Sherraden (Eds), *Service Enquiry in the 21st Century*. Johannesburg: Global Service Institute and Volunteer and Service Enquiry Southern Africa, pp. 47–60.

Bruzas, C. (2004) 'The role of the service partner in service learning'. Unpublished Master's thesis, University of KwaZulu-Natal, Durban, South Africa.

Bruzas, C. and O'Brien, F. (2001) 'Interim institutional narrative report of the University of Natal', Durban. Unpublished overview for the Joint Education Trust of CHESP Service-Learning Projects.

Butin, D.W. (2003) 'Of what use is it? Multiple conceptualizations of service learning within education', *Teachers College Record*, Vol. 105 No 9, pp. 1674–92.

Charmaz, K. (2006) *Constructing Grounded Theory*. Thousand Oaks: Sage.

Council on Higher Education (Ed.) (2010) *Community Engagement in South African Higher Education*. Kagisano No 6. Auckland Park: Jacana Media.

Erasmus, M.A. (2007) 'Service learning: Preparing a new generation of scientists for a mode 2 society', *Journal for New Generation Sciences*, Vol. 5 No 2, pp. 26–40.

Evans, L. (2008) 'Professionalism, professionality and the development of education professionals', *British Journal of Educational Studies*, Vol. 56 No 1, pp. 20–38.

Fourie, F. (2006) 'Towards a South African scholarship of engagement: Core and supplemental tasks of a university?' Paper presented at the community engagement in higher education conference, Cape Town, September. Retrieved 5 November 2009 from http://www.che.ac.za/documents/d000153/

Gee, J.P. (1990) *Social Linguistics and Literacies Ideology in Discourse*. London: Falmer Press.

Gee, J.P. (1999) *An Introduction to Discourse Analysis*. London: Routledge.

Gee, J.P. (2000) 'Identity as an analytic lens for research in education', *Review of Research in Education*, Vol. 25, pp. 99–125.

Glaser, B.G. and Strauss, A.L. (1967) *The Discovery of Grounded Theory: Strategies for Qualitative Research*. New York: Aldine Publishing Company.

Goduka, M.I. (1999) *Affirming Unity in Diversity in Education: Healing with Ubuntu*. Cape Town: Juta.

Grossman, J. (2007) 'Social responsiveness and workers' knowledge in our own backyards: The blunted challenge of service learning'. Paper presented at the fifth international conference on researching work and learning, Cape Town, December.

Henning, E. (1998) 'Service learning in the university curriculum: Partnerships in community education', *South African Journal of Higher Education*, Vol. 12 No 1, pp. 44–53.

Higher Education Quality Committee (2006) *Service-Learning in the Curriculum: A Resource for Higher Education Institutions*. Pretoria: Council on Higher Education.

Mahlomaholo, S. and Matobako, T. (2006) 'Service learning in South Africa held terminally captive by legacies of the past', *Alternation*, Vol. 13 No 1, pp. 203–17.

McMillan, J. (2002) 'The sacred and profane. Theorising knowledge reproduction processes in a service-learning curriculum', in S.H. Billig and A. Furco (Eds), *Service-Learning through a Multidisciplinary Lens*. Greenwich, CT: Information Age Publishing, pp. 55–70.

Mitchell, C. and Rautenbach, S. (2005) 'Questioning service learning in South Africa: Problematising partnerships in the South African context. A case study from the University of KwaZulu-Natal', *South African Journal of Higher Education*, Vol. 19 No 1, pp. 101–12.

Muller, J. and Subotzky, G. (2001) 'What knowledge is needed in the new millennium?' *Organisation*, Vol. 8 No 2, pp. 163–82.

Neefjes, K. (2000) *Environments and Livelihoods: Strategies for Sustainability*. Oxford: Oxfam.

Netshandama, V. and Mahlomaholo, S. (2010) 'The role of community engagement in higher education: Focus on the discourse relating to knowledge development'. Paper presented at the third global conference: 'Intellectuals: knowledge-power', Prague, Czech Republic, May.

O'Brien, F. (2001) 'Sites for service-learning'. Seminar presentation to the School of Community Development and Adult Learning, University of Natal, Durban, April.

O'Brien, F. (2005) 'Grounding service learning in South Africa', *Acta Academica Supplementum*, Vol. 3, pp. 64–98.

O'Brien, F. (2009) 'In pursuit of African scholarship: Unpacking engagement', *Higher Education*, Vol. 58, pp. 29–39.

O'Brien, F. (2010) 'Grounding service learning in South Africa: The development of a theoretical framework'. Unpublished PhD thesis, University of KwaZulu-Natal, Durban.

Osman, R. and Attwood, G. (2007) 'Power and participation in and through service learning', *Education as Change*, Vol. 11 No 3, pp. 18–21.

Strauss, A. and Corbin, J. (1994) 'Grounded theory methodology', in N.K. Denzin and Y.S. Lincoln (Eds), *Handbook of Qualitative Research*. London: Sage, pp. 273–84.

University of Natal (2002) 'CHESP pilot service learning modules narrative report: Community placement project'. Unpublished report, University of Natal, Pietermaritzburg.

van Rensburg, W. (2004) 'Writing partnerships: Academic writing and service-learning'. *Education as Change*, Vol. 8 No 2, pp. 134–45.

von Kotze A. and Cooper L. (2000) 'Exploring the transformative potential of project-based learning in university adult education', *Studies in the Education of Adults*, Vol. 32 No 2, pp. 212–28.

Webster-Wright, A. (2009) 'Reframing professional development through understanding authentic professional learning', *Review of Educational Research*, Vol. 79 No 2, pp. 702–39.

12

Community engagement in Africa: Common themes, challenges and prospects

Julia Preece

An African university must not only pursue knowledge for its own sake, but also for the ... amelioration of conditions of life and work of the ordinary man and woman. It must be fully committed to active participation in the social transformation, economic modernization, and the ... upgrading of the total human resources of the nation. (Wandira, 1977, p. 22, cited in Seepe, 2004, p. 21)

The above statement was first cited in 1977, but is still reflected in Seepe's publication some thirty years later. It constitutes the thread of all the chapters in this book – that of the need for universities to be relevant and connected to their societies, albeit recognising that connection is to an increasingly complex world. Seepe highlights the need for scholarship to address, among others, issues of hunger, disease, poverty, crime and racial divisions. The pursuit of truth, he argues, must be 'imbued with a sense of social responsibility' (p. 27). But he also stresses that this pursuit must be from African perspectives grounded in African experiences 'so that the African experience should be a source of ideas leading to public policy' (p. 31).

The focus of this book has been on eliciting a multiplicity of African experiences and perspectives that may contribute to the wider global debate on universities and engagement. Thematic concerns that run through most of the chapters include a desire to develop Africa-centric engagement strategies for collaboration, fostering lifelong learning, knowledge building, enhancing the university curriculum, creating opportunities for mutual learning, and repositioning the university within its environment to achieve these strategies. The first part of the book addresses these issues under the broad label of learning cities and regions. The second part provides some practical examples and speculative notions of engagement as community-based initiatives, often involving the concept of service learning as a means of encouraging critical reflection among student participants.

This chapter compares perspectives and challenges on some of the most common themes (engagement, collaboration, lifelong learning and knowledge) in the context of wider literature.

Engagement

The literature is not short of definitions for engagement for universities, as chapter 1 shows. It has been associated with active citizenship (Department of Education, 1997; UNESCO, 2009), the expansion of learning as a lifelong project (Longworth and Allwinkle, 2005) and the co-production of knowledge (Muller and Subotzky, 2001).

Two chapters in this book offer conceptual frameworks for how engagement appears to operate. The first, in chapter 8 (Preece *et al.*), suggests that it can be plotted on a sliding scale or continuum of working relationships that starts from engagement as a unidirectional outreach activity led by universities and often encompassing formal course provision to the world outside the university's walls (see also Openjuru and Ikoja-Odongo, chapter 9). The most extensive form of engagement on this continuum is one where staff and students are involved and which includes a service learning process to ensure the activities are embedded in the university curriculum. In relation to the associated activity of service learning with engagement, O'Brien (chapter 11) provides a conceptual framework or typology of four strands of engagement.

These strands reflect many of the activities across the chapters, irrespective of their service learning component, and the typology offers a way of positioning them as follows.

'Scholarly' engagement focuses on knowledge generation and integration of service learning into academic programmes. The Malawi case study in chapter 8 and Tagoe's positioning of service learning within experiential learning pedagogy in chapter 10 are indications of this type of engagement.

'Benevolent' engagement positions service learning and other activities within a philanthropic mode, focusing on 'doing good', volunteerism and acting as a service provider to community needs. Many of the project activities described in chapter 8 fit into this mode. For instance, all the projects involved volunteering by staff and students with a view to benefiting community identified need.

'Democratic' engagement perhaps reflects the aspirations of three of the Botswana chapters. Dube, in chapter 5, and Molebatsi, in chapter 4, both talk about democratic participation in public decision making and Ntseane, in chapter 2, stresses the consultative nature of engagement that leads towards ownership of decision making and social action or change. O'Brien also stresses that this form of engagement focuses on assets rather than needs – again reflecting Dube's concern with developing indigenous assets for sustainable development. In the context of the Malawi case study in chapter 8, there is also evidence that the service learning students, through their Theatre for Development activities, contributed to increased social awareness and motivation to challenge oppressive structures.

'Professional' engagement is understood as a formal arrangement between institutions, but in the context of managerialism and organisational structures. There is evidence that the Botswana learning city initiative reflects this aspect of engagement through its formal memorandum. Similarly, Openjuru and Ikoja-Odongo, in chapter 9, describe a number of formal arrangements that signify professional engagement.

It can therefore be seen that while engagement can be subdivided into different typologies, in practice one engagement initiative may embrace more than one typology.

The practice of engagement, however, seems to share a common characteristic. One of the most commonly used concepts throughout all the chapters is that of 'collaboration'. Although Dube (chapter 5) does not refer explicitly to this word, it is worth exploring in a little more depth what, in the different chapter contexts, is meant by collaboration as a feature of engagement.

Collaboration

Within the wider literature, collaboration is often a theme of the caring professions. So, for instance, Bruner *et al.* (2011, p. 2), in the context of promoting patient health care, describe the core features of collaboration as embracing 'sharing, mutual respect, complementarity and interdependent roles'. They cite interprofessional collaboration as a process of 'promoting and optimizing active participation'.

Schmied *et al.* (2010, p. 3518), again in relation to the nursing profession, suggest that collaboration also operates on a continuum, starting from a position of 'coexistence', where there is no formal relationship between services, to 'cooperation,' which may involve *ad hoc* sharing of information, to 'coordination', which entails some shared decision making. Finally 'integration' and 'co-ownership' collaboration entails formal arrangements 'based on common values, where there is no differentiation between services'. Schmied *et al.* argue that this level of collaboration requires 'high-level vertical and horizontal integration' of agencies working together at all levels of service delivery.

These interpretations translate across to community engagement. For instance, Schmied *et al.*'s rendering of high-level collaboration bears similarities to the more integrated aspects of engagement described by Charles and Benneworth (2009) and cited in chapter 8 by Preece *et al.* Schmied *et al.* (2010, p. 3522) elaborate on their understanding of successful collaboration systems by highlighting some key elements which include 'shared vision and values'; 'clearly stated aims'; valuing different contributions; attention to power issues in relationships; conflict-resolution mechanisms; sufficient resources and time to build the necessary relationships between participants; suitable communication and information sharing systems; and an understanding of participants' value systems. Other features include the use of multidisciplinary teams, collegial respect and trust, and a willingness to overcome pre-existing assumptions about each other in order to develop a shared framework for action. Thune and Gulbrandsen (2011) emphasise the complexity of collaboration. They argue that its coordination feature is an evolutionary process that must also take into account power relations.

So how does collaboration manifest itself in community learning regions and community engagement activities? Walters (2007), cited in chapter 1, summarises one of the characteristics of a learning region as having high levels of collaboration and networking. Kearns and Ishumi in chapter 7 also stress the need for broad partnerships between the different actors. In reality, though, as authors in chapters 6 and 7 point out, very few universities have formal collaboration relationships with their constituencies. One example of a formal arrangement is cited by Openjuru and Ikoja-Odongo in chapter 9, where there are a number of institution-wide, vertical and horizontal structures to facilitate coordination and integration of partnership activities between private and public agencies to address regional development needs. Here, there is a university-wide strategy that partners with local government at district leadership levels as well as with the private sector which, in turn, actively participates in university policy structures. While many of the activities described reflect traditional extra-mural work, there are some interesting interdisciplinary university interventions such as the model village project, which encourages self-sustainability by developing skills in building, sanitation and agriculture.

Botswana is one of the few exceptions to demonstrate Schmied *et al.*'s (2010, p. 3522) 'co-ownership' end of the continuum where there is a formal arrangement that has undergone a variety of stages in order to build up sufficient trust and relationships. The extent to which information sharing systems are sufficiently embedded to sustain the collaboration has yet to be tested, as chapters 3 (Modise and Mosweunyane) and 4 (Molebatsi) highlight.

Other chapters – for instance chapter 8 by Preece *et al.* – show that collaboration is rather more at the level of 'cooperation' where *ad hoc* activities, such as individual projects set up for particular purposes with selected stakeholders, entail some shared decision making. But Preece *et al.* emphasise that collaboration at community level also requires a community, needs-led approach, perhaps going some way towards addressing the issue of power and control that Thune and Gulbrandsen (2011) talk about. The different strands of engagement cited by O'Brien in chapter 11 could also be plotted across Schmied *et al.*'s collaboration continuum so that 'democratic engagement', for instance, represents the most sophisticated form of collaboration. However, O'Brien stresses that collaboration also entails recognition of 'assets that each sector can contribute to the collaboration'. This is an important feature of engagement, which focuses on reciprocity rather than philanthropy and positions universities as partners rather than sole providers in collaboration relationships.

A theme that only emerges in part 2 of the book is the notion of service learning as a student-focused feature of community engagement. Chapters 10 and 11 focus on this issue in some detail. Tagoe, in chapter 10, links it ideologically to pedagogy and as a resource for collaboration, particularly drawing on the heritage of adult education extra-mural work. Service learning is often sold as a reciprocal, mutual learning experience, though, as chapter 1 highlights, there is much criticism about how effectively reciprocity and mutuality are realised in practice.

In a number of chapters, collaboration is emphasised with a specific contextual focus of drawing on African communication styles. Mwaikokesya, for instance, in chapter 6, first positions Tanzania's learning cities origins within the nation's historical heritage of Nyerere's socialist development goals of the 1960s. Kearns and Ishumi, in chapter 7, also advocate an African learning city network that draws on traditional methods of learning. Ntseane, in chapter 2, emphasises the need to do things 'the African way', particularly with regard to public consultation and consensus building to ensure collective ownership of ideas and plans. In African contexts this takes time. Modise and Moswunyane (chapter 3) suggest that part of the responsibility lies with universities taking a proactive step to create a more attractive public image of themselves in order to position themselves as partners in development. Molebatsi, in chapter 4, reinforces the need for 'interactive and reciprocal partnerships'. In the context of urban planning, this is manifested by promoting opportunities for participatory decision making concerning the city's ongoing urban developments and the consequences of non-consultation.

However, partly due to the emerging nature of these collaborations, none of the chapters addresses the complexity of human relationships in collaboration. Fryer (2010, p. 172), in the context of Canadian university projects, asserts that engagement is 'all about relationships'.'Successful community-university engagement is not only a function of what people do … but also … it is a function of *who people are*'. A primary issue for collaboration in university–community engagement is the fact that all stakeholders are influenced by their cultural world view and internalised norms – including the situation where different institutions have their own practices and work cultures. For example, a for-profit business operates on different value systems from a not-for-profit department of education. There is a need for ongoing tolerance and willingness to understand the cross-cultural dynamics of interactions and willingness to 'co-create hybrid cultural spaces' (*ibid.*, p. 174) where people can collaborate to develop shared visions. Fryer emphases the need, therefore, for strong communication links and awareness of the unequal power differentials between the different players. Ntseane (chapter 2), in support of this, highlights the need for dialogue. This, Fryer asserts, includes being persistent with negotiations but also maintaining respect for the 'emergent power' (Fryer, 2010, p. 177) of untapped resources in the community itself and in students who can be partners in decision making.

Other challenges in relation to collaboration include those summarised by Wergin (2006, pp. 25–6) in relation to academic staff not being 'accustomed to the messiness of direct engagement in societal problems', their lack of experiential knowledge and the need for participating stakeholders to spend time together to build mutual trust. Finally, he also suggests – perhaps controversially – that collaboration 'is not always beneficial'; not all partners in a partnership are useful and sometimes results could be achieved more effectively through other strategies.

In spite of these challenges and caveats, it is important to recognise the inextricable relationship between the university engagement-as-collaboration philosophy, and lifelong learning.

Lifelong learning

Chapter 1 has already highlighted that lifelong learning as a concept is not well defined in policy documents on the African continent, though the term is often referred to in relation to universities. (Chapter 8, for instance, cites policy documents from Botswana, Lesotho, Nigeria and Malawi which all link lifelong learning to community service in relation to universities.) We have also noted that education-sector strategic plans often reduce lifelong learning to a basic education and literacy focus (see chapter 6), largely because of the influence of donor funding policies.

Longworth (2012) points out, however, that learning cities and learning regions are essentially about a notion of lifelong learning for all, understood in its broadest sense – to embrace a wide range of competencies, attitudes and skills which can address environmental and humanistic issues as well as economistic concerns.

For the African continent, this vision for lifelong learning must also connect with African identities. For many this means recognising the traditional heritage of lifelong learning that was interrupted by colonialism (Fordjor *et al.*, 2003; Omolewa, 2002; Amutabi and Oketch, 2009). The challenge is to reflect on how such traditions impact on the value systems that are part of lifelong learning in contemporary contexts (Mbigi, 2005; Lekoko and Modise, 2011). There are overlapping features between those articulated in Africa and those articulated in the political north in relation to engagement and learning cities (Longworth, 2012). The emphasis in both cases is on a holistic view of learning – the role of heritage and culture as arenas for learning and building community and the organic nature of learning that draws upon its living heritage and communal life (as cited by Kearns and Ishumi in chapter 7). Mwaikokesya, in chapter 6, also highlights the life-wide and life-deep nature of learning. All these aspects take us away from the dominant, individualistic and economistic focus of most policy documents (CEC, 2000; OECD, 2004; World Bank, 2003, for instance).

Nevertheless, writers such as Avoseh (2001), Mbigi (2005), Preece 2009 and Lekoko and Modise (2011) emphasise additional features of learning in African contexts that reflect a collective and spiritual vision of learning that, when drawing on African traditions, functions on the basis of a close connection between the living, the dead and those yet to be born. In other words, the emphasis is on our interconnectivity and the interrelations that link learning to practical issues but also take learning into the realm of spirituality, context and identity. Lekoko and Modise (2011, pp. 28–9), for instance, highlight a distinction between Western and African identities in the form of I/we. 'I' is the individualistic concept of the self in Western ideology, but 'we' is the more collective notion of the self in African ideologies:

> *The African philosophy of 'I am because we are' (Mbiti, 1988) encourages a culture of learning in which the learner's success is attributed to the entire situation within which she/he learns and lives ... This ideal is central to any learning that recognizes that an African has a past that can be tapped into to further his/ her learning. It is also important to remember that experiences in the social environment serve as an index of relevant learning and as a measure of how one applies what he/she has learned. This further validates the importance of learning for social living.* (Lekoko and Modise, 2011, pp. 28–9)

Of course, such internalised rationales for existence are no longer universal for all Africans or specific to Africa, but they provide the basis from which to conceptualise lifelong leaning for community engagement that reflects an Africanised learning context.

Dube, in chapter 5, particularly emphasises the need to harness such indigenous aspects of learning in order to instil a sense of connectivity to the issues of sustainable development:

> *A western ... school system, isolated African children from their knowledge context – that is, from the family and community knowledge base – and starved them of a whole system of lifelong learning (Omolewa, 2002). This served to break down the system for transferring knowledge and skill, and erode confidence in African society.* (Dube, chapter 5)

Dube argues strongly for a lifelong learning approach that captures different knowledge systems to facilitate sustainable environmental engagement. She also recognises the complexity of contemporary society, which requires an evolution of traditional knowledge systems to facilitate connections with globalisation and take us beyond the immediate environment. This, of course, is part of the project of regional engagement – to develop networks and links that respect the local but also relate to wider international connections. Chapter 7, by Kearns and Ishumi, encourages such networking, utilising cyberspace as a resource. Chapter 2, by Ntseane, highlights the experiential value of such networking in Botswana's own lifelong learning project.

Lifelong learning is a feature of ongoing knowledge production, dissemination and application. Knowledge in African contexts includes the construction of knowledge that takes place outside the formal, scientific community.

Knowledge

The extent to which lifelong learning can be Africanised in the way that Seepe (2004) highlighted at the beginning of this chapter depends partly on its relationship to knowledge production. Indigenous knowledge is referred to specifically by six chapters in this book, though only Dube elaborates on the challenges of a development agenda that 'excludes locally adaptive systems in place of imported knowledge systems'.

Dube addresses the Africanisation theme in relation to traditional knowledge systems. This is the most comprehensive exposition in the book of how indigenous knowledge can both inform and be informed by the present and contribute to culturally sensitive development. She provides examples of the dynamics and tensions between modernisation demands for commercialisa-tion of resources and resultant over-exploitation of those resources in the face of competitive Western demands to produce at undervalued rates. She positions universities as potential think tanks with resources for research that can address sustainability issues in context. Apart from chapter 8, this is the only chapter that discusses how knowledge disciplines might work together to address the complexity of development issues. But Dube elaborates on this notion, emphasising the co-production of knowledge through collabora-tive learning that uses the social capital of traditional community ties. This perspective is also referred to in the wider literature on collaboration for engagement, as Fryer (2010) demonstrates.

There is another feature of knowledge, however, that is often articulated as mode 2 knowledge (Gibbons *et al.*, 1994). Mode 2 knowledge, particularly in African contexts, has been highlighted as a relevant feature of engagement scholarship because it allows for practice-based knowledge that develops in context and is not confined to disciplinary boundaries.

Waghid (2002), for instance, cites extensively from Gibbons *et al.* (1994) to distinguish between the more conventional notion of mode 1 knowledge as scientific, discipline-based knowledge that is more commonly associated with university knowledge production and that of mode 2 knowledge. Mode 2 is differentiated by its context-specific framework, rather than its disciplinary framework. It is associated with transdisciplinary production – or socially distributed knowledge. That is, the knowledge is problem based, and develops as a result of reflexivity and interaction with real-life situations. The knowl-edge producers may be teams of actors working across a variety of social groups and organisations to focus on addressing a specific problem, the solu-tions or products of which are accountable to a broader range of actors. Mode 2 knowledge thus steps out of its discipline and is socially produced as an outcome of dialogue and meaning making.

In acknowledging that mode 2 knowledge has been received with some scep-ticism in the light of its validity in relation to science, and amid criticisms of relativism, Nowotny *et al.* (2003) attempt to reposition mode 2 knowl-edge as possessing five characteristics. First, as already stated, it is context specific. For community engagement activities, therefore, much of the knowl-edge described in chapter 8, for instance, was context specific. Second, it is transdisciplinary (as opposed to interdisciplinary or multidisciplinary, since these two concepts still present knowledge as framed within separate disciplines). Examples of acceptable transdisciplinary knowledge locations within universities include newly formed, non-discipline specific areas of study such as women's studies or social justice. Third, Nowotny *et al.* assert that mode 2 knowledge is an inevitable product of interactions between different sites of knowledge, facilitated by cyber interconnectivity and the crossing of transnational boundaries. Therefore knowledge producers are inevitably networking to produce 'new kinds of "knowledge" organisations' (*ibid*, 2003, p. 187). A fourth characteristic, as mentioned above, is that knowledge production is no longer confined to scientific experiment. It is often the product of a dialogic process, an ongoing conversation between researchers and the actors with whom they interact. The learning city or learning region, as a collaborative project, is a prime example of this ongoing dialogic process, as is highlighted by Ntseane in chapter 2. Finally – and associated with the dialogic process – the quality-control process of assessing knowledge validity inevitably moves us beyond the laboratory into the realm of peer discussion from a broad range of participants. In chapter 5, Dube emphasises the challenges to environmental awareness when we fail to interface conventional and local knowledge systems. In chapter 8, Preece *et al.* demonstrate how knowledge is shared and adopted differently by participating actors in the different community engagement projects. This latter aspect is elaborated further in the ITMUA project report (Preece, 2011). The projects demonstrate, for instance, how simultaneous learning occurs on different levels in the same activity. Students may learn about negotiation and planning skills, staff members learn about adult education pedagogy, and community participants learn how to adapt their indigenous farming practices for better productivity.

Engagement at any level, however, is not without its challenges. While some have already been mentioned in relation to the specific themes, we conclude with some more general observations.

Challenges and prospects

Some of the broader challenges to community engagement in African contexts reflect those on a global scale. Schuetze (2010, pp. 19–20), for instance, identifies several that are relevant to Africa. These include confusions about terminology of community and regional engagement; poor experiences of unrealised partnerships; the increasing emphasis on quality and competitiveness among higher education institutions, which tends to pull academics back to their core activities of teaching and research; cutbacks in funding; and the prevailing culture of not rewarding academics for engagement work. African universities are increasingly being drawn into managerialist approaches to university competitiveness. Openjuru (2011) highlights this trend for Makerere University in Uganda and it is also evident across the South African higher education sector (DoHET, 2012). Furthermore, the battle to position lifelong learning as a holistic endeavour is not peculiar to Africa, as Inman articulates:

> *The greatest challenge to society today is the creation of genuine learning communities that encourage lifelong learning and celebration of relationship. This is differentiated from an individual lifelong learning agenda. ... lifelong learning ... is collaborative and defined by diverse stakeholders.* (Inman, 2010, p. 116)

But the historical circumstances outlined in chapter 1 – and the nature of national economies on the African continent alongside the vast inequalities that exist among its populations – require added resilience and resourcefulness to overcome them. Furthermore, the simultaneous plundering, exploitation and undermining of indigenous knowledge systems has the effect of belittling and denying African identity – ultimately taking away the African potential for agency (self-determination) and innovation.

Engagement, in whatever form, poses many challenges as the chapters have demonstrated. They include inadequate resources (material, technological and human); issues around political will, motivation and institution-wide infrastructure and systems to support engagement activities; and questions of conceptual understanding. But, as the chapters have equally shown, the African university has a strong historical mission to participate 'in the social transformation, economic modernization, and the … upgrading of the total human resources of the nation' (Seepe, 2004, p. 21). In the South African context, this mission is enshrined in government policy (Department of Education, 1997) as part of the drive to eliminate racism and other forms of oppression and instil a social conscience in the younger generation of future citizens. As such, community and regional engagement are predictably an element of university life that is likely to grow, rather than diminish.

The more effort that is made to publicise what is already happening, the more opportunity there is to develop the very scholarship and critical mass that are necessary for credible legitimacy of community engagement in higher education institutions.

References

Amutabi, M. and Oketch, M. (Eds) (2009) *Studies in Lifelong Learning in Africa: From Ethnic Traditions to Technological Innovations*. Ceredigion: Edwin Mellen Press.

Avoseh, M.B.M. (2001) 'Learning to be active citizens: Lessons of traditional Africa for lifelong learning', *International Journal of Lifelong Education*, Vol. 20 No 6, pp. 479–86.

Bruner, P., Waite, R. and Davey, M. (2011) 'Providers' perspectives on collaboration', *International Journal of Integrated Care*, Vol. 11, pp. 1–11.

Charles, D. and Benneworth, P. (2009) *Benchmarking The Regional Contribution of Universities*. Newcastle University: HEFCE.

Commission of the European Communities (2000) *A Memorandum on Lifelong Learning*. Brussels: SEC(2000) 1832.

Department of Education (1997) *White Paper on Higher Education*. Pretoria: Department of Education.

Department for Higher Education and Training (2012) *Green Paper for Post-School Education and Training*. Pretoria: Department for Higher Education and Training.

Fordjor, P.K., Kotoh, A.M., Kpeli, K.K., Kwamefio, A., Mensa, Q.B., Owusu, E. and Mullins, B.K. (2003) 'A review of traditional Ghanaian and Western philosophies of adult education', *International Journal of Lifelong Education*, Vol. 22 No 2, pp. 182–99.

Frycr, M. (2010) 'How to strengthen the third mission of the university: The case of the University of British Columbia learning exchange', in P. Inman and H.G. Schuetze (Eds), *The Community Engagement and Service Mission of Universities*. Leicester: NIACE, pp. 165–80.

Gibbons, M., Limoges, C., Nowotney, H., Schwartzman, S., Scott, P. and Trow, M. (1994) *The New Production of Knowledge: The Dynamics of Science and Research in Contemporary Societies*. London: Sage.

Inman, P. (2010) 'Institutionalising community engagement', in P. Inman and H.G. Schuetze (Eds), *The Community Engagement and Service Mission of Universities*. Leicester: NIACE, pp. 103–18.

Lekoko, R.N. and Modise, O.M. (2011) 'An insight into an African perspective on lifelong learning: Towards promoting functional compensatory programmes', *International Journal of Lifelong Education*, Vol. 30 No 1, pp. 5–18.

Longworth, N. (2012) *The Changing Scope of Learning Cities and Regions*. Retrieved 19 January 2012 from http://pascalobservatory.org/pascalnow/blogentry/changing-scope-learning-cities-and-regions

Longworth, N. and Allwinkle, S. (2005) 'The PALLACE project: Linking learning cities and regions in Europe, North America, Australasia and China'. Final report to the European Commission. Edinburgh: Napier University.

Mbigi, L. (2005) *The Spirit of African Leadership*. Randburg: Knowres.

Muller, J. and Subotzky, G. (2001) 'What knowledge is needed in the new millennium?' *Organization*, Vol. 8, pp. 163–82.

Nowotny, H., Scott, P. and Gibbons, M. (2003) 'Mode 2 revisited: The new production of knowledge', *Minerva*, Vol. 41, pp. 179–94.

OECD (2004) *Lifelong Learning: Policy Brief*. Paris: Organisation for Economic Cooperation and Development.

Omolewa, M.R. (2002) 'The practice of lifelong learning in indigenous Africa', in C. Medel-Añonuevo (Ed.), *Integrating Lifelong Learning Perspectives*. Hamburg: UNESCO Institute for Education, pp. 13–17.

Openjuru, G. (2011) 'Lifelong learning, lifelong education and adult education in higher institutions of learning in Eastern Africa: The case of Makerere University Institute of Adult and Continuing Education', *International Journal of Lifelong Education*, Vol. 30 No 1, pp. 55–70.

Preece, J. (2009) *Lifelong Learning and Development: A Southern Perspective*. London: Continuum.

Preece, J. (Ed.) (2011) *Community Service and Community Engagement in Four African Universities*. Gaborone: Light Books.

Schmied, V., Mills, A., Kruske, S., Kemp, L., Fowler, C. and Homer, C. (2010) 'The nature and impact of collaboration and integrated service delivery for pregnant women, children and families', *Journal of Clinical Nursing*, Vol. 19, pp. 3516–26.

Schuetze, H.G. (2010) 'The "third mission" of universities: Community engagement and service', in P. Inman and H.G. Schuetze (Eds), *The Community Engagement and Service Mission of Universities*. Leicester: NIACE, pp. 13–32.

Seepe, S. (2004) *Towards an African Identity of Higher Education*. Pretoria: Vista University and Skotaville Media.

Thune, T. and Gulbrandsen, M. (2011) 'Institutionalisation of university–industry interaction: An empirical study of the impact of formal structures on collaboration patterns', *Science and Public Policy*, Vol. 38 No 2, pp. 99–107.

UNESCO (2009) *Conference Statement*. World conference on higher education, 'The new dynamics of higher education and research for societal change and development', UNESCO Paris, 5–8 July 2009. Paris: UNESCO.

Waghid, Y. (2002) 'Knowledge production and higher education transformation in South Africa: Towards reflexivity in university teaching, research and community service', *Higher Education*, Vol. 43, pp. 457–88.

Walters, S. (2007) 'Building a learning region: Whose framework of lifelong learning matters?' in D.N. Aspin (Ed.), *Philosophical Perspectives of Lifelong Learning*. Hamburg: Springer, pp. 275–92.

Wergin, J.F. (2006) 'Elements of effective community engagement', in S.L. Percy, N.L. Zimpher and M.J. Brukardt (Eds), *Creating a New Kind of University: Institutionalising Community–University Engagement*. Bolton Massachusetts: Anker Publishing, pp. 23–42.

World Bank (2003) *Lifelong Learning in the Global Knowledge Economy: Challenges for Developing Countries*. Washington, DC: The World Bank.

Endnotes

Chapter 1

1 Sec http://pumr.pascalobservatory.org and http://pure.pascalobservatory. org as well as earlier publications, of which this present book is a part, most particularly Inman and Schuetze (2010).

Chapter 4

2 Botswana's population is estimated to be around 2 million.
3 The Department of Architecture and Planning falls under the Faculty of Engineering and Technology.
4 Wards are sub-units of neighbourhoods in urban areas. Ward development committees are statutory bodies made up of local residents and function mainly to coordinate local community development projects.
5 See Joseph Molefe (2003) 'Urban planning aspects of street vending in Gaborone City, Botswana', unpublished dissertation submitted for the award of MPhil in Urban Planning, University of Botswana.

Chapter 7

6 Dar es Salaam has one of the highest growth rates of African cities, although many African cities are experiencing strong urban growth with problems of the kind illustrated by Dar es Salaam. The UN-Habitat Agency has forecast that the population of Dar es Salaam will grow by over 80 per cent between 2010 and 2025, with a number of African cities forecast to increase by over 60 per cent in this period. (*The Economist*, 13 December 2010).
7 See the 'Responding to social change' theme on the PIE website (PASCAL Observatory, 2010–11).
8 A paper for the May 2010 International Forum on Lifelong Learning, Shanghai, drew on a 2009 survey conducted by the Chinese Ministry of Education to estimate that there were, by the end of 2007, 114 national pilot learning community initiatives in 30 provinces, autonomous regions and municipalities, with more than 4,000 pilot learning communities organised by provincial authorities (Keming, H., 2011, p. 64).

9 Enquiries in this matter may be directed to the coordinator of PASCAL PIE, Peter Kearns, at p.kearns@netspeed.com.au

Chapter 8

10 The MDGs address universal primary education, poverty reduction, reduction of diseases such as HIV/AIDS and malaria, maternal and infant mortality, gender inequalities, sustainable partnerships, literacy and environmental awareness.

Index

Index

Index

Index

Index